# The Boleyns

# The Boleyns

## The Rise & Fall of a Tudor Family

### DAVID LOADES

AMBERLEY

First published 2011
Amberley Publishing
The Hill, Stroud
Gloucestershire, GL5 4EP

www.amberleybooks.com

British Library Cataloguing in Publication Data.
A catalogue record for this book is available from the British Library.

ISBN 978 1 4456 0304 9

Typeset in 10pt on 12pt Sabon.
Typesetting and Origination by Amberley Publishing.
Printed in the UK.

# CONTENTS

# PREFACE

The Boleyns were not a great family. They traced their origins to Geoffrey and Alice, parish gentry in Norfolk at the turn of the fourteenth and fifteenth centuries. They made their way by a mixture of business acumen and well planned marriages, which gave them access to the court. Sir Geoffrey, Lord Mayor of London and the founder of their fortunes, married (as his second wife), Anne the daughter and co-heir of Lord Hoo and Hastings. His son, William, married Margaret, the daughter of Thomas Butler, Earl of Ormond, and their son, Thomas, married Elizabeth, daughter of Thomas Howard Earl of Surrey. This last marriage brought them into the ranks of the higher Tudor nobility, because Surrey became Duke of Norfolk in 1514, and his son, Elizabeth's brother, became the third Duke in 1524. The second daughter of this marriage, Anne Boleyn, notoriously became Henry VIII's second queen in 1533, a circumstance which spelled first triumph and then disaster for her family. There they might have remained, among the wreckage of Tudor politics, if the accidents of mortality had not brought Anne's daughter to the throne as Queen Elizabeth I in 1558. Although not Boleyn by name, Elizabeth was very much a Boleyn in her behaviour, and particularly in her sexuality. She reigned in the way which no king could have done, and left a dazzling image to posterity. The other third generation Boleyn was Henry Carey, Elizabeth's cousin by way of his mother Mary, who was Anne's sister. Henry served his kinswoman faithfully, and it was through him that the Boleyn genes were transmitted into the seventeenth century and beyond.

It was through the sexuality of his daughters that Sir Thomas Boleyn became a great man – temporarily at any rate – and by the same means that he was brought low. This was not typical of the Tudor nobility, but it does make them a fascinating study for the twenty-first century, and a source of endless entertainment. Philippa Gregory has colonised this territory in a number of books, and at least one film, but those are fiction and her chronology is imaginative. This work is history, and is an attempt to reconstruct the fortunes of a remarkable family from the records. It will, hopefully, be none the less interesting for that, because the marriages and sexual adventures which lay at its heart were real enough. These exploits caused fascination and scandal at the time, and Henry's relationship with Anne not only brought about a political revolution at home, but outrage all over Europe. It was not by accident that 'Anna Boleyna' featured as a carnival demon in Spain until well into the twentieth century.

In a sense a lifetime of working on Tudor history lies behind it, and I have incurred more debts of gratitude that I could possibly list. The most recent is to the History Faculty of Oxford University, which has extended its hospitality to me, and to the graduate seminars which I have been privileged to attend. My thanks are also due to my wife, Judith, who has been an unfailing source of inspiration, and to Jonathan Reeve of Amberley Publishing who suggested this as a subject worthy of attention.

DL
Burford, Oxfordshire
January 2011

# I

# ORIGINS – THE BLICKLING YEARS

The founder of the family fortune was Sir Geoffrey, who was Lord Mayor of London in 1457–8. Geoffrey was the son of another Geoffrey and Alice his wife, who were parish gentry at Salle, between Aylsham and Reepham in Norfolk.[1] He was born in 1405, but nothing is known of the circumstances, or whether he had siblings. He may have been taught his letters at home, or by the local priest, and he was apprenticed to a hatter in the City of London at some time about 1420. This suggests that he was a younger son, and that his father had some contacts in the City, but the evidence does not survive. A grant of the manor of Stiffkey in Norfolk to Cecily Boleyn and Thomas Boleyn, clerk, in 1455 suggests the possibility of siblings, but the name was not uncommon and they may have been no relations.[2] Geoffrey must have prospered, because he appears for the first time in the records when he transferred to the more prestigious Mercer's Company in February 1436. Unlike the hatters, the mercers were a Livery Company, and it was from the Livery Companies that the aldermen and other officers of the City were drawn. This move then suggests that Geoffrey, in addition to being prosperous, was also an ambitious young man. He became one of the aldermen for Castle Barnard Ward, and served as Sheriff of London in 1446–7. By that time he had also married, but nothing is known of his first wife beyond the fact that her name was Denise, and that she had died by 1448. In, or slightly before that year he had remarried and his second wife was Anne, the daughter and co-heir of Thomas, Lord Hoo and Hastings, through whom he established for the first time a link with the aristocracy.[3] How they encountered is not known, but by 1462 he was acting as trustee of the Hoo estates, presumably in the right of his wife, and it may well have been his business acumen which first attracted his Lordship's attention. In the pardon roll of 1462 he appears as 'Alderman of London, alias merchant, alias tenant of the manors of Lord Saye and Sele, alias late Sheriff, alias late Mayor, alias tenant of the lands of Sir Thomas Hoo deceased ...'[4]

There are indications that he was also acting as a business agent for other well connected gentlemen at the same time, because in March 1448 he received a grant of some shops in St Clements Danes, which he passed on to Sir John Fortescue in July 1449. Also in February 1449, being an ex-sheriff and of sufficient seniority, he was elected as one of the four members to represent the City in the House of Commons.[5]

In the mid-1450s Geoffrey appears frequently in the records going about the business of a wealthy citizen. For example, in February 1451 he was one of those listed as contributing to a loan of £1,246 made to the King 'towards the expenses of Sir Richard Wydville going to Gascony to resist the malice of the king's enemies', a fruitless expedition as it turned out. Whether the citizens ever got their money back is not recorded.[6] In 1457, for reasons which may have been connected with a change of residence, he moved his base of operations from Barnard Castle ward to Bassingshaw ward, and remained an alderman there until he died in 1463. In 1457–8 he served his turn as lord mayor, and was duly knighted. On 28 November 1457 he was commissioned as mayor to raise 1,100 archers from the city and its suburbs for the service of the Crown. Nevertheless, he is described as being a man of Yorkist sympathies, and that would fit with his appearing as a representative on a delegation which was sent by the city to Henry VI in 1460 in an attempt to dissuade him from raising an army against the Duke of York. Since the army deployed at Wakefield was already in the north at the time, it may be presumed that these representations were (in a sense) successful.[7] Sir Geoffrey was by this time an elder statesman of the City, and may have been entertaining thoughts of retirement. At some time before 1460, probably while he was mayor, he had purchased the manor of Blickling from Sir John Fastolf, having rented it for several years, and by the end of that year had replaced the existing dwelling with 'a fair house of brick'.[8] The citizens of London were generally sympathetic to the Duke of York and his sons, or perhaps more accurately, were appalled by the lack of justice under Henry VI's partisan regime. It was the unwillingness of the City to admit them which turned Margaret of Anjou and her northern army back after their victory at St Albans on 16 February 1461. On the other hand they welcomed the advent of Edward, Earl of March on 27 February, and that was the turning point of the campaign. As King Edward IV he took pains to cultivate that loyalty. He was generous with pardons in the first year of his reign, and carefully entertained the aldermen and their wives at court. It may be presumed that Anne, with her aristocratic background was particularly welcome. Several years later this generosity was repaid when the city supported him on his return from exile in 1471.[9]

At the time of his death on 17 June 1463, Sir Geoffrey was a rich man, with lands in several counties in addition to his Norfolk estates. His heir at that time was his elder son, Thomas, who may have been Denise's child. Thomas was still alive in 1466, when his father's executors entered into a bond to deliver jewels to the value of £236 when he reached his twenty-fifth birthday. However, he disappears thereafter, and must have died, perhaps without achieving his majority, because Anne, who lived until 1484, administered the estate in the name of Geoffrey's second son, William. William, born in 1451, would have achieved his majority in 1472, and that would be consistent with his appearing before the Court of Aldermen to acknowledge satisfaction for his patrimony as a citizen of London in May 1473.[10] Geoffrey also left a daughter, Alice, who in 1466 was also to have received £30 and 'certain jewels' on her marriage, or attaining the age of twenty-five, whichever came sooner. What happened to Alice we do not know. William's upbringing and schooling are as obscure as his father's, but his mother seems to have decided that he was more suited to the life of a country gentleman than to that of a London merchant. He was not apprenticed, and after suing out his freedom, seems to have had no further connection with the City. Anne may have introduced him to the court, but if so he never obtained any position there. What he did achieve was a good marriage, because in about 1475 he wedded Margaret, the daughter and co-heir of Thomas Butler, soon to be Earl of Ormond.[11] The Butlers were a family based in Ireland, but had many estates and properties in England and Wales, which Thomas was licensed to enter in October 1476. When he died in 1515 his son-in-law was to engage in a long legal battle for his mother's inheritance. William Boleyn had properties in Kent as well as in Norfolk, and appears to have divided his time and attention between Hever Castle and Blickling. It is thought that his two sons, Thomas and James were born at the latter in 1477 and 1480 respectively. William served on various commissions in Norfolk, including one with Anthony Earl Rivers in November 1482 for the adjudication of certain disputes, which were presumably felt to be beyond the reach of the normal courts, and another with Sir William Hopton in September 1483 for the security of the sea coasts of Norfolk and Suffolk.[12] At some point between these two dates he was knighted, which may indicate that he was, or was thought to be, sympathetic to Richard of Gloucester's coup of June 1483. The Duke of Norfolk, to whose affinity William Boleyn belonged, had served as Earl Marshal at Richard III's coronation, and played an important part in frustrating the Duke of Buckingham's supporters in East Anglia from linking up with those in Surrey when Buckingham rose in rebellion in the autumn of 1483. It may well have been for service in that connection that William received his knighthood.

When the threat from Henry Tudor began to mount in 1484, Richard again called upon the Howard affinity for support, and commissions of array were issued to the Duke in both May and December of that year. To both these commissions Sir William Boleyn was named, as well as to the Commissions of the Peace for both Norfolk and Kent.[13] When the threat became real in July 1485, John Howard led his men from Norfolk to the King's support, and it may be presumed that Sir William was among them. If so, his part in the decisive battle of Bosworth is obscure – probably deliberately so in view of the outcome. The Duke of Norfolk led the King's vanguard, and perished in the fighting. He was subsequently attainted, and his massive estates were confiscated, but William seems to have returned quietly to Norfolk and laid low for a while. Because he never received a pardon, his very presence at the battle is uncertain, although how he could have avoided it is unknown. As early as December 1486 his wife was given custody of some of the Ormond lands in Devon, Somerset and Cornwall, and it is difficult to see how that could have been allowed if he had been under suspicion. In 1489 he served as Sheriff of Kent, and that even more argues that he was in good standing at that time.[14] On 29 October 1489 he also received a grant of the manors of Buxton and Hengham in Norfolk, in the King's hands since the attainder of the Duke, and in 1490 served again on a commission of array for the county, although this time it was headed by John de la Pole, the Duke of Suffolk.[15]

Meanwhile, Thomas Howard was trying to rebuild his father's affinity. As Earl of Surrey he had been attainted with his father following the fiasco at Bosworth, but had earned remission by good behaviour, and in 1489 was restored to his title and precedence. He was not permitted to inherit the dukedom, and his lands were severely curtailed, but he still enjoyed a great deal of goodwill in East Anglia, and among those who welcomed his restoration was Sir William Boleyn. However, Sir William was a public figure, and a man with a career in the royal service to maintain, so it would not have done for him to commend himself to Surrey in the traditional fashion. Henry VII was very averse to his servants becoming the retainers of noblemen, and it is obvious from his selection for so many commissions that he regarded Boleyn as his own man. No nobleman was permitted to retain men outside his own household and family, but in this case Surrey found an original way around this difficulty. By offering his daughter Elizabeth to William's son Thomas in marriage, he established a legitimate kinship between them that not even the King could object to. In about 1495 therefore Thomas, who was about eighteen at the time, married Elizabeth and thus brought the Boleyns into the family circle of one of the great noble houses

of England.[16] It was a dazzling achievement for the son of a
London alderman, and the foundation of much of the fortune and
misfortune which subsequently overtook the family. Thomas was
brought up to regard himself as a soldier and a courtier. Nothing
is known about his education, except that it corresponded to the
norm for a well connected young gentleman, and would have
been conducted at home by a private tutor. He probably shared
his lessons with his brother James, who was about two years his
junior, and possibly with the sons of other gentlemen who were
in Sir William's service.[17] Someone also taught him arms, because
later he was a skilled jouster, although this may have happened
only after his arrival at court in about 1500, when he joined the
circle around the young Duke of York – the future King Henry
VIII. In 1497 he served with his father against the Cornish rebels
at Blackheath, which earned them both further commendations.
William was Sheriff of both Norfolk and Suffolk in 1499 in spite
of his close association with the Howards, but signed off that
service in 1502 when he was granted a life exemption from the
office.[18] He continued to sit on other commissions, such as Oyer
and Terminer and Gaol Delivery until within a few weeks of his
death in 1505.

By that time Thomas, who had started his court career as
Yeoman of the Crown had advanced to the status of Esquire of
the Body. This was not a position carrying with it any access to
the King's more intimate moments; in spite of its title it was a
second ranking chamber appointment, but it did carry with it the
right to be fed at the royal table (bouge of court) and a salary of
about £30 a year. Thomas later complained that his father had
made him an allowance of only £50 a year, and that his wife had
given him 'every year a child', but that was stretching the truth.[19]

He also had the use of Hever Castle, which was conveniently situated for access to London, and his salary from the court. Elizabeth may have suffered from a number of miscarriages and still births, but the only three children that we know about were Mary, born in about 1499, Anne (*c.*1501) and George (*c.*1504). We do not know where these children were born. The natural assumption is that it was at Hever, but many years later Mathew Parker, who in Henry VIII's reign was Anne's chaplain, spoke of her coming from Norfolk, so perhaps she at least was born at Blickling.[20] About their education and early up-bringing nothing is known, but once Thomas had been licensed to enter all the lands which his father had held as tenant-in-chief of the Crown, an event which occurred on 3 February 1506, he would have been a rich man, well able to afford a suitably qualified tutor. The tradition is that they were brought up at Hever under the watchful eye of their mother. Thomas himself would have been frequently absent because of his duties at court. He is known to have been present at the celebration of the nuptials of Prince Arthur and Catherine of Aragon in November 1501, and to have accompanied Princess Margaret when she went to Scotland to marry James IV in 1503. In addition to the lands which he inherited directly, William appears to have left certain manors in Norfolk in trust for him by an arrangement known as feofment to use. This had presumably been done while he was still a minor, and on 15 May 1506 these foefees were licensed to alienate the lands concerned to Thomas, being of full age and *compos mentis*.[21] According to the writs of *diem clausit extemum* issued in November 1505, which would have constituted his original title, he held lands in Norfolk, Suffolk, Kent, Bedfordshire, Hertfordshire and Sussex, by a variety of different tenures and some in full ownership.[22] A considerable estate which bears witness to the acquisitiveness and management skills of his father and grandfather. William may not have been a courtier, but through marriage and patronage he had many of the advantages of that status, and had given his son a flying start in life.

Thomas's younger brother James, who was born in 1480, has always been overshadowed by his sibling. In his youth he may well have received some legal training, and he served on the commission of the peace for Norfolk from 1511 until his death in 1561, but he seems to have been handicapped through most of his career by his lack of lands.[23] Although described as 'of Blickling' he used that house by courtesy of his brother, and most of the successes of his life can be attributed to the latter's patronage. He was knighted in 1520 for no obvious reason, and was a Knight of the Body by 1533, a position which did not involve regular attendance at court, and was largely honorific. In 1529 he sat for Norfolk in the Reformation parliament, and may also have sat in 1536, for which the returns do not survive.[24] He survived the storm which destroyed his niece and nephew in 1536 and the death of his distinguished brother in 1539, his own favour not having been notable enough to have attracted the attention of his family's enemies. He attended the third Duke of Norfolk, who was his kinsman by marriage, at the reception of Anne of Cleves in January 1540, and in February of the same year was granted livery of his brother's lands as his heir male, although he was not permitted to claim the earldom of Wiltshire, which remained in abeyance.[25] The following month he exchanged Thomas's former lands in Kent with the Crown for other properties in Norfolk, thus confirming his intention to retain his local base, and resolving his relative lack of property in the county. In 1542 he received a grant of all the moveable property which Jane Rochford had left at Blickling. Jane was the widow of James's nephew George, Viscount Rochford, who had been executed in 1536 for treasonable incest with his sister Anne. She had presumably lived at Blickling after that disaster, when she was not at court. Jane had herself been attainted and executed for acting as a pander in Queen Catherine Howard's infidelities during the summer of 1541, so her goods were in the hands of the Crown, but not apparently, considered to be of sufficient value to be worth retaining.[26] James was also considered to be sufficiently trustworthy to serve on the jury which in 1546 indicted his kinsman Henry Howard, Earl of Surrey for high treason, and as *custos rotulorum* for Norfolk from 1558 to 1560. He lived to see his great niece ascend the throne in November 1558, and when he died in 1561 left various things to her in his will. There is no evidence of any particular favour from Elizabeth, but his will was overseen by his kinsman, Henry Carey, Lord Hunsdon. James had married, at some time before 1520, his wife being Elizabeth, the daughter of one John Wood of East Barsham in Norfolk, but she presumably predeceased him and they had no children who survived.[27] He was a very advanced age by the time that he died, and with him the direct male line of the Boleyns became extinct.

Meanwhile, with the accession of Henry VIII, Thomas's career at court had taken off. The origin of his favour seems to have lain in his skill at the joust, because in spite of being a man in his thirties, and thus too old to have been a companion to the Prince of Wales, he had nevertheless tilted with the Prince and won his regard. He was knighted at Henry's coronation, and took part in all the 'feats of arms' which attended that event, being particularly conspicuous at the tournament called to celebrate the birth of the short-lived Prince Henry in January 1511.[28] He was given a number of minor offices, not individually significant but enough to indicate that he was well thought of, and probably quite close to the King. He was close enough at any rate to make his support for Henry's warlike ambitions audible, and to impress the King with his excellent knowledge of French. He served as sheriff of Kent in 1510–11, which is another indication that his principal base was at Hever, and in 1512 was selected to lead an important diplomatic mission to the court of Margaret of Austria, the regent of the Low Countries. Henry had been spoiling for a fight since coming to the throne, and his target was the King of France. There was no objective political reason for this desire, but it had a great deal to do with the King's self image, and his relations with his own aristocracy. Henry was young, and anxious to make his mark as quickly as possible. This, he judged, could be best done upon the field of battle, as his great ancestor Henry V had done.[29] It was also true that his nobles, and particularly the younger ones, still saw their service to the Crown primarily in military terms, and there had not been a decent war for many years. Henry VII's expedition to Etaples in 1492 hardly counted, because there had been no fighting. So they shared Henry's chivalric dreams, and urged him on. Sir Thomas Boleyn would have been typical in this respect, and may even have been a mouthpiece for his mentor, the Earl of Surrey. Constrained by his council, which was dominated by clergy and not at all bellicose, in the spring of 1510, the King renewed his father's treaty with France, but he had no intention of abiding by it.[30]

However, even Henry realised that he could not fight the French on his own. Allies would be needed, and he naturally looked first to his father-in-law, Ferdinand of Aragon. Perhaps he had even married Catherine within weeks of his accession with that very thought in mind. Catherine had been his brother Arthur's wife, and had been a widow since 1502. Some thought that she was forbidden fruit, but the King had swept all obstacles aside, and driven either by desire for her or by ambitions for a link to her formidable father, had wedded her.[31] In the summer of 1511 he signed a treaty with Ferdinand, which was a direct breach of his obligations to Louis XII. Fortunately, Pope Julius II then stepped in to save him from any moral embarrassment by falling out with Louis himself. The origins of this contretemps lay in the collapse of the League of Cambrai, formed in 1508 against the Venetians, at that time deemed to constitute a threat to the papal patrimony. That League had consisted of the Emperor Maximilian, Ferdinand of Spain and Louis XII in addition to the Pope, but by the summer of 1510 Julius had concluded that the French constituted a bigger menace than the Venetians, and was trying to turn the League around. Getting wind of what was afoot, Louis struck back, first by convening a council of French clergy to make Gallican and anti-papal noises, and then by calling a general council of the Church to meet at Pisa in the spring of 1511 for no less a purpose than the deposition of the Pope.[32] Needless to say, the council never met, but Louis' action had given Julius the pretext that he needed to convert the League of Cambrai into a Holy League against France. The negotiations went on throughout the summer, and in October the League was signed in Rome. Originally it consisted of Ferdinand, the Venetians and the Pope, but Henry VIII was quick to join, and in November, having delivered an ultimatum to the French king, he declared war.[33] So keen was he to display his intentions, and keep his aristocracy on their toes, that this had been preceded earlier in 1511 by two small military expeditions – one to support a strike which the King of Spain was proposing to make against the Muslims of North Africa, and the other to assist the Emperor against the rebellious Duke of Gueldres. Both of these were goodwill gestures, and although the latter was militarily successful, it failed of its diplomatic intention to persuade Maximilian to adhere to the Holy League. The expedition to Spain failed for the quite different reason that Ferdinand cancelled his proposed crusade, leaving Lord Darcy, the commander, with the problem of maintaining discipline among his unemployed troops. In that he was deplorably unsuccessful, and his small army returned home in considerable discredit. It was not a good omen for future collaboration.[34] Against this background of large aspirations and limited attainment, Sir Thomas Boleyn was given his first diplomatic assignment.

# 2

# THOMAS AT COURT – THE HEVER YEARS

When Henry needed someone to undertake the delicate task of coaxing Maximilian into the Holy League, he was naturally looking for his own man – someone with a commitment to the war upon which he was now embarked. That man was Sir Thomas Boleyn. Sir Thomas was a courtier to his finger tips, a man who had been made a Knight of the Bath at Henry's coronation, who had jousted with him, and who had been a pall bearer at the funeral of Prince Henry in February 1511, the latter a mark of particular intimacy.[1] He was too old to be one of the King's mignons, but as a Knight of the Body was as close as it was possible to get. He was also one of those who swung the council in favour of war after the formation of the Holy League, and was actively involved in the preparations for the Marquis of Dorset's expedition to Guienne, which was to open hostilities in April 1512. He was not, however, destined to accompany that army. Instead, on 17 May, he was sent on embassy to Margaret of Austria, the Regent of the Low Countries.[2] This was an indirect way of approaching the Emperor, because Margaret was thought to be sympathetic to the war, and was know to have great influence with Maximilian. An embassy based in her court at Mechelen was therefore likely to stand a greater chance of success. It was also a French-speaking court, and Sir Thomas's command of the language was an additional reason for choosing him for the mission. He was accompanied by Richard

Wingfield, but it is obvious from the reports sent back that he was in charge. The negotiation got off to a slow start. The Emperor was very poor, Boleyn wrote on 7 June, 'which my lady knows right well', and was therefore probably going to need a hefty subsidy before he would move.[3] Although Margaret had written in support of the English request, this had produced no result and at the end of June it was decided that a direct approach might be better. On the 29th Sir Thomas set off in search of Maximilian, but this turned out to be frustrating hunt, because the Emperor kept on the move, and no one seemed to be able to anticipate where he would go next. However, he caught up with him eventually, and a sequence of some half dozen letters in late July and early August outline the progress which had been made. So confident was Boleyn of ultimate success that he returned to the Low Countries, where on 20 August he reported that he had struck an amicable wager with the Regent that there would be an agreement within ten days – her Spanish courser against his hobby.[4] He probably lost his wager, because it was 4 September before he was able to report that agreement had actually been reached. In spite of this, the Emperor was in no hurry to conclude, and on 10 November Boleyn wrote in some frustration that there was still no word of his final decision. It was April 1513 before he finally signed the coveted treaty, and within a couple of weeks Sir Thomas was on his way home. The cost to Henry was 35,000 crowns, due one month after Maximilian's declaration of war, and which was duly paid in June.[5]

Throughout this mission he had reported directly to the King, and although this probably means in effect to the council, it is sufficient indication that Thomas Wolsey, although rising in the King's favour, had not yet acquired that general control of business which he was to display a year or so later. It was also part of Sir Thomas's business to recruit mercenaries for Henry's service, in anticipation of the campaign which he was to launch in 1513, and on 4 July 1512 he was able to report that he had paid retainers to 2,000 such, although he did not say where he had got them from. Presumably they had come courtesy of the Archduchess Margaret, with whom he seems to have been on friendly, even familiar terms from the beginning.[6] It is possible that Boleyn was becoming anxious as his mission dragged on, of the influence which Thomas Wolsey was beginning to acquire over the King, but in terms of his own affairs, he need not have worried. In spite of a somewhat sinister reference to 'debts owed to the late king' in November 1512, in March of the following year he was released of all such accruing from his service at Sheriff of Kent in 1510–11, including the bond of £40 which he had entered into on assuming office. The remainder were not pursued, and in January 1513 he was duly paid the 200 marks which were due to him for his ambassadorial expenses, the kind of favour which most diplomats had to wait until their return to enjoy.[7] Henry had been more than a little dismayed by the chaos which accompanied the Marquis of Dorset's expedition to Guienne in the early summer of 1512, which had been aborted on account of Ferdinand's failure to provide the expected back up, and even more annoyed by the latter's decision to sign a truce with France in direct breech of his obligations under the Holy League. 1513 had not been a good year for English arms either. Sir Edward Howard, the Lord Admiral, had been killed in a foolhardy attack on some French galleys near Brest, and his fleet had retreated in confusion.[8] Consequently the King was even more determined to take advantage of the Treaty which Sir Thomas had negotiated with Maximilian, in order to redeem some honour from two otherwise unfortunate seasons. In the high summer he mustered an army royal of some 40,000 men, and invaded Hainault via Calais at the beginning of July. Accompanying him in the 'middle ward' of this host were about 800 members of his household under arms, and one of these would have been Sir Thomas Boleyn.[9]

The nature of Sir Thomas's service in this connection can only be guessed at, because he does not feature in the surviving records, but as a Knight of the Body he must have been with Henry, and may well have acted as an interpreter during the constant discussions which went on between the English and Burgundian forces. He may not have had any active military role, because in spite of his chivalric skills, his only field experience had been at Blackheath nearly twenty years before. Maximilian duly put in an appearance at the siege of Therouanne in August, offering to serve under Henry's command in return for another hefty dollop of cash, and when the town surrendered on the 23rd, it was handed over to him and largely destroyed.[10] In the wake of this victory, Henry took himself off to Lille to celebrate with his ally Margaret of Austria, and it is hard to imagine that her friend Sir Thomas Boleyn was not of the company. Apart from any other consideration, it would have given him a chance to visit his younger daughter Anne, whom he had successfully established as a *demoiselle d'honneur* in her household before his departure in the spring. Indeed it is very likely that Anne herself was involved in the endless discussions which resulted in Henry turning his next attentions to the town of Tournai, a place in which Maximilian's interest was more marked than his own. This time, however, there was no hand over. When the town surrendered on 23 September it was on the understanding that the citizens would acknowledge

Henry as King of France, which was a polite way of choking off the Emperor's ambitions.[11] Maximilian seems to have swallowed the rebuff with equanimity and the town remained in English hands for the next five years. About a week later Henry returned to England, and his household travelled with him. The King seems at first to been determined to fight another campaign in the summer of 1514, and mobilised ships and men for that purpose, but he changed his mind. It may have been doubts about the effectiveness of his ally, and the expense of maintaining him, or it may have been disgust at the withdrawal of Ferdinand from the alliance, but most probably it was because the Pope was anxious to abandon the Holy League. Julius II had died in February 1513 and his successor Leo X was not committed to the war. By the beginning of 1514 he was putting pressure on the belligerents to settle, and after some hesitation, Henry responded positively.[12] This may have been because he was beginning to appreciate the fearsome cost of hostilities, but more likely it was on account of the influence of Thomas Wolsey, his almoner, who was rising very fast in the royal favour during 1513 and 1514. Wolsey had been responsible for the logistics of the Tournai campaign, and had been rewarded with the revenues of the see after its fall. It was consequently Wolsey who organised the peace negotiations which took place in the summer of 1514, and in which Sir Thomas Boleyn seems to have played no part. As one of the councillors most committed to the war, he was probably omitted deliberately. Wolsey was, however, careful to ensure that the latter's services did not go unrewarded, and in May 1514 Sir Thomas was granted four lordships in the hundreds of Wayland and Greymanshaw in the county of Norfolk, for which he was required to pay an annual rental of £71 6s 8d.[13] This would have been a very profitable deal for its recipient, and would have strengthened considerably his hold upon the landed estates of the county.

There are a number of indications that Sir Thomas Boleyn was in high favour at this point. In spite of his known opposition to the peace he was able to take advantage of it in one very significant way. His elder daughter, Mary, was one of those named to accompany the King's sister when she went to marry Louis XII, by the terms of the treaty. This was certainly an appointment which owed more to Sir Thomas than it did to any qualities in the girl herself, because although she was attractive to look at, she seems to have had no gifts either of character or ability which would qualify her for such a posting.[14] It may be that the King regarded the Boleyns as a trustworthy family, because at about the same time their father wrote a somewhat embarrassed letter to the Archduchess, asking her to release Anne for the same service. He would hardly have done this of his own volition, and we must assume that Henry had for some reason decided that both the Boleyn girls should accompany his sister to France. Sir Thomas and Lady Boleyn both took part in the mumming at the Christmas revels in 1514, along with the Guildfords, the Duke of Suffolk and 'Mistress Elizabeth Blunt', which was again a mark of particular favour.[15] Unfortunately Mary Tudor's reign as queen of France came to an abrupt end only weeks after it had started, because Louis died on 1 January 1515, leaving her and her entourage stranded in a France now run by the twenty-year-old Francis of Angouleme. Mary solved this problem tidily by marrying Charles Brandon, the Duke of Suffolk whom Henry had sent to bring her home. There is much controversy surrounding this marriage, with which the King was alleged to be offended, but which Wolsey seems to have approved. Did Mary take the initiative? Was she trying to escape the unwelcome attentions of Francis? The French king approved of the union because he was anxious to prevent Henry from deploying her on the international market, and it may have been for that reason that Henry was annoyed.[16] Anyway, when she returned to England in May 1515 it was as the Duchess of Suffolk, and the couple faced stiff financial penalties until the King was placated. At the same time, Anglo-French relations began to deteriorate, not least because the two kings were now alike in their age and ambitions. The Boleyn girls, however, did not return. Sir Thomas must have enjoyed some especial favour at the French court because he was able to transfer both his daughters to the service of the new Queen Consort, Claude, who was a girl not much older than themselves. Given the competition which must have existed within France for such positions, it is remarkable that Claude chose to retain two English girls among her personal attendants, but so it was.

In spite of Wolsey's rise to power, Sir Thomas remained a leading member of the council, and may well have been one of those most suspicious of the Bishop of Lincoln, as Wolsey had now become. In February 1515 Thomas Spinelly, in the Low Countries warned the bishop that a certain Don Diego, a 'subtle fellow' on an exploratory mission from Spain, would secretly visit the Duke of Buckingham and the Marquis of Dorset, who were known opponents of Wolsey. He would also be calling on Sir Thomas Boleyn.[17]

Perhaps because of the exposed position of his daughters, Sir Thomas had abandoned his opposition to improved Anglo-French relations, and supported Wolsey when he re-negotiated the peace of 1514 in April. This was necessary because the original treaty had been scheduled to expire one year after whichever of the kings died first – which would have meant January 1516. Consequently, in spite of Henry's grumbling, a quarrel over the return of Mary's jewels, and French meddling in Scotland, the peace was renewed.[18] Henry seems to have deluded himself that this gave him some control over Francis. If such was his thinking, then he was disabused in September when the French king crossed the Alps with a large army, and defeated the Swiss at Marignano – a victory which left the King of England both impressed and envious. In October he reconciled himself to Ferdinand, but this was a defensive measure only, and when he began to look for potential allies, he looked instead to the Swiss, whom he rightly believed to be anxious to redeem the defeat of Marignano. During the autumn and winter Richard Pace went backwards and forwards, but in the event Henry paid the Swiss a substantial sum and they acted in alliance with Maximilian rather than England. The campaign fizzled in the spring of 1516, and Henry began to rethink his French strategy. After all his main quest was for honour, which could be achieved just as well by peace as by war. With Wolsey's encouragement he began to see himself as the arbiter of Europe, and when Pope Leo proposed a general truce as a preliminary to a great crusade against the Turks, he quickly moved into a position of support for his minister's scheme to hijack the papal proposal in his own interest.[19] Sir Thomas Boleyn does not feature in all this diplomatic activity, although as a member of the council he must have been aware of what was going on. In March and November 1515 he was named again to the commission of the peace for Norfolk, and in December was granted the constableship of Norwich Castle in survivorship with Sir Henry Wyatt. In February of 1516 he sold the manor of Newhall to the Crown for £1,000, and acted as a canopy bearer at the christening of the Princess Mary on the 21st. All signs of favour, but not of much political significance.[20] More important, perhaps, Thomas Butler, Earl of Ormond, died without lawful issue on 3 August 1515. This triggered a dispute over the inheritance between his cousin, Sir Piers Butler, and the two daughters of his brother and predecessor, John Butler, Anne St. Leger and Margaret Boleyn. Margaret was, of course, Sir Thomas's mother. The Earl of Kildare wrote to Henry on 1 December, notifying him that the ladies had entered a suit as heirs general against Sir Piers, who was claiming as the male heir. On 12 December livery of the lands was granted to the petitioners, but that was not the end of the story.[21] Piers had assumed the title of Ormond, and the council in Ireland backed him. He had physical control of the Irish estates and was not prepared to concede. Meanwhile the English and Welsh estates had been placed under the control of a body of trustees, headed by the Bishop of London. The legal battle ground on, complicated by the fact that the English government could not afford to offend Piers, who on the basis of his Irish lands alone was a major magnate. Sir Thomas naturally used all his influence on his mother's behalf, because he stood to inherit anything which she gained, but the issue was not resolved until February 1528, when Piers accepted the earldom of Ossory in lieu.[22] He appears to have retained control of most of the Ormond lands in Ireland.

While this was going on, there was trouble in Scotland, where John Stewart, Duke of Albany, had returned in 1515, and immediately set out to re-establish French influence against the Queen Mother, Margaret Tudor and her second husband, Archibald Douglas, Earl of Angus. In 1516 he imprisoned her in Stirling Castle and took control of the Regency government in the name of her son, James V. Later in the same year she escaped and fled to England, seeking the support of her brother Henry VIII, and there she was joined by her husband. Henry was not reluctant, but he realised that he needed to provide 'conduction' for her, not least as a safeguard against attempts at kidnap or assassination. This duty was probably undertaken in relays by trusted courtiers, and of these Sir Thomas Boleyn was one. In May 1517 he was paid £10 for fulfilling this duty for forty days, although it is not quite clear when he undertook his stint.[23] Margaret shortly after returned to Scotland on the understanding that she would play no further part in the government, a condition only enforceable as long as Albany remained in the country. However, as negotiations for a general peace got under way in 1518, Francis recalled him as a good will gesture, and the Queen Mother resumed her thankless task of trying to manage the aristocratic factions, which did duty as Scotland's domestic politics. Meanwhile, Sir Thomas was rewarded with other small gestures of favour. In May 1517 a recognisance which he owed to the Crown was cancelled and he was granted a license to export timber from his estate at Rochford in Essex. In November he was pricked a second time as Sheriff of Kent – not much of a favour in view of the expenses of the office, but he was selected ahead of such local worthies as Sir John Fogge.[24] Obviously he was not spending all his spare time in Norfolk. His wife, Elizabeth, was present at the christening of the Duke and Duchess of Suffolk's daughter Frances on 17 July. At some time before 1519, Sir Thomas also recalled his elder daughter from France. Unlike her sister, Mary had not taken comfortably to the service of the French court. Perhaps she found the language difficult, or perhaps she was not sufficiently adept at fending off the attentions of the male courtiers. She acquired a reputation for easy virtue, and that was bad news from her father's point of view, so at some time, probably in 1518, he called her home before any more damage should be done. Fortunately her reputation had not preceded her, and he was able to secure a place for her in the household of the Queen, Catherine of Aragon. This must have required considerable tact on Sir Thomas's part, because the King's favour was by no means an automatic passport to the Queen's. Relations between the royal couple were strained on account of Henry's liaison with Elizabeth Blount, which by the end of 1518 had resulted in her pregnancy. The Queen was expected to pay her own servants out of her jointure of over £4,000 a year, and had exclusive control over whom she appointed to her chamber, so Henry was in no position to plant the daughter of a favoured courtier.[25] Sir Thomas, however, was man with many diplomatic skills.

The treaties which were signed in London on 2 and 4 October 1518 were Wolsey's triumph. Leo X had proclaimed a general truce throughout Europe in 1517, and sent his legates out to whip up support for his crusade. Wolsey, by this time Cardinal Archbishop of York and Lord Chancellor, was prepared to welcome Lorenzo Campeggio to England, but only on condition that he was joined in commission with him, and given equal status – that of Legate de Latere. This took several weeks to negotiate, and when Campeggio at length arrived, he found that his main mission had been sidelined.[26] Henry was fully supportive of the general truce – there was in any case no war going on in Europe at the time – but determined to convert it to his own purposes. He made polite noises in response to the Cardinal's appeal, and pressed on with his own plan. This was for a new Anglo-French alliance, to be sealed with a marriage between his own two-year-old daughter, Mary and the even younger Dauphin, Francis, which was also to be an open treaty, to which all princes of good will were invited to adhere. In other words a general declaration of peace and reconciliation.

The French king was easy to persuade, but Wolsey had to work extremely hard to win the acceptance of the Emperor Maximilian, and of the young King Charles of Spain. Charles had inherited his throne on the death of his grandfather Ferdinand in February 1516, and was having considerable difficulty establishing himself in his kingdom.[27] However, in spite of these preoccupations he agreed at length, and so did the Emperor. Indefatigably, Wolsey trawled Europe for other signatories, and swept in most of the lesser powers, from Denmark to Genoa. The result was a diplomatic tour de force, which sent Henry's (and Wolsey's) reputations soaring. He had at last secured the position to which he aspired – that of arbiter of Europe – and it had cost his exchequer less than a medium sized military campaign. His council, inevitably, was divided over this treaty, but no one was prepared to resist the combined enthusiasm of the King and the Cardinal, and they duly signed this grandiose declaration, Sir Thomas Boleyn among them. This is the only indication that we have of his direct involvement in the negotiations, but we may reasonably conclude that he used his good offices with Margaret of Austria to get the Emperor's agreement. Maximilian was a sick man, and maybe was unwilling to commit his successor to anything so sweeping. However, it would not have required much persuading to convince him that he was committing him to nothing. Although a worthy statement of intent, and accepted by the Pope for that reason, such a treaty was bound to be at the mercy of circumstances. The solid core, the Anglo-French treaty was signed just two days later, and again Sir Thomas appended his signature, this time, we can be sure, with a good will.[28] Tournai was returned to French control, and his daughter Anne would now be safe at the French court for the foreseeable future.

By January 1519, Sir Thomas was back in France. The recent treaty had alluded to a meeting between the two kings, to take place within the next year, and it is reasonable to suppose that he was being sent to begin negotiations for that meeting. However, his mission had hardly begun when the news arrived of Maximilian's death, and on 9 February he wrote that Francis would enter the ensuing election. This was a decision entirely consistent with the French king's ambitions, but it did not bode well for the security of the peace treaty which he had signed less than six months earlier.[29] His principal rival was Charles, King of Spain and the late Emperor's grandson and heir. Whichever of these two was successful, it was likely to lead to conflict. So Pope Leo thought, and he began the quest for a third candidate who might be able to take advantage of any deadlock in the Electoral college. He probably had in mind the Elector of Saxony, who had all the right credentials, but he did not name him, and when he wrote to Henry VIII about this possibility, Henry took it as an invitation to enter the lists himself. Success in such a venture would also, as he might have calculated, guarantee the security of the treaty of London. So in May he announced his intention to stand for election also, and with Wolsey's encouragement Richard Pace set off on a canvassing tour of Germany.[30] Such actions must have made Sir Thomas Boleyn's sojourn at the French court an uncomfortable one, but at least it could be agreed that no meeting between the kings would be possible while the election was pending, and that it would be better to postpone it until the following year. When the election took place on 12 and 13 June, it became apparent at once that Henry was not a serious contender. Francis was, but it soon appeared that he had been out-bribed by Charles, who had the great banking house of Fugger behind him, and the King of Spain emerged victorious. On the 14th, probably before the news had reached him, Francis wrote a friendly letter to Henry, informing him that his ambassador had stood godfather on his behalf at the christening of the new Duke of Orleans, and had performed at the ceremony 'with all possible honour'.[31] When he learned of Charles's success, Francis was deeply chagrined, but he could not blame Henry for his failure as the latter had failed to secure a single vote!

Meanwhile, it had been agreed that the meeting between the kings would take place in the summer of 1520, probably at Guisnes on the borders of the Calais Pale, and the diplomatic preliminaries were put in place. There is no indication that Sir Thomas had failed to perform satisfactorily in his embassy; indeed he had done an exceptionally good job in keeping relations amicable in the run up to the Imperial election, but the decision was taken early in 1520 to replace him with Richard Wingfield. He was recalled on 21 February. This may have been on Wolsey's initiative, but more likely because Henry had decided that he needed Sir Thomas as a part of his entourage for the impending meeting, and on 26 March he was appointed to be one of those to 'ride with the king at the embracing of the two kings'. This was not only a great honour, but also an indication that Wolsey, who was responsible for the arrangements, appreciated just how great his favour was at that time.[32] So Sir Thomas attended the Field of Cloth of Gold. What he did there is not apparent, because he was at forty-three too old to take part in the 'feats of arms' which were part of the festivities. It is possible that he acted as interpreter for his linguistically challenged colleagues, but most probable that his function was the background one of political adviser. He also accompanied Henry to his meetings with the new Emperor both before and after the Field, and they were both more amicable and more fruitful in political terms. The encounter with Francis, for all its flamboyant embracing and declarations of goodwill, was primarily an exercise in social competition. The two kings, as one Venetian observer wrote, detested each other cordially.[33] Their meeting, however, must also have served as something of a Boleyn family reunion, because both Sir Thomas's wife and elder daughter were among the ladies accompanying Queen Catherine, while Anne was among the attendants of Queen Claude. When the queens encountered, Anne must have been worked quite hard, because although Catherine's own French was adequate, most of her ladies did not speak the language and none of Claude's other servants (as far as we know) had a word of English. English was not yet the international language that it would eventually become, but it had become long since the language of the court, and of domestic business in general.

While engaged in this high social and political activity, Sir Thomas did not neglect his own interests. He had apparently been promised the office of Comptroller of the Royal Household, but Wolsey secured the office for Sir Henry Guildford. Whether this was the result of a misunderstanding, or evidence of some hostility on the Cardinal's part is not apparent. He may have held the post briefly in 1520 before being persuaded, or compelled to step aside in Guildford's favour. This could have been on the understanding that he received the reversion to the superior position of treasurer. That became vacant on the death of Sir Thomas Lovell in 1522, when Boleyn was duly appointed in his place.[34] At the same time he was pursuing the marriage negotiation between Anne and James Butler. James was resident at the English court at the time, but it was no use trying to put pressure on him, because it was his father who was in control, and in September 1520 the King himself wrote to the Earl of Surrey, the Lord Deputy in Ireland, urging the expediency of the match and offering to 'advance the matter' with Sir Thomas. Surrey replied to Wolsey on 6 October, agreeing about the advantages of the match, but referring to Sir Piers as the Earl of Ormond, which must have given the cardinal pause for thought.[35] Meanwhile, Margaret Boleyn, Sir Thomas and Elizabeth his wife were granted a pardon in September 1520 for the alienation of Fritwell manor in Oxfordshire, a parcel of the Ormond estate, which suggests that the legal status of the lands was still unsettled. As late as November 1521 Wolsey could write to the King about the desirability of the marriage, and offering to talk to him about the matter 'on his return', because he was in Bruges at the time.[36] Whether Anne herself had been consulted at this stage is unclear, because her residence in France might have made that difficult. It was a delicate matter to be entrusted to paper, and as far as we know she was not written to upon the subject. All that was about to change, because Sir Thomas was well enough aware that Wolsey's negotiations in Bruges had resulted in a treaty with the Emperor committing Henry to war with France in 1522. In January, Francis wrote suspiciously to his envoys in England that 'the English scholars have returned home, and also the daughter of Mr. Bullen'. Something was clearly brewing, and Sir Thomas had retrieved Anne about Christmas 1521.[37] There would now be a chance for her to express herself directly about the Butler marriage proposal, and the indications are that she did not like what she saw.

In May 1521 Sir Thomas served on the juries for London and Kent which had indicted the Duke of Buckingham of high treason, which was not any particular indication of favour, but simply that he was regarded as a safe pair of hands. In September he returned to his favourite occupation when he was sent on mission to the Emperor in preparation for Wolsey's trip to Bruges, and stayed to take part in those discussions, which is how he came to know about the intention to make war before the King of France was aware of it. However, the preparations for war hung fire. Henry was short of money, and Scotland was again causing concern, so apart from a plundering expedition by the Earl of Surrey against Brittany, nothing was done.[38] In May the Emperor came on a visit, ostensibly one of goodwill, but in fact to assess the situation in England and the reasons for the delay. Sir Thomas was among those who welcomed him at Canterbury, and was a signatory of the agreement eventually concluded on 20 June, whereby Charles acknowledged that there would be no English campaign in 1522, and Henry renewed his commitment to hostilities in 1523. At the end of August Sir Thomas followed the Emperor back to the continent, where he had the unenviable task of trying to keep Charles in a good mood while Henry struggled with his financial problems.[39] In that he was no doubt aided by the breakdown in relations between Francis I and one of his chief vassals, the Duke of Bourbon, which resulted in the Duke putting out feelers to the Anglo-Imperial alliance. Unfortunately, his chief need was for money, and that neither Henry nor Charles was in a position to supply. In March 1523 Sir Thomas and Richard Samson, his colleague in the mission, followed Charles to Spain, but on 6 May the former was recalled, an event which attracted a letter of commendation from the Emperor to Cardinal Wolsey.[40] At least by the time of his return Bourbon's pretensions had become sufficiently convincing to persuade Henry that he must make a supreme effort to return to the continent in military guise before the year was out. Meanwhile, he may have been raised to the peerage. A letter from Richard Hales to Lord Darcy, dated 28 April 1523 states unequivocally that in the parliament then sitting Sir Arthur Plantagenet had been created Viscount Lisle, and Boleyn, with several others had been made barons.[41] Unfortunately, there is no confirmatory evidence for that, and he continued to be referred to as Sir Thomas, even in official documents until 1525.

Following up Boleyn's efforts, at the end of June the ambassador in the Low Countries was instructed to contact Bourbon and to offer him an English subsidy in return for a joint campaign. This was just what Charles had been pressing for, and at the end of August the Duke of Suffolk led an army of some 10,000 men out from the Calais Pale as England's contribution to the united effort. Henry Jerningham, Sir Thomas's replacement in Spain, did not arrive until late July, and in reporting this to the King, Wolsey observed that the Emperor was planning an expedition against Langedoc in support of Bourbon, which was not at all the kind of collaboration that Henry had in mind.[42] Whether Jerningham was right or not, the Imperial thrust from the east towards Paris, which Suffolk was expecting, never materialised, and Bourbon, of whom great things were expected, similarly failed to show up. This left the Anglo-Burgundian army in the north to its own devices, and faced with heavy French mobilisation north of Paris, they decided to retreat. By the time that they reached this decision, they had crossed the Seine and encountered only sporadic resistance, but it was already October and in view of the lateness of the season, it was the only rational decision to make. Even so, they got caught in a ferocious cold snap during November, which must have been one of the worst freezes of the century. Men and horses died of the cold, and others lost fingers and toes to frostbite – not at all the kind of conditions one expects in northern France before the turn of the year.[43] The Burgundians simply went home, and discipline collapsed. Having led out a well equipped fighting force, the Duke of Suffolk returned at the head of a demoralised rabble, which shipped itself back to England in dribs and drabs as shipping became available. Henry was both distressed and annoyed by this debacle, which had cost him money which he could not afford, but he did not blame the Duke. The Emperor was responsible and relations between the allies became frosty. However, his mood fluctuated, and by Christmas he was upbeat again, talking of a new campaign by Bourbon, and of leading an army to France in person. He was, reported the Spanish ambassador, confident that he could conquer the northern provinces of France – even as far as Paris – irrespective of what the Emperor might do.[44] However, as 1524 wore on, nothing happened, and unofficial peace feelers from France were even entertained. The problem, as Wolsey knew full well, was money. He had attempted to get a double subsidy out of the 1523 parliament, but had been forced to settle for a single one, and that spread out over two years. Even the subsidy to that most useless of allies the Duke of Bourbon, had had to be borrowed on the Antwerp market. Henry was in no position to lead an army royal to France, no matter how belligerent he might be feeling.

Sir Thomas Boleyn had contributed in a small way to this stand-off between the allies, because when he returned from Spain, he had been accompanied by some kind of special envoy from Charles. This person, whose name was Bewreyn, cannot have been an official ambassador, because if he had been he would have gone straight to court, presented his credentials and been assigned accommodation. Instead he was apparently abandoned by Boleyn in London, and left to find his own lodgings. Not surprisingly, he complained, and when Jerningham wrote to the Duke of Suffolk in October, he passed on these complaints.[45] It seems that the ambassador felt bound to tell someone, but was reluctant to be thought bearing tales to Wolsey against one so high in the King's favour. It may be that Sir Thomas felt that Bewreyn had been foisted on him, and felt no responsibility for him. The whole episode is mysterious, because Boleyn clearly lost no favour as a result. Shortly after the complaint was lodged he received £100 towards the expenses of his mission, and livery of the lands of Anne Tempest, whose wardship he had been granted. By the beginning of 1524 Sir Thomas was a very rich man. When the household was assessed for the subsidy in February, he was rated as treasurer on lands, wages and fees at £1,100.[46] This was to place him in the same league as the major nobility. By comparison, the Comptroller of the Household, Sir Henry Guildford, was assessed at £300. In December 1524 he appears for the first time on the commission of the peace for Sussex, an indication of how far his landed interests then extended.

In spite of his poverty, and of the peace negotiations which were quietly going ahead, news of the war continued to provoke moods of belligerence in Henry. In August, when the Duke of Bourbon appeared (at last) to be making some progress, he started talking again about an invasion, and of sweeping up the Rhone to link up with the Duke. It all fizzled out because Charles was not ready for any quick action, and because his own ministers were reluctant, having heard these outbursts before, but it should serve to warn us that Henry had not given up on the war, and still saw himself riding in triumph into Paris – a feat which not even Henry V had achieved.[47] Consequently when Charles won his stunning victory at Pavia in February 1525, and captured Francis in the process, his ambitions were immediately rekindled. Let the allies seize their opportunity, and partition the leaderless kingdom. Charles could take what provinces he liked, Bourbon's patrimony could be resurrected, and Henry would take the rest, as lawful King of France. Unfortunately the Emperor was unmoved by such extravagance. He had achieved his objective and would be able to squeeze a favourable treaty out of his captive. He had no money for further campaigning, and if Henry wanted to take advantage of the situation, then by all means let him do so – on his own.[48] The King was mortified, and extremely angry, but he recognised defeat when he saw it, and Sir Thomas Boleyn was no longer in Madrid or Brussels to soften the blow. However, he did the only rational thing, and resurrected the peace process with France, finding the Queen Mother's regency government only too willing to respond. Wolsey, and probably Boleyn, were relieved by this change of mood, because since Pavia it no longer made sense to be on the same side as so great a power as the Emperor had now become. Better by far to come to terms with France, and even to help her to modify the adverse treaty which Charles was bound to extract. In August 1525 a treaty was signed to that effect at the More, Wolsey's residence in Hertfordshire, and Sir Thomas Boleyn was one of the English signatories.[49] It was just as well that a settlement had been reached, because Henry's finances were going from bad to worse. In March, Wolsey had tried to raise an 'Amicable Grant' on the basis of the subsidy assessments of 1523, the idea being to bypass the parliament which had been so obstructive in that year. Whether Sir Thomas approved of this levy or not we do not know, but as a councillor and treasurer of the Household he cannot escape a share of the responsibility. He was one of the commissioners named to collect the Grant in Kent, and one of the eighty commissioners who gathered in Canterbury on 2–3 May to report the difficulties that they were having.[50] Many of those assessed at £20 or more had come in professing their willingness to pay, or to serve the King in many other ways, but alleging that they simply did not have the money. Warham, the Archbishop of Canterbury, Lord Cobham, Sir Henry Guildford and Sir Thomas Boleyn wrote a number of letters to Wolsey, making their case. The concessions already granted to London had done nothing, they pointed out, to make the situation in Kent any easier. It grew tense as the protesters turned out in force to make their point. Lord Cobham sent one man to the Tower for his evil words, and Sir Thomas Boleyn was roughly treated by an assembly at Maidstone.[51] It was, the Duke of Norfolk reported, 'almost a rebellion', and in the event the King backed down, initially making concessions and finally cancelling the demand altogether. Wolsey, who had been the main manager of the business, loyally took the blame for this fiasco, but in fact it was the King who was responsible, and he learned a salutary lesson. The 'taxpayers strike' of 1525 demonstrated one of the limitations upon his power. It was all very well to claim that he was answerable only to God, when it came to money, the commons were in the driving seat. Forced loans were illegal, and this did not even pretend to be a loan. The Cardinal's credit with the King was undoubtedly shaken by these events, but they seem to have done Sir Thomas no harm at all. In the midst of the crisis, in April 1525 he was appointed to yet another office of profit, this time the stewardship of the lordship of Swaffham in Norfolk, which was part of the honour of Richmond.[52] His father had been a client of the first Duke of Norfolk, and later of the Earl of Surrey who became the second Duke in 1514. However, the third Duke, who succeeded to the title in 1524, was his brother-in-law, a friend and ally rather than a master, and in terms of their estates they must have been well nigh equal.

Henry spent a fair part of 1525 trying to get his mind straight. Rebuffed by the Emperor, he made peace with France. Rebuffed by his own subjects, he cancelled the Amicable Grant. Frustrated in his attempts to get a male heir, he convinced himself that his marriage had offended against the laws of God, and began to contemplate his options for the succession. One possibility was to legitimate the son whom Bessy Blount had borne him. Henry Fitzroy had always been acknowledged, and had been brought up in a quasi-royal establishment apart from his mother. Now the King decided to ennoble him and on 18 June in a well publicised ceremony, created him first Earl of Nottingham and then Duke of Richmond and Somerset.[53] There is no conclusive evidence that the King ever intended to include him in the succession, and it may have been that his elevation had more to do with Wolsey's plans for governing the 'dark corners' of the land than with any plan of Henry's. The child was soon despatched to the north of England with a suitable council to govern in the king's name, but his headship was purely nominal, and the person to whom that council answered was Wolsey. At about the same time his nine-year-old sister, Mary, was sent to the Welsh Marches, similarly equipped and for the same purpose.[54] However, Richmond was a royal title and the gesture was a significant one. Other peerage creations and promotions at the same time are equally suggestive. Henry Brandon, his nephew and the son of the Duke of Suffolk, was created Earl of Lincoln, the title born by John de la Pole, Richard III's designated heir. Henry Courtenay, his cousin, was promoted from the earldom of Devon to the marquisate of Exeter, and Thomas Boleyn was created Viscount Rochford. There is nothing in the contemporary record to suggest that Henry was doing any more than honouring his chosen favourites, but all in different ways proposed answers to the succession dilemma. It is a little early to imagine that Thomas Boleyn was being identified as the father of a potential alternative to Catherine, but the chronology of the King's relationship with Anne is highly uncertain, and in any case he was certainly the father of Henry's last mistress. Henry appears to have parted with Mary Boleyn on amicable terms, and that may have been in no small part due to Thomas's calming influence. In any case Sir Thomas (or possibly Lord Boleyn) had long since earned his promotion by years of diligent and effective service. He was also one of the first peers created whose elevation owed nothing to their lineage and everything to their function at court, in diplomacy and in administration. In spite of his wife's connections, he was a new man. A few months later Lord Rochford and Elizabeth his wife were assigned lodgings in the King's house 'when they repair to it', a privilege which only those close to the King could ever hope to enjoy.[55]

# 3

# MARY & THE KING'S FANCY –
# IN & OUT OF FAVOUR

Mary was the oldest of Sir Thomas's three children, born probably in 1499. There is no concrete evidence for this, but nearly a century later in 1597 her grandson George, the second Lord Hunsdon, petitioned for the Boleyn earldom of Ormonde on the grounds that Mary was the oldest child.[1] Circumstantial but convincing evidence points to a birth date for Anne in 1501 and for George in 1504, so that indicates 1499, or possibly 1500, as the relevant date for Mary. Lord Hunsdon is unlikely to have been mistaken since the daughter of her sister Anne was none other than the Queen herself, who would have had a prior claim if Anne had been the elder. George Carey's petition was unsuccessful, but that was for other reasons. There has been over the years a great deal of controversy about the respective ages of the Boleyn siblings. George Cavendish, for example, a near contemporary source, makes George the eldest, and he was followed recently by Philippa Gregory in her fictional reconstruction of Mary's life, *The Other Boleyn Girl*. However, Eric Ives sets out the evidence for the order adopted here persuasively, and he has been followed very recently by George Bernard, so I have taken the scholarly consensus.[2]

It is not known where she was born. Tradition says Hever Castle in Kent, and that is probably right because her grandfather William was Sheriff of Norfolk in 1499, and therefore likely to have been resident at Blickling. Both Thomas and Elizabeth were much about the court over the next few years, but it is not known whether their children were with them. Nothing is known of Mary's upbringing or education except what can be deduced from her later life. She was literate, and presumably numerate, but never followed her father's and sister's gift for languages. Nor did she correspond with the learned, or exchange ideas with humanist divines. Her books, if she ever had any, have been long since dispersed and were never recorded. She was not intellectually precocious, and the chances are that she was trained mainly in those domestic and courtly accomplishments which would have made her an attractive bride for some aspiring courtier. At the age of about fifteen, when her father secured for her a place among the ladies accompanying the King's sister Mary to France, she was probably already known about the court.[3] She was pretty, and had perhaps already begun to attract attention in an undesirable way, so Sir Thomas may well have felt that a few years in the well-chaperoned entourage of the Queen of France would provide a safe environment in which she could finish growing up. If such was his thinking, he was disappointed because King Louis lasted only a matter of weeks. Moreover, immediately after his wedding he had taken the precaution of dismissing some of his wife's more senior attendants on the ground that they were interfering in the relationship.[4] Mistress Boleyn was one of those retained, but it is likely that her intended chaperone was not, and that left the girl rather more exposed than she should have been. Queen Mary, who at eighteen was not very much older than her namesake, was similarly exposed, and quickly found refuge in the arms of Charles Brandon, the Duke of Suffolk, whom Henry had sent to bring her home. After 1 January 1515, Mary Boleyn may therefore have witnessed more sexual manoeuvring than was good for her. It is possible that the ex-Queen took the initiative in her relationship with Brandon, and having got him into bed, left him with no option but to marry her. It is also possible that King Francis, who was a notorious womaniser, was fishing in that same pool, and that Mary acted to forestall him. The evidence as to what happened is conflicting, because according to one story Henry had anticipated and approved some such outcome, while another version has the King seriously put out by his friend's effrontery.[5] The truth seems to have been that Henry had extracted from Brandon a promise that he would do nothing until the couple were back on English soil, and that it was the breaking of that promise which caused his anger. King Francis, whose intentions (if they ever existed) were strictly dishonourable, seems to have approved of the match, and even to have expected it; but he was anxious to prevent Henry from deploying his sister on the international market, and that may have contributed to Henry's annoyance.[6]

Sir Thomas, however, was not to be deterred. He had sent his daughter to France to learn some courtly polish in a reasonably safe environment, and when that household turned out to be anything but safe, he withdrew her. When the King's sister, now the Duchess of Suffolk, returned to England in May 1515, Mary Boleyn did not accompany her. With her sister Anne, who had joined her in the Queen's service sometime before Christmas, she was transferred to the household of the new Queen of France, Claude, who was a girl of exactly her age.[7] This argues extraordinary favour, because the competition for such places among the French nobility would have been fierce. Either Francis was impressed by Sir Thomas, who he can scarcely have met, or he was impressed by Mary, and the latter is more likely. A few years later, a Venetian envoy described Sir Thomas as 'much hated' at the French court because he was suspected of retailing information to the Archduchess Margaret, although there is no hint of that in Francis's correspondence with Henry.[8] Claude's chamber, in short, was anything but a safe place for a young girl to be. The Queen was enduring annual pregnancies and was unavailable to her husband for long periods of time. We do not know that Francis amused himself with her attendants in consequence, but it is a reasonable assumption. Anne quickly learned to fend off these unwelcome attentions, but Mary may have been less successful. Rightly or wrongly she acquired a reputation for easy virtue, '*per una grandissima ribaldaa et infame sopre butte*', as one observer put it, and her father read the warning signs.[9] If she was to secure an acceptable marriage, either in France or in England, such reports could do her inestimable harm. So at some point, probably before his next diplomatic mission in 1519, he called her home. He seems to have acted in time, because rumours of her misdemeanours had not yet crossed the Channel, and he was able to secure a place for her in the strait-laced chamber of Queen Catherine. Catherine had been recently forced to endure her husband's infidelity with Elizabeth Blount, and had been shamed by the birth of her son, probably in July of that year, so it is unlikely that she would have been wanting to put more temptation in his way. Perhaps he pressed her to accept Mary, or perhaps not. Probably Sir Thomas exercised his charms on the Queen, or, even more likely, his wife Elizabeth, who had been a member of that charmed circle for a number of years, persuaded Catherine to accept her daughter. By 4 February 1520 she was well enough established to be married, her groom being William Carey, an up and coming member of the King's Privy Chamber, and the King was the principal guest at their wedding.[10]

These facts have caused endless speculation about the nature of Mary's relations with the King. That she later became his mistress is authenticated by Henry's own admission, but it is usually thought that that did not happen until 1522, when the beginning of a number of grants to William Carey indicate a special interest in his wife. Mary used her influence to get Thomas Gardiner appointed to the priory of Tynemouth, but that is an event which cannot be securely dated.[11] It did not happen before 1520, but then Mary was not in a position to exercise any influence until the latter part of 1519. She took part in a number of courtly entertainments in 1520 and 1521, but that proves nothing beyond the fact that she was a well-established lady of the court. She also accompanied the Queen to the Field of Cloth of Gold in the summer of 1520, but there is no record of what she may have done there, apart from assisting the Duchess of Suffolk by looking decorative. The first indication that she might have been in any way special comes on Shrove Tuesday 1522, in the Burgundian style masque of the assault on the Chateau Verte. The King's sister in the guise of *Beauty*, led the defenders, among whom Mary featured in the significant role of *Kindness*. Her sister Anne, then newly returned to England, also took part as *Perseverence,* but it has been rightly commented that Mary's designation was the more suggestive.[12] If Mary was sharing the royal bed in 1522 and 1523, then she must have had some contraceptive knowledge, which no well brought up young lady was supposed to possess. Henry had inflicted well nigh annual pregnancies on Catherine between 1509 and 1518, and another on Bessy Blount in the latter year. So whatever may have happened later, there is no reason to suppose that in the early 1520s, the King's potency was any the less. Yet Mary survived anything between three and five years as the royal mistress without becoming pregnant. Where she had learned this art is another matter, but presumably in France, where those adventures which had earned her a reputation may also have taught her a lot about ways in which to manage her body. Henry may well have been mystified, because this was a skill which only whores were supposed to possess. On the other hand, he may not have cared, because another bastard was not going to solve the succession problem which was increasingly gnawing away at his mind.[13]

Mistress Carey's charms may have faded, or been replaced by those of her sister, but the indications are that Mary was handed over to her husband at some point in the summer of 1525. Her son, Henry Carey, was born on 4 March 1526, and that suggests that she began to sleep with William at some time in June or July of 1525. Although it was soon being suggested that Henry was the King's son, those tales came from the anti-Boleyn political camp of the 1530s and need not be taken too seriously.[14] If there had been any doubt at the time about Henry's paternity, there was no reason why the King should not have claimed him. He had just made a great fuss of ennobling his only acknowledged bastard, Henry Fitzroy, and would no doubt have been willing to do as much for a second – if one had appeared. The token which Mary did leave to the King was not a child but a ship. The *Mary Boleyn* was a vessel of 100 tons, which was deployed in the Irish Sea in September 1523, and appears to have been a royal ship which the King had named after his mistress. Unfortunately, no such ship appears in the King's inventories of the time; the only vessel of 100 tons in service with the navy was the *Katherine Pleasaunce*, which had been built in 1518. We are therefore left with the intriguing possibility that Henry renamed a ship originally called after his wife in honour of his mistress![15] More mundanely it is possible that the *Mary Boleyn* belonged to Sir Thomas, and had been 'taken up' for some particular service in Irish waters. The records do not make this clear, and the *Katherine Plesaunce* goes on being mentioned down to 1525. From 1526 onwards Mary is overshadowed by her sister Anne, and glimpses of her in the records become few. She must have spent quite a lot of her time on pregnancy leave, because a few months after Henry's birth she had conceived again, and bore William's second child, a daughter Catherine, at some time in 1527. Then in the summer of 1528, the sweating sickness visited the court. Henry immediately panicked, as was his wont in such situations. Anne was sent down to her father's house at Hever, where she and Sir Thomas both fell ill, but recovered. The King took himself off into the country, moving his lodging frequently to avoid infection, and somehow or other escaped. William Carey was less fortunate, and on 28 June 1528 he died.[16]

William, although he has only a walk-on role in this context, was a person of consequence in his own right. Born in 1500, he was the son of Thomas Carey of Chilton Foliot, Wiltshire, and a grandson of Sir William, an eminent Lancastrian who had been beheaded after the battle of Tewksbury in 1471. His mother had been Margaret, a granddaughter of Edmund Beaufort, first Duke of Somerset, and he was thus a very distant kinsman of the King.[17] He appeared at court as a protégé of the Earl of Devon, some time about 1515 or 1516, and seems to have been a formidable tennis player. It may have been this quality which attracted the King's attention because he became a founder member of the Privy Chamber, and was well enough placed to marry Mary, as we have seen. Perhaps the King already had his eye on her, because their marriage was morganatic for the first five years. William was rewarded with grants of land from the King in 1522, 1523, 1524 and 1525, so he died possessed of a considerable estate in addition to his patrimony.[18] These lands would have been inherited by his two-year-old son, Henry, who became a ward of the Crown. Mary seems to have passed into limbo, because at some time before December 1529 his wardship was granted to his aunt Anne, who would consequently have enjoyed the profits of the estate, and what provision she made for her sister is not known. In December 1531 Mary Carey was granted an annuity of £100 out of the Treasury of the Chamber, which suggests that she was suffering a degree of hardship.[19] Anne may have conceded the right to educate and bring up Henry and Catherine to Mary on an unofficial basis, because there is no sign of her having sold or otherwise disposed of the wardship, but the relationship between the two women can hardly have been an easy one, particularly while Anne was so high in favour. Over the next two or three years Mary can be glimpsed as a member of her sister's entourage, in which capacity she no doubt attended Anne's creation as Marquis of Pembroke in September 1532, and she certainly accompanied her when she went with the King to Calais in October. What she may have done there can only be conjectured, but she took part in the masked dance which followed Anne's ceremonial entry at the banquet on 28 October, when she was one of the six 'gorgeously apparelled [ladies] with visors on their faces who came and took the French king, and the other Lords of France by the hand; and danced a dance or two ...' However, after the masquing was over 'they departed to their lodgings' and we are told no more.[20]

This is a pity, because it was probably at Calais that she first met a dashing young man named William Stafford, who was then an officer of the garrison there. Stafford was the second son of Sir Humphrey Stafford of Blatherwick, Northants., and was a distant kinsman of the last Duke of Buckingham. He seems to have been quite a lot younger than the thirty-three-year-old Mary, probably

about twenty.[21] At any rate, she fell in love, and he followed her
back to England, where he became a hanger on at court, and was
a servitor at Anne Boleyn's coronation. Mary seems to have taken
the initiative in their relationship, because Stafford at this point is
a shadowy figure, seen mainly in the light of her opinion. Early in
1534 she became pregnant by him, and they were secretly married.
For some reason this caused mortal offence to her family. Anne
was particularly alienated, although whether by her extra-marital
pregnancy or by the marriage which followed it is not apparent.
As the Queen's sister, Mary should have gained official permission
for this marriage, and that she clearly failed to do so may have
been the cause of the angst. Anne may well have felt that, having
survived several years in the King's bed, her decision to conceive
at this point was a statement of some kind. The Queen, who was
pregnant herself in the spring of 1534, may also have felt betrayed
when her sister had to withdraw from attendance on her due to
her own condition. An Imperial report of December 1534 declares
that 'the Lady's sister was ... banished from Court about three
months ago ... because she had been found guilty of misconduct
...'[22] William Stafford, for all his exalted kindred, seems to have
been thought unworthy to marry a Boleyn. Her annuity of £100 a
year was cancelled, and Anne withdrew whatever favour she had
extended in respect of the children. So distressed was Mary by
these rejections that she wrote to Thomas Cromwell in December,
lamenting her plight and begging for his assistance. Her husband
was young, and did not deserve so much disfavour. She saw much
honesty in him, and he loved her as truly as she did him. 'For well
I might have had a greater man of birth and a higher, but I assure
you that I could never have had one that should have loved me so
well nor a more honest man ...' Her problem, she implied, was not

with the King but with her family. Not only was Anne rigorously against her, but her brother and her uncle the Duke of Norfolk were 'very cruel' as well.[23] She did not name her father, but the suggestion is that he shared the family's aversion.

Cromwell appears to have done his best. The King wrote to the Earl of Wiltshire inviting him to make suitable provision for his daughter, being, presumably, unwilling to offend Anne by doing so himself. It is not clear that anything happened immediately, but after the catastrophic fall of Anne and George in May 1536, the remaining Boleyns were reconciled and Thomas allowed Mary and her husband the use of Rochford Hall in Essex, which was part of his estate.[24] The wardship of Henry and Catherine would have reverted to the Crown on Anne Boleyn's attainder, and was regranted to Mary. On 3 April 1537 the Prior of Tynemouth wrote to Cromwell, begging permission to cancel the annuity of 100 marks which she had been granted for obtaining the preferment of his predecessor, because 'the said lady can now deserve no such annuity as she can do no good for me or my house ...' But this somewhat pusillanimous request was clearly refused, and the annuity went on being paid – at least it was paid out of Augmentations after the Priory was dissolved.[25] Between 1539 and 1542 Mary inherited most of her father's lands, albeit in trust for her son, including Rochford Hall. It was William who obtained in 1541 a licence to alienate the manor of High Roding in Essex, but this did not take effect, presumably because his wife objected. Nor did the Staffords go on being frozen out of the court. 'Young Stafford that married my lady Cary' was one of those gentlemen appointed to attend of Anne of Cleves when she arrived to marry King Henry in January 1540, while Catherine Carey, then aged thirteen, was named among the ladies of the new Queen's Privy

Chamber.[26] Mary was now at last in control of William Carey's estate, and she and her husband disposed of quite a lot of it by sale over the years 1539 to 1543. In October 1542 they were pardoned for having alienated 700 acres at Fulborne in Cambridgeshire without license.[27] Although Mary did not occupy any position in the Queen's chamber, William Stafford was a gentleman Pensioner by 1540, and a Esquire of the Body by 1541. He was also named to lead 100 footmen in the 'army for Flanders' which was notionally assembled in July 1543, and actually served in the Boulogne campaign of the following year, when he was accompanied by six men.[28] Intriguingly, a William Stafford, who was probably the same man, was imprisoned in the Fleet in April of that year for having eaten meat in Lent. This William Stafford was discharged by the council on 1 May, and his brush with the law does not seem to have done him any harm at all. Presumably his evangelical attitude was sympathetically regarded by the dominant party.[29] This modest level of favour continued and in May 1543 he and his wife were granted livery of the lands of Margaret Boleyn, deceased, who was Mary's grandmother, and had outlived her son and grandson. Mary's son, Henry, being still underage, the lands were allowed to come to her. At the same time the Staffords received livery of the lands of Jane Rochford, George's widow, who had been executed in 1542 and whose possessions were in the hands of the Crown by virtue of her attainder.[30] Perhaps the Duke of Norfolk was now reconciled to her marriage, because someone was looking after their interests, and it was not Thomas Cromwell, who had fallen to the executioners axe in 1540. At some point before July 1543 Mary, but not her husband, was granted the wardship of William Bailey, together with lands in Wiltshire, Kent and Hertfordshire.[31]

Mary died at Rochford Hall in July 1543, and the legal position in respect of her estate appears to have been exceedingly complex. Lands held jointly with William remained to him, but those which were in her name alone reverted to the Crown, together with the wardship of Henry and Catherine, who were seventeen and fifteen respectively at that point. Catherine may already have been married to Sir Francis Knollys, because her wardship does not feature in the records, and Henry was taken into the royal household, where he appears in 1545. Presumably his estates were released to him at about that time. As might be expected from his brush with the Act of Six Articles, William emerged as a Protestant once Henry was dead, and warmly supported the policy of the new Protector, the Duke of Somerset. He had by that time acquired something of a reputation as a soldier, having served in 1544 as a member of the Royal Household. He also went briefly to Scotland in 1545, in a punitive raid which the Earl of Hertford (as Somerset then was) had launched in September. On the 23rd of that month he was knighted.[32] As a known supporter of the regime, Somerset found a place for him in the parliament of 1547, in which he sat for the borough of Hastings – a town with which he had no known connection. At the age of about thirty-five, his career was taking off, and from 1548 to 1553 he served as Standard Bearer of the Gentlemen Pensioners, a position of some standing in the court. Nevertheless he seems to have gone on selling lands, because in February 1544 Sir John Gresham and Sir John Williams were granted lands in Kent 'lately held by William Stafford and Mary his wife', which had been purchased by the King. In 1545 he was released of a debt of 200 marks to the Crown, which also suggests continued financial difficulties, as well as the favour which was already developing.[33] At some time between 1545 and 1550 he married again, his second wife being Dorothy, the daughter of Henry Stafford, first Lord Stafford, and hence a distant kinswoman, who presented him with three sons to continue his line. Dorothy was also a daughter of Ursula Pole, granddaughter of George, Duke of Clarence, so these sons would have had a distant claim to the throne. The child which Mary had been carrying in 1534 presumably died, and his first wife may well have been too old to conceive again. In 1551 he was sufficiently well known to accompany the Marquis of Northampton when he went to France to bestow the Order of the Garter on King Henry. As late as 24 June 1554 he was paid £900 in respect of his services; services which presumably dated back to before July 1553.[34]

Sir William was distinctly uncomfortable with the restored Catholicism of Mary's reign, and when it became obvious that persecution was looming, at the beginning of 1555, he quitted the realm without license and went with his extended household to Geneva, where he was received as a resident on 29 March. Apparently he soon became embroiled in the politics of the city, and was set upon and almost killed in the aftermath of the May rising of that year, for which reason he was shortly thereafter permitted to wear a sword. When the English congregation was organised on 1 November 1555, William and his household became members, and his son John, to whom Calvin stood as godfather, was the first child to be baptised there on 4 January 1556.[35] He must presumably have had an agent or agents in England to make sure that the revenues of at least some of his lands reached him in exile, because an establishment of some half a dozen people, with their servants, would have been expensive to maintain. He had lost his position as Standard Bearer of the Gentlemen Pensioners at the beginning of the reign, but was presumably one of those who benefited when a government bill for the confiscation of the property of all such exiles, as he was defeated in the House of Commons in November 1555. The Privy Council was sufficiently interested in him to attempt to prevent other money from reaching him 'by exchange or otherwise' in May 1556, but by the time that order was enforced (if it was), Sir William was dead. He died on 5 May 1556, and after a quarrel with his brother over the custody of young John, Dorothy withdrew to Basle, taking the child with her. She was received as a burgher of her newly adopted city on 3 November 1557.[36] She returned to England in January 1559, to an appointment as Elizabeth's Mistress of the Robes, and died at a very advanced age in 1607.

Whether Mary had been in any way sympathetic to William's nascent Protestantism we do not know. That could have explained the hostility of the Duke of Norfolk, and even of the Earl of Wiltshire to her marriage, but is unlikely to account for the animosity of Anne or of Lord Rochford. In fact very little is known for certain about Mary as a person. Her surviving letters are few, and almost all relate to business. She seems to have been a woman steered by her emotions rather than by her intellect, and that may have been why Henry tired of her in the summer of 1525. Although reputed beautiful she seems to have been somewhat vapid as a person, and the scholarly and artistic accomplishments of the French court made little impression upon her. Once Henry had discarded her, she showed few of the skills necessary for survival in that context, and depended first on the goodwill of Thomas Cromwell and after on the tolerance of the Duke of Norfolk. We do not even know how good she was as a manager either of men or of money, because the signs left in the records are ambiguous. It is perhaps significant that William's career only appears to have gained momentum after her death. In the context of the Boleyn story she is important first as a foil for her sister, and secondly as the means by which the Boleyn genes were transmitted into the seventeenth century and beyond.

# 4

# ANNE & THE GRAND PASSION – THE PARIS YEARS

Anne was the first of the Boleyn girls to leave home. Her father had got on exceptionally well with the Regent, Margaret of Austria, during his diplomatic mission to the Low Countries in 1512–13, and had managed to secure for his daughter a place as one of Margaret's eighteen *filles d'honneur*. When he returned to England in the early summer of 1513 therefore, Anne was promptly despatched under the care of one of the Regent's Esquires, Claude Bouton. The Regent's first impressions were favourable, and she wrote: 'I find her so bright and pleasant for her young age that I am more beholden to you for sending her to me than you are to me …'[1]

At twelve, Anne may well have been the youngest of her attendants, but Margaret had other young charges to care for and employed a tutor named Symonnet to look after them and teach them their letters. Anne began to write in French at the dictation of her tutors, and then wrote independently to her father, expressing all the right sentiments, but in a language which was more idiomatic than accurate. As Eric Ives has observed, she really did need to work on her written French, however fluently she may have spoken it. Sir Thomas had obviously set out some guidelines for her, and Anne responded:

'... you desire me to be a woman of good reputation when I come to court, and you tell me that the queen will take the trouble to converse with me ... This will make me all the keener to persevere in speaking French well ...'[2]

The objective was clearly to give her a head start at the English court, and how long her sojourn in Mechelen was intended to last is uncertain. Probably the intention was to bring her home after two or three years, when she would have been ripe for the marriage market. The Regent's court was the great exemplum of the Burgundian tradition, and the finest place in Europe to learn deportment.

So Anne would have learned a lot, apart from improving her French. The elaborate dances which occupied such an important place in court festivities and entertainments would have been on the curriculum. A court presided over by a woman was expected to make much of the courtly love tradition, and the chivalric traditions flourished there. The pageants featured imprisoned damsels, noble knights (to rescue them), wild men, mythical beasts and ships in full sail, each with its point to make in the subtle diplomacy of the renaissance.[3] So Anne would have learned the bass dance, that graceful staple of courtly revels, how to play a number of musical instruments, and how to conduct that game of artificial flirtation which was expected of all the maidens at the court. Margaret was a rigid chaperone, and was much concerned that these games did not get out of hand. They were to be played in strict accordance with the conventions, and any genuine by-play with the gentlemen of the court was strictly forbidden. At thirty-three the Regent was an old hand in these arts, and quite capable of expressing her views in graceful verse:

Trust in those who offer you service,

And in the end, my maidens,

You will find yourselves in the ranks of those

Who have been deceived ...[4]

The remedy lay in a quick wit:

Fine words are the coin to pay back

Those presumptuous minions

Who ape the lover ...

So Anne learned to flirt, not with her body, but with words
and gestures in a manner which would have been well enough
understood by those who approached her with tokens and looks
of love. Margaret's original training had been in France, where she
had been sent at the age of three as the intended bride of Charles
VIII. However, in 1491 Charles had decided to marry Anne, the
heiress of Brittany, and at the age of eleven, Margaret had been
returned to the Low Countries, where Maximilian had arranged
tutors to continue her education.[5] Her background has therefore
been described as 'Franco-Flemish', although there were no strains
between the two cultures. Brief spells in Spain and in Savoy did
nothing to disturb that orientation, and when she returned to
the Low Countries as regent after the Archduke Philip's death in
1506, she established her court at Mechelen in that mould. Her
palace was resplendent with tapestries and with rich fabrics of all
kinds, and the finest artists and calligraphers also displayed their
work there. Music, both in its sacred and its secular forms was
cherished, and the best composers of the day were patronised; so
Anne would have learned the most discriminating taste in every

aspect of courtly life, while preserving the 'precious jewel' of her chastity.[6] In her turn, she made an impression which lasted many years. Lancelot de Carles later recorded:

> la Boullant, who at an early age had come to court, listened carefully to honourable ladies, setting herself to bend all her endeavour to imitate them to perfection, and made such good use of her wits that in no time at all she had command of the language ...[7]

Altogether a better start for an ambitious damsel would be hard to imagine.

Anne also seems to have made herself useful, because on 30 June, not very long after her arrival, Henry VIII arrived at Calais at the beginning of the campaign which would culminate in the taking of Tournai on 23 September. His allies, the Emperor Maximilian and the Archduchess Margaret, needed to keep in touch with him, and English speakers were at a premium, so there is every chance that Mistress Boleyn was called into service as an interpreter. When Margaret joined the victors at Lille in September to celebrate their success, she was certainly accompanied by her ladies, and there Anne would have had a chance for a brief reunion with her father, who had accompanied the King.[8] At first Henry had every intention of renewing hostilities in 1514, but in the course of the spring he changed his mind. The Holy League was falling apart, because not only had Ferdinand defected, but the Pope was now pressing for peace. So a treaty was signed in August which had serious implications for Anglo-Burgundian relations. Henry's sister Mary was committed to marry the fourteen-year-old Charles of Ghent, Maximilian's grandson and Margaret's nephew, by the terms of their alliance. Now she was suddenly switched to the fifty-two-year-old Louis XII. Her own feelings were not consulted, and Margaret was seriously offended. Sir Thomas Boleyn may well have felt that the court at Mechelen would be an uncomfortable place in future for a young English girl, and he took advantage of the creation of a new household for Mary to withdraw her. He wrote a somewhat embarrassed letter to Margaret on 14 August announcing his decision, and the Regent, as he anticipated, was not pleased.[9] What Anne thought of the new arrangement we do not know. She had been happy at Mechelen, but the thought of serving the new Queen of France, and one whose command of French was definitely inferior to her own, may well have been an exciting one. Unfortunately, we do not know how, or just when, the transfer was made, because only one Mistress Bullen features in the wedding list, and that was her sister Mary. It is possible that Margaret raised objections, or put obstacles in the way of her departure. However, that is not likely and the chances are that Anne joined her sister in Paris at some time before Mary's coronation on 5 November. Later memories of her presence are quite explicit, but no contemporary list survives to confirm it.[10]

Mary's reign, however, was a brief one, and on 1 January 1515 she was a widow. For the time being, her household held together, and both the Boleyn girls would have had the chance to observe at close quarters the behaviour of the Duke of Suffolk as he played the game of courtly love in earnest with the nineteen-year-old dowager. What Mary Boleyn may have learned we do not know, but Anne almost certainly learned the difference between the conventional game and the real thing, especially when the ex-Queen actually got into bed with her lover. Charles Brandon was an old hand at courtly love. He had even played it with the Archduchess a couple of years before, but this time the chances are that he got more than he had bargained for.[11] The couple were secretly married, but is unlikely that either of the sisters was a witness to that clandestine occasion, because the fewer who knew about it the better. Meanwhile, as we have seen, Henry was genuinely annoyed, and it was May before he was sufficiently placated for them to return to England, and to a public renewal of their wedding vows. Whether Sir Thomas was responsible for what then happened in France, we do not know – he was reportedly unpopular at the French court, so perhaps it is unlikely – but his two daughters were transferred to the service of Queen Claude, the consort of the new French king, Francis I. Lancelot de Carles, writing in 1536, was quite clear in recalling that Anne, at least, was retained by the express wish of the Queen.[12] The two girls were of an age, and it is quite likely that Claude, who had a warm and gentle nature, was genuinely fond of her. Equally, with much future diplomatic business between England and France in prospect, and with many English visitors to entertain, either she or her husband might have thought it expedient to have some English speaking ladies on hand. Mary, as we have seen, left under something of a cloud about two or three years later, but Anne served for something like seven years, and that was as formative a period of her life as the year which she had spent at Mechelen, although in a rather different way.

Most of the evidence which we have for her years at the French court is either circumstantial or retrospective. Culturally there was little difference, but serving a girl who was almost constantly pregnant must have been a very different experience from attending the urbane and widowly Margaret. Having no family base in France, Anne must have been permanently resident in the household, which spent most of its time at Amboise or Blois on the Upper Loire.[13]

This meant that in courtly terms her life was much less public than it had been before. Francis was a frequent visitor, and he brought his attendants with him, so it is not safe to assume that Anne was free from unwelcome attentions, but courtly love, as that would have been practised in a full court was not on the agenda. Nor were lavish entertainments as frequent as might be supposed. She may have taken part in the ceremonial journey which Claude and the Queen Mother, Louise of Savoy, made to welcome back Francis after his victory at Marignano in October 1515, and would certainly have been present when the Queen (in an interval between pregnancies) was crowned at St Denis in May 1516. However, she was most in demand, naturally, when there was a significant English presence, as in December 1518 when an English mission arrived to negotiate a marriage between Henry's two-year-old daughter Mary and the one-year-old Dauphin.[14] A magnificent banquet was held in the Bastille, when there was much dancing, and the ladies appeared at midnight, dressed in the latest Italian fashions. The next day there was a tournament, followed by more dancing, and Anne would have been in heavy demand as an interpreter. As we have seen, Sir Thomas was himself on mission in France in 1519, and although there is no direct evidence of the fact, he would have taken some time to spend with his daughter, whom he had scarcely seen for five years. She was now a poised and self assured eighteen-year-old. More obviously we know that Anne was called into service at that great Anglo-French junketing known as the Field of Cloth of Gold. She was among the Queen's ladies, and must have played an ambiguous role in the 'beauty competition' which developed between her compatriots and the attendants of Queen Catherine. Richard Wingfield, who had recently taken over from Sir Thomas as resident ambassador, warned Henry of what to expect in that connection:

Your Grace shall also understand that the Queen here, with the King's mother, make all the search possible to bring to the assembly the fairest ladies and demoiselles that may be found ... I hope at the least, Sire, that the queen's Grace shall bring such in her band, that the visage of England, which hath always had the praise, shall not at this time lose the same ...[15]

The two queens and their entourages met for the first time at the jousts which were held on Monday, 11 June, where their competition was given edge by the favours of the jousters. The noble ladies were, we are told:

... all vieing with each other in beauty and ornamental apparel, and for the love of them each of the jousters endeavoured to display his valour and prowess in order to find more favour with his sweetheart ...[16]

Neither Catherine, who was running to fat, nor Claude, who was thirty-one weeks pregnant, were parties to this game, but it is to be assumed that the Duchess of Suffolk and Mary Boleyn were on the English side, and Margaret of Angouleme (the King's sister) and the daughters of Lorraine on the French side. In this glittering company, Anne passed quite unremarked, but she was certainly present, and Sir Thomas probably took advantage of the opportunity to present her to Henry VIII. There must have been something of a Boleyn family reunion.[17] Contemporary commentators, the Venetians in particular, preferred the French style of beauty, describing Catherine's companions as neither very graceful nor very handsome, but Polydore Vergil writing later on the English side, disagreed. Such things are a matter of taste.

One of the things that Anne did do while in the court of France was to make the acquaintance of Margaret of Angouleme. Whether there was any real friendship between them is a matter for speculation. Similar tastes in religious matters would argue that there was, but the difference in their rank makes it unlikely.[18] That Margaret was aware of the young Englishwoman, and may have shown her some favour, is very probable, but the suggestion of intimacy in Anne's later correspondence is almost certainly wish fulfilment. It used to be thought that Anne served some time in the Duchess of Alencon's household, but recent research has demolished that thesis.[19] Anne stayed with Claude until the later part of 1521, when her father decided to call her home. Sir Thomas was aware, as Francis was not, of the terms of the treaty of Bruges which Wolsey had recently signed with the Emperor, which committed England to war with France in the summer of 1522. In January 1522, the King of France noted that she had gone, and that the English scholars studying in Paris had likewise departed. These, he rightly adduced, were signs of a deteriorating relationship. The court of France would soon be an impossible place for Anne to be, and although Queen Claude may have regretted it, her English bird had flown.

There was also, however, another reason for her recall. In August 1515, Thomas Butler, Earl of Ormond, had died, leaving two daughters as his heirs general and a cousin, Piers Butler, as his heir male. One of these daughters was Margaret, Sir Thomas Boleyn's mother. Livery of her share of the estate was granted within four months, and as far as the English lands of the earldom were concerned, appears to have been effective.[20] Ireland, however, was a different matter. Gerald FitzGerald, the Earl of Kildare, Lord Deputy at the time, and the Council of Ireland, favoured Sir Piers, recognised him as Earl of Ormond, and made the Irish lands over to him. A legal tussle and a political row ensued, because Henry declined to recognise the *soi disant* earl, and the latter showed no inclination to give way. Then Sir Thomas's brother in law, the Earl of Surrey, was appointed Lord Lieutenant, and in 1520 he came up with bright idea for solving the conflict. If Sir Thomas's daughter, Anne, were to marry James Butler, Sir Piers' son and heir, then the present situation could be frozen and the two claims united in their children.[21] What Anne St Leger, Margaret's sister, thought of this proposal is not known. Wolsey, in whose household James Butler was living, was enthusiastic, the King undertook to advance the proposal with Sir Thomas, and Wolsey was still writing from Bruges as late as November 1521, expressing his desire to talk it through with the King when he returned from his embassy.[22] Anne said that she would not agree to marry any man that she had never met, and that may have been an additional reason for her recall. It may also have been a sign of impending reconciliation that Piers was appointed Lord Deputy of Ireland on Surrey's recall in 1521, although the ambiguity over his status appears to have continued. The marriage, however, never took place. Either the young people themselves were opposed or, more likely, Sir Thomas went off the whole idea. Eventually Sir Piers lost patience and discontinued the negotiation, even threatening to resolve the conflict by violence.[23] It was eventually settled in 1529, when he conceded the title of Ormond and accepted that of Ossory instead, together with the Irish estates. The English and Welsh lands remained in the hands of Margaret Boleyn and Anne St Leger.

So Anne made her debut at the English court at the beginning of 1522, having been placed alongside her sister in the household of Queen Catherine. Her French manners and general courtly panache seem to have made an instant impression, but since Mary was almost certainly the King's mistress by this time, the Queen's reaction to her advent can only be speculated upon. Anne's first public appearance was at York Place on 1 March when she took part in that Burgundian extravaganza, the siege of the chateau verte, in which she played the part of *Perseverance*, one of the eight female defenders of the chateau. We have a long and detailed description of the development of this siege, which was laid by the King and seven other 'male virtues' – *Nobleness*, *Loyalty*, and so on – all magnificently attired.[24] Having summoned the castle to surrender in due form, and received a suitably scornful response, the besiegers bombarded it with dates and oranges, to which the besieged responded with sweetmeats and rosewater. Inevitably the male virtues prevailed, and led out their captives to the dance, after which their masks were removed and they all sat down to a sumptuous banquet. We do not know that Anne made any particular impact in the entertainment – indeed she would scarcely have had a chance to do so – or even just what she looked like. Unlike Mary, who was fair and pretty, she seems to have been dark, and not noticeably beautiful, except for her eyes, which were frequently remarked upon. The only detailed description comes from that Elizabethan recusant polemicist Nicholas Harpesfield, who could not have known her, and who was concerned to expound the 'monster' myth which arose from her later fate:

Anne Boleyn was rather tall of stature, with black hair and an oval face of sallow complexion, as if troubled with jaundice. She had a projecting tooth under the upper lip, and on her right hand six fingers. There was a large wen under her chin, and therefore to hide its ugliness, she wore a high dress covering her throat ...[25]

The family tradition of course was quite different, conceding only a trace of a nail upon one of her fingers, but even George Wyatt, who represented that tradition, did not claim that she was great beauty.[26]

About her attractiveness and sexuality, however, there can be no doubt, and that soon brought admirers. Among these was Sir Thomas Wyatt, the diplomat and poet, who recorded his infatuation sadly and in cryptic verse several years later, at the time of her fall. However, exactly when this flirtation occurred, and how far it went is the subject of much learned controversy.[27] Sir Thomas was estranged from his wife, and may well have sought agreeable female company, but the story of his warning the King off a loose-living woman belongs to the anti-Boleyn propaganda of later years. It would also have to date the affair to after 1525, and that is almost certainly too late. If Wyatt was actually involved with Anne at all, it would have had to be between 1522 and 1525, at which time we know that she was conducting a relationship with Henry Percy, the son of the fifth Earl of Northumberland. The principal source for this story is the account written in 1557 by George Cavendish. However, Cavendish, unlike Harpesfield, would have been an eye witness of the events which he recorded, having entered Wolsey's service in 1522, and been a Gentleman Usher at the time. Having commented upon her 'gesture and behaviour', Cavendish went on:

In so much [that] my Lord Percy, son and heir of the earl of Northumberland, who then attended upon my Lord Cardinal ... when it chanced the Lord Cardinal at any time to repair to the court, the Lord Percy would then resort for his pastime unto the Queen's Chamber and would there fall in a dalliance amongst the Queen's maidens ...[28]

By that means he became 'conversant' with Anne Boleyn, and their relationship grew closer, until at length they were 'insured' together, intending to marry. There were, however, a number of snags to this hopeful plan. Sir Thomas, who would not have objected to having the future Earl of Northumberland as his son-in-law, was still at this stage hoping to match her with James Butler, while Percy was pledged to Mary Talbot, daughter of the Earl of Shrewsbury. Beyond this point, however, Cavendish is not a reliable guide because these events must have occurred in the autumn of 1522, whereas he represents the King as being offended with the liaison on the grounds of his own interest in the lady, which had not developed by that time.[29] Wolsey's hostility, of which Cavendish makes much, was not therefore based upon any knowledge of the King's mind, but rather upon his knowledge of the Talbot commitment and of the Earl's intentions in that respect. If the King was offended by the idea, it was on account of his knowledge and approval of the Butler marriage, upon which he had bestowed a certain amount of time and effort. In an invented exchange of speeches, Cavendish has Wolsey berating Percy for having offended both his father and the King by seeking to bind himself to an unworthy spouse, and Percy replying that he was of full age to chose for himself, and that in any case Anne Boleyn was not unworthy of a nobleman. Her father, indeed, was mere knight, but her mother and grandmother came of noble houses, and he besought the Cardinal's favour with the King. In any case, he declared, he had gone too far in the matter to withdraw with a good conscience.[30] Whether this means that he had actually slept with Anne, or that he wished Wolsey to think that he had is not known. Consummation of such a union would have been a very hazardous business, as both parties would have been aware, and it is unlikely that Anne would have permitted such intimacy, however smitten she may have been by young Henry. The Cardinal duly sent for the Earl of Northumberland and appraised him of the situation, whereupon the Earl roasted his son as 'proud, presumptuous, disdainful and a very unthrift waster' which scarcely seems justified by the alleged offence. Cowed by this exhibition of paternal ire, and threatened with disinheritance, the young man had given way, and cancelled whatever understanding he had with Anne.[31] Instead he went ahead and married Mary Talbot in the summer of 1525, and the marriage was a complete disaster, but that cannot have been much consolation to Anne, who was, according to Cavendish 'greatly offended', as well she might have been. He traces Anne's subsequent hostility to Wolsey to this sequence of events, but in that he is surely using hindsight, because at this juncture she would have had no particular influence, and there is abundant evidence later of her attempts to ingratiate herself with the Cardinal at a time when his influence seemed to be crucial to her own chances of success. It would, in any case, have been foolish to manifest enmity to Wolsey in 1523, when these events probably occurred. Because he was then at the height of his power; and Anne was not foolish.

However, it would have been her intention to secure an advantageous marriage, and in that so far she had been conspicuously unsuccessful. James Butler was not to her taste, and Henry Percy, who clearly was, was forbidden by forces which were too powerful for even the most accomplished seductress to master. A prolonged courtly love affair with Thomas Wyatt, if it actually occurred, would have been no substitute for a marriage bed, and other suitors do not seem to have been queuing at her door. This may have been because of the Butler negotiation, and the King's known interest in it, or it may have been down to Anne herself.

Accomplished as she was in the courtly arts, she was also highly intelligent, and possessed a mind of her own, not qualities which would have endeared her to the average early Tudor nobleman. A wife was supposed to be docile, and above all faithful, neither of which was to be expected of this free-spirited and flirtatious damsel.[32] There was one man, however, who would not be put off by this combination of attributes, and that was the King. At what point Henry began to manifest an interest in her, and what the level of that interest was, has been the subject of much speculation.[33] The chances are that it began as a conventional courtly love exercise. Henry had played these games with numerous ladies in the past, and each time it had set tongues around the court wagging and kept the diplomatic gossips busy. There was usually nothing in these tales, except that the King was amusing himself in his customary fashion, and even Catherine did not take them seriously. However, at some time, probably in the summer of 1525, Henry decided that Anne was different. It may well have been that her responses were wittier than usual, and the sidelong glances more convincing. At any rate he was sufficiently attracted to end his relationship with her sister, and set out on the uncharted waters of soliciting a girl who was his intellectual equal. It may well have been an exhilarating experience.

Calendaring the development of that experience is, however, a difficult matter, because it is necessary to work backwards from the known events of 1527. In April of that year the King began a secret consultative process aimed at securing the annulment of his eighteen-year-old marriage to Catherine, and in May began a collusive suit in Wolsey's Legatine court to obtain such a verdict, on the basis of his conviction that by wedding his brother Arthur's widow he had offended against the law of God set out in the Book of Leviticus.[34] Wolsey was understandably anxious to keep these proceedings secret, especially from Catherine. The Queen was the aunt of the Holy Roman Emperor, Charles V, and if she got wind of what was intended would undoubtedly invoke his aid to get Wolsey's proceedings quashed in Rome. Henry, however, was in a highly emotional state, and in June confronted his wife with the news that they had never been truly married, thus anticipating the verdict, and sending her messengers scurrying off to Valladolid to request that intervention which Wolsey had dreaded.[35] In spite of these adverse developments, and the fact that the collusive case had been dropped, in August Henry sent to the Pope to request permission to marry a woman related to him in the first degree of affinity, once his present marriage was dissolved. This was the degree of affinity which existed between Henry and Anne as a result of his liaison with her sister, and indicates that he had proposed marriage to her by that time, and that she had accepted him. As a way ahead it was useless because of its proviso, but at least it indicates the state which the couple's relationship had reached by that time. It has been reasonably deduced that Henry had first proposed at Easter that Anne become his mistress on some recognised and stable basis, and that she had turned him down.[36] By the summer she would have known of the breakdown of the King's relationship with Catherine, and intimated to him that she would be prepared to become his second queen. He had accepted her on those terms, and that explains his approach to Rome. Neither of them at that time appears to have expected a long wait.

However, the way in which they had got to that point is much more problematical. Henry seems to have given up sexual relations with his wife at some time in 1524, presumably on the grounds that there was no point now that she was passed the menopause and he had a satisfactory partner in Mary Boleyn. In the summer of 1525 he passed Mary over to her husband, and thereafter had no partner that anyone knows about, which perhaps explains his developing ardour for Anne. Between then and the spring of 1527 the interpretation of that ardour depends upon a sequence of undated letters, because even the usually sharp eyed Imperial ambassadors did not notice anything out of the ordinary until the summer of 1527, and the Venetians did not associate him with Anne until the spring of 1528.[37] The first three of these letters show the King trying to turn a conventional courtly love attachment into something more meaningful. The first accompanied the gift of a buck, the fruit of a recent hunting expedition, and chides his mistress with not having replied to his earlier epistles, or kept her promise to write. It is signed 'written with the hand of your servant … HR' and has been tentatively dated to the autumn of 1526.[38] Some time later, and after an exchange of letters now lost, he wrote again, complaining that he had been 'now above one whole year struck with the dart of love', and asking that she 'certify me of your whole mind concerning the love between us two'. He promised to 'take you for my only mistress … to serve only you'. This could have been a proposition in the crude sense, or it could have been another manoeuvre in the complicated game. Anne apparently took it in the latter way, and responded with coy professions of chastity.[39] If she was playing hard to get, she was doing it convincingly, and the next sequence of letters begins with one of apology from the King for having offended her. She had apparently absented herself from the court, and this had caused Henry some soul searching. Faced with the unusual situation of having to court a woman rather than having her provided by diplomatic means or *droit de seigneur*, he had rushed her defences in an unacceptable manner. Realisation of this fact, and of his need for her, then forced the King to reconsider his position. At some point during the summer of 1527 he offered her marriage, and that changed her attitude entirely. Hitherto, we may imagine, she had been placed in a very difficult situation, overawed in a sense by the size of the fish which she had (probably inadvertently) hooked. He could, as her sovereign, simply have commanded her to his bed, but he had not done so, playing instead the courtly gallant, and taking her coy professions of reluctance seriously.[40]

She responded, not by letter or by word of mouth, but by sending him a token loaded with meaning in the manner loved by Tudor courtiers. It was a small model ship with a woman on board, and a pendant diamond. The message would have been clear to the recipient, because the ship had for centuries been the symbol of protection, a protection which she, as the occupant, was now giving over to her Lord and Master. In other words, Anne was accepting his offer.[41] Henry was delighted, and not a little relieved by the

> ... good intent and too humble submission vouchsafed by this
> your kindness, considering well that the occasion to merit it would
> not a little perplex me, if it were not aided therein by your great
> benevolence and goodwill ...

He went on to reassure her that his heart belonged to her alone, and that he was 'greatly desirous that so my body could be as well, as God can bring to pass if it pleaseth him ...'[42] This exchange can probably be dated to July 1527, just a few weeks before the King launched his appeal to Rome for permission to remarry. Henry was intending to take his sexual abstinence seriously on the assumption that it would not be of long duration. Anne was obviously away from the court at the time of this last letter, because he goes on to urge her to persuade her father to let her return earlier than had hitherto been planned, because he was missing her company. Meanwhile, the Pope had been incarcerated in the Castel de San Angelo by a mutinous Imperial army which had sacked the city of Rome in March, and this had created the opportunity for Wolsey to set up an interim government for the Church while Clement was out of action. If that could be brought about, the Pope's opposition to Henry's annulment plea could be circumvented, and Wolsey set off for France on 22 July with the intention of calling a congregation of the 'free' cardinals – those not with the Pope in San Angelo – in order to bring this about.[43] He knew well enough about the King's intention to seek a dissolution of his marriage, and that was clearly high on his agenda, but he appears not to have known about Anne Boleyn's position. He knew of her existence, of course, and of Henry's affection for her, but he did not know of the King's commitment, in spite of keeping eyes and ears about the court. This suggests that Anne's trinket arrived at about that time, or a little after, because part of his purpose in going to France was to sound out the possibility of a French bride for Henry. This would have cemented the Anglo-French amity which was the current foreign policy, and made any agreement with the Emperor more difficult to achieve. Such a prospect would also ensure French diplomatic backing for his plans with regard to the Church, because only by out-flanking both the Pope and the Emperor could Henry be free to marry again.[44] The timing is tight, given that Catherine's message about her plight could only have reached Charles towards the end of June, but a lot was happening in the crowded summer of 1527.

If this timetable of events is accurate it means that Henry began his courtly pursuit of Anne at sometime early in 1526, possibly in February. He appeared at the Shrovetide jousts in that year bearing the device of a heart in flames and the motto 'Declare I dare not', which would have been just the sort of gesture expected of a courtly gallant.[45] It would also be consistent with his statement in February 1527 that he had been in the 'toils of love' for upwards of twelve months. It is not very satisfactory trying to piece an emotional relationship together in this fashion, but it is the best that the evidence permits. It is also a one-sided story because Anne's reactions can only be reconstructed from the King's responses. Was she as committed as he was? At what point did it become clear to her that his intentions were more serious than those of a mere gallant? Was she holding out on him in the spring and summer of 1527 in anticipation of getting a better offer than that of *maitresse en titre*? The long frustration which followed is also capable of more than one interpretation. Now that marriage was a commitment on both sides, did she go on resisting pressure to share his bed, or did he not press her very hard? Even if they begot a bastard who was subsequently legitimated by their marriage, that would not necessarily solve the succession problem because the Beauforts, begotten in similar circumstances by John of Gaunt in the later fourteenth century, had subsequently been barred from the Crown in a precedent which would have been well enough remembered.[46] It would be better to wait until they were properly married, then there could be no question of the legitimacy of their children. Perhaps it is also worth remembering that Anne had pledged her virginity to her future husband, and was more serious in that intention than she is usually given credit for. Because of the circumstances of her fall a decade later, Anne's virginity was the subject of much ribald speculation among her enemies, but there is no reason not to take it seriously. In any case, Henry already had a bastard son, and although he had made a great thing of ennobling the child in the summer of 1525, there is no real evidence that he seriously intended to include him in the succession.[47]

So they waited ... and waited. Henry had a case in canon law, but it was not a strong one and would have needed exceptionally skilled management, and a degree of luck, to be accepted. The crux of the matter was the dispensation issued by Julius II in 1503. No one denied that the canon law forbade a man from marrying his brother's relict, but equally it was generally accepted that the Pope had the power to dispense from that law, which was what Julius had done. Henry based his case on the argument that the prohibition derived, not from the canon law but from the Book of Leviticus, thus making it a part of the Divine Law, which no pope has the power to dispense.[48] This was arguable, but was not accepted by Clement because it imposed undesirable limitations upon the papal authority. In taking this stand he was supported by the Emperor, who had a vested interest in the case, and by a majority of the College of Cardinals. The politics of the situation also favoured Imperial influence. Wolsey's attempt to set up an interim government came to nothing because only a handful of cardinals responded to his call, and the Pope from his prison fulminated against it. So the English attempt to circumvent him failed. When Clement first escaped to Orvieto in December 1527, he was indignant at his recent treatment, and very hard up, so that diplomatic and financial assistance, rapidly deployed, might for a few weeks have won Henry his will, but he allowed the opportunity to slip.[49] Moreover, repeated French failures to defeat Charles led the Pope in the course of the following months to reassess his position. The Emperor was the likely winner in the battle for the military control of northern Italy, and it would be folly to provoke his displeasure. So repeated English missions were put off with empty words. What Henry wanted was a so-called Decretal Commission, which would have enabled Wolsey to hear the case in England without any possibility of appeal. At length, in the summer of 1528, he apparently got what he desired – a commission to Wolsey and Lorenzo Campeggio to hear the case in London – but it rapidly transpired when Campeggio arrived in the autumn that it was not a decretal commission. Moreover, which did not transpire, Campeggio was under secret instructions under no circumstances to find for the King.[50] In other words the commission was a time-wasting sham, designed to cheat Henry of his expectations. The King's public position was that his conscience was troubled. Anne was not mentioned and Catherine continued to preside at the court. A curious *ménage a trois* was established, with Anne being given lodgings close to those of the King and easy of access, but Catherine presiding at all public occasions including the christmas celebrations of 1528. Meanwhile, rumours of the King's intentions had got out, indeed no particular attempt at secrecy was made, and it soon transpired that the Queen had widespread aristocratic and popular support. This was particularly true among women, who identified with her as the wronged spouse, and could not find words bad enough to describe the 'other woman'. From time to time, as in September 1528, Henry felt constrained to send Anne home to Hever Castle, more for her own security and peace of mind that for any advantage to himself.[51] On 8 November in order, as he said, to discharge his conscience, he addressed an invited assembly of nobles and citizens at his palace of Bridewell:

For this only cause, I profess before God and in the word of a Prince, I have asked Council of the greatest clerks of Christendom, and for this cause I have sent for this Legate [Cardinal Campeggio] as a man indifferent only to know the truth and to settle my conscience ...

Nothing would give him greater pleasure (he declared mendaciously) than to have his marriage declared good by the Law of God, if only his scruple could be resolved. The response was not what he either desired or expected:

... for some sighed and said nothing, others were sorry to see the king so troubled ... Others that favoured the Queen much sorrowed that this matter was now opened, so everyman spoke as his heart moved him ...[52]

Meanwhile Anne, although partly out of sight, was by no means out of mind. She was, for good reason, the councillor most insistent that Henry persevere in his quest. She even briefed ambassadors, as she did with Stephen Gardiner and Edward Fox, who were sent to Rome in February 1528. The King, for his part, did his best to curb her impatience, insisting that he was doing his best and that these things take time. He wrote sweetly during their tactical separations, urging her to be sensible,

... Wherefore, good sweetheart, continue the same, not only in this but in all your doings hereafter, for thereby shall come both to you and to me, the greatest quietness that shall be in this world ...[53]

and then went on tactfully to discuss plans for their wedding!

By the end of 1528, however, her intransigence was serving a different political purpose. Discouraged by the reception of his 'scruple', and increasingly baffled by the complexities of Roman politics, Henry appears to have been on the point of giving up and reverting to his earlier suggestion that she become his mistress. It was this crisis of confidence which brought out the best in Anne. Tough and determined, she stiffened his resolve, and insisted that he persevere with his efforts to the bitter end. She did not know, any more than he did, that the Legatine Commission was a sham, and if she had known, that would not have deterred her. Her success can be measured by the fact that by 9 December 1528 she was not only back at court (after a strategic absence) but was again lodged grandly 'near to the king' according to the French ambassador. When the court moved to Greenwich for Christmas, she was given her own separate suite in the palace, but Catherine held pride of place.[54] There was lot still to be done.

# 5

# THOMAS, EARL OF WILTSHIRE – THE WESTMINSTER YEARS

Sir Thomas had given up his treasurership of the Household upon his creation as Viscount Rochford in June 1525, but remained a favoured courtier. Over the next few years his position, both at court and in council, was determined by the developing relationship between the King and his daughter Anne, particularly when that turned decisively in the direction of marriage in the summer of 1527. Anne was naturally inclined to be pro-French, and as the Emperor's opposition to the King's suite for annulment became increasingly obvious during the autumn of that year, the whole logic of the Boleyn position shifted in that direction. Francis was naturally anxious to keep the English council in the same frame of mind, and by November the Duke of Norfolk was in receipt of a French pension of 437 crowns per year, while Lord Rochford received 262, a difference reflecting their ranks rather than their perceived usefulness.[1] Wolsey, of course, received far more, but the Cardinal's influence was slipping. While he was still in France that summer he received news that the King was throwing lavish parties at New Hall at which the Viscount was a favoured guest, and even worse, that Henry's regular supper companions included the Dukes of Norfolk and Suffolk, the Earl of Devon, and Viscount Rochford. Worse still he was listening to their advice.[2] When he returned from his mission in September he found the King closeted with Mistress Anne, and was forced to wait upon her convenience. It is unlikely, however, that these noblemen's counsel would have differed significantly from his own. If the King wanted the Pope to annul his marriage, the diplomatic support of France was essential.

Francis had been constrained in January 1526 to sign the treaty of Madrid with his captor, surrendering his sons as hostages and giving up all his claims to Northern Italy. Wolsey was sceptical: 'I cannot persuade myself,' he wrote, 'that the king of France is determined to perform the same ...', and he was right.[3] By May the League of Cognac had been signed, aligning the Papacy and Venice with France to put pressure on Charles to modify his terms. England did not at first join this League, because Wolsey was anxious to appear as an honest broker, to mediate the new treaty which was perceived to be necessary. Fighting broke out in Italy, and the Emperor showed no sign of yielding. In October Henry was constrained to offer the League 35,000 ducats (about £10,000) as a prop to its finances, but he did not join. It was not until December that Charles professed himself willing to participate in an international peace conference, and even then it was not clear that he was prepared to submit to English arbitration. Partly in order to rack up the pressure still further, a new Anglo-French treaty was signed in April 1527, which was celebrated at Greenwich with feasts, jousts and disguisings as though it were a great triumph.[4] The core of this treaty was a marriage agreement between Mary, Henry's daughter, then aged eleven and one of the princes of the French royal house. Charles himself had facilitated this negotiation by abandoning his treaty claims on Mary in order to wed Isabella of Portugal during the previous year. The treaty also proposed another 'summit meeting' between Francis and Henry, in which Charles was welcome to join if he was so minded. A joint mission was sent to Spain, bearing these terms, and the prospects for peace suddenly seemed good. Then on 6 May this hopeful scenario was rudely disrupted when a mutinous Imperial army under the nominal command of the Duke of Bourbon took and sacked the city of Rome. This immediately changed the agenda. The release of the Pope from the Castel San Angelo became a top priority, or alternatively, as we have seen, the establishment of an interim government for the church. It was with these objectives in mind that Wolsey set out to meet King Francis on 2 July.[5] By which time the whole issue had become entangled with Henry's search for an annulment of his marriage, and with the fact that his queen 'identifies herself entirely with the Emperor's interests'. Difficult international and domestic issues thus became interlocked, and Boleyn interest at court saw the former in terms of the latter. Unless Wolsey's scheme for a temporary take over of the papal authority could be made to work, peace would best serve their interests too.

While Wolsey was in France, the King sent his secretary William Knight on an independent mission to Rome, bearing a draft bull for the Pope's signature. This was the document which would have authorised him to marry a woman within the first degree of affinity, provided his existing marriage had been annulled.[6] It is highly unlikely that any of his council were privy to this initiative. In the first place, it spelled out the nature of the affinity from which he was seeking dispensation in highly explicit terms, which is unlikely to have been acceptable to Lord Rochford, and secondly it could not take effect until the major impediment was removed. In other words, as it stood it was useless. Henry's attempt is more significant in terms of his relationship with Wolsey than in advancing his cause. The Cardinal did not know of Knight's mission, and when he found out his attempt to abort it was overridden by explicit instructions from the King. Not only was the King's 'secret matter' about to be divulged to the Courts of Europe, but the Cardinal now had good reason to fear that his mission to broach the possibility of a marriage with Renee, Francis's sister-in-law, would be so much wasted breath.[7] The significance of Viscount Rochford's place in the Royal councils now became apparent. He was the father of the woman whom Henry planned to make his queen, and Wolsey was not a party to that secret. He also picked up rumours that it was being said behind his back that he was less committed to the King's Great Matter than he pretended. In early September he wrote to Henry:

> Assuring your highness that I shall never be found but as your most humble, loyal and faithful obedient servant ... enduring the travails and pains which I daily and hourly sustain without any regard to the continuance of my life or health ...[8]

Henry replied with soothing expressions of confidence and goodwill, but his deeds spoke louder than his words, and they were not reassuring.

In international terms, 1528 was occupied by the search for an annulment. The Anglo-French mission to Spain and Wolsey's peace initiative having alike come to nothing, in January an English herald delivered a declaration of war to the Emperor at Burgos. This was a purely diplomatic move, as no hostilities followed, or were intended. It was symbolic of the anti-Imperial stance which the King was now taking up, and a means of putting extra pressure upon Charles to allow the pope to settle the marriage business. It had no effect. In March Wolsey was optimistic of a settlement, and in May an envoy was sent to Madrid. However, after waiting six weeks to see the Emperor, he found him non-committal, and by early November was back in France empty handed.[9] Meanwhile, in domestic terms it was the year of the great sweat. In June both William Carey and Sir William Compton died of the disease, and one of Anne's ladies became infected, so that she was sent down to Hever, and Henry set off on his travels. In July both Anne and her father caught the illness, but recovered. Her frequent absences from the court, which we have already noticed, were as much caused by fear of infection as they were tactical in terms of her position, and it is often hard to tell which was which.[10] In November, Henry broached his 'scruple' to the assembly of notables, and, disconcerted by the response, may have considered giving up his quest. However, by that time Cardinal Campeggio had arrived bearing the deceptive commission which Gardiner and Fox and worked so hard to achieve, and the King was clearly torn between hope and apprehension. At the end of October Campeggio reached the court, to find Henry insistent on swift action. This however, was precisely what the Cardinal was instructed not to allow. He engaged in lengthy discussions with the King, and became impressed by his grasp of the issues, if not by his conclusions. Even an angel from heaven, he wrote, could not persuade him that he was mistaken.[11] With Wolsey, his conversations were more practical – the annulment was a political necessity, and if it were not granted not only would the English Cardinal be finished, but England might well throw off the papal allegiance entirely. Such a prospect was too terrible to contemplate. Campeggio was, however, extremely reluctant to allow the issue to come to a trial, and suggested instead attempting to persuade Catherine to enter religion. This would not have offered a cut and dried solution, but a respectable body of theological opinion maintained that if a married person took vows, then that automatically ended their relationship, and that the other party was free to marry again. This had the obvious advantage that their child, Mary, would have remained legitimate, whereas an annulment would have bastardised her. It was also consistent with Catherine's renowned piety, but the Queen turned a deaf ear to all pleas. Henry's wife she was, and Henry's wife she would remain.[12] There was no option but to convene the Legatine court, and let the issue be tried openly. What part the Boleyns may have played in all these manoeuvres remains shadowy, probably by intent. Anne was the recipient of a number of passionate letters from her beloved, and returned to the court for Christmas. Lord Rochford, as a member of the council, must have been aware of all the public and semi-public moves which were being made, but, equally aware of the hostility which his daughter was generating, probably kept as low a profile as was consistent with his position. If he expressed any opinions he did not write them down, or confide in anyone else who might have committed his thoughts to paper.

Meanwhile, Henry's carefully devised strategy was in danger of falling apart because a different version of Julius's brief had turned up in Spain. He had hitherto concentrated his arguments upon the inadequacies of that brief, as a means of avoiding the direct issue of papal competence, but the new version (of which Catherine had been sent a copy) remedied most of those inadequacies. This left Henry with the bleak alternatives of confronting the issue of authority head on, or giving up. He naturally tried to argue that the Spanish version was a forgery, which was a plausible thesis given that Charles would not surrender the original and no copy could be found in Rome.[13] English envoys were sent to the Curia to verify this notion, and when they were unable locate it, their case found some credibility. Unfortunately it was not enough to budge Clement, who was politically hamstrung, but it was sufficient to convince those who wanted to be persuaded, including Henry himself. By the spring of 1529, Henry was consumed with impatience, and quite unaware of the fact that Campeggio had secretly requested Charles to petition Clement to revoke the case to Rome, which he had in fact done, unknown to anyone in England.[14] On 29 May the King issued a licence for the case to proceed, and the Legates named Friday, 18 June for the commencement of the hearing. Campeggio knew, but Wolsey did not, that their ordeal would be a short one, because the case was bound, sooner or later, to be revoked. On the 18th Henry appeared by proxy, but Catherine turned up in person, only to challenge the judges and announce her appeal to Rome. Campeggio kept his counsel, and when three days later both the royal couple were in court, announced that they had overruled the Queen's protest. She repeated her appeal and withdrew, declining all requests to return, whereupon she was pronounced contumacious.[15] It was the nearest that Henry was to get to success, because as the pleadings went on, Bishop John Fisher built up a formidable case on Catherine's behalf, and tore the King's representations to shreds. Henry had taken his courage in both hands in insisting that the court proceed, and now it looked as though he would be faced with defeat. He was spared that humiliation because on 13 July Clement yielded to Imperial pressure and revoked the case to Rome, citing Catherine's appeal (of which he had been made aware) as the reason. Swiftly and secretly, Campeggio was appraised of that decision, and deliberately slowed down the proceedings with technical quibbles, which even Wolsey found baffling, and then announced on 31 July that since his court was a papal one, it would follow the

Roman timetable and go into recession until October.[16] It never re-convened because long before then the papal letters of inhibition arrived, citing the King instead to appear in Rome.

It would be difficult to say who was the more angry: Henry, whose expectations had been so cruelly abused, Anne, who was again cheated of her expectation, or Cardinal Wolsey who had been deliberately deceived by his colleague and was now left to face the wrath of the King and the Boleyns without any visible means of support. Wolsey was notoriously the first victim, because the weakness of his position was that he had always been exclusively dependant upon the King. Unpopular in the country at large, he had been actively hated by the leading nobles on the grounds that he had usurped their confidential relationship with their monarch. This had been the theme of John Skelton's attacks several years before, when he had been in the pay of the Duke of Norfolk, and it was revisited now.[17] They had thought that they had him in the summer of 1527, when the King's confidence was visibly slipping, but he recovered because he seemed to offer the only realistic prospect of getting an annulment through the Rota. Now that hope was gone and Anne, who had hitherto maintained amicable relations with the Cardinal, turned against him. The failure of the Legatine court was the principal reason for this, but it was not the only one. Preoccupied with the King's Great Matter, Wolsey had failed to take the Franco-Imperial peace negotiations going on at Cambrai seriously, so that England, although technically a belligerent, was not represented at the conference table. Too late he realised his mistake, and rushed a delegation out, which arrived in time to sign the 'Ladies Peace' on 5 August, but not to make any input into its content. England's interests were effectively ignored, and the diplomatic backing which had been guaranteed by the continuing war, now seemed likely to be withdrawn.[18] When the Cardinals arrived at court on 19 September for Campeggio to take his leave, Henry dismissed them briefly and then went off hunting with Anne. Two days later, Wolsey was commanded to hand over the Great Seal, and on 9 October *praemunire* charges were filed against him. He confessed and was pardoned, but rehabilitation was still a long way off.

Lord Rochford's role in these proceedings is unrecorded, except that he was a member of that aristocratic group in the council, headed by the Dukes of Norfolk and Suffolk, that was most opposed to the Cardinal. His son George was sent in embassy to France on 8 October as replacement for Sir Francis Bryan, and that is probably an indication of his continuing influence within that group.[19] On 8 December, perhaps to demonstrate that all was well with the machinery of State in spite of Wolsey's abrupt departure, Henry promoted a new batch of peers; George Lord Hastings became Earl of Huntingdon, Robert Ratcliffe, Viscount Fitzwalter became Earl of Sussex, and Viscount Rochford became Earl of Wiltshire and of Ormond. The creations took place, perhaps symbolically at Wolsey's former residence of York Place, now in the King's hands, with rituals similar to those which had accompanied the elevation of Henry Fitzroy in 1525. Significantly, these were all 'new men', without peerage ancestry, promoted exclusively for services to Henry VIII, and they were political allies.[20] The elevation of Rochford to the earldom of Ormond was particularly significant, representing as it did the end of a protracted legal and political argument. Sir Piers Butler had been defeated, and was constrained to accept the earldom of Ossory in lieu. However, it was no bad deal for him, and it is unlikely that he regretted losing patience over the marriage negotiations. This group of new peers also constituted what might loosely be described as the 'Boleyn party' within the council, who had recently worked with the two dukes against the Cardinal. The following month, when the King decided to translate Cuthbert Tunstall from the see of London to the distant posting of Durham, he handed the Privy Seal to the new Earl of Wiltshire. For the first time Thomas Boleyn was a senior officer of state, and a member of the inner ring of the council.[21]

Meanwhile, in spite of his disappointment, Henry had not given up on his search for an annulment, and pressed by an increasingly frustrated Anne, decided to try some new initiatives. One of these was to take advantage of the anti-clerical mood of the House of Commons to pass acts against probate and mortuary fees, and another was to canvass the theological opinions of the universities. This latter was originally suggested by an obscure Cambridge don named Thomas Cranmer, in conversation with his old friend Stephen Gardiner (the King's secretary) during a visit by the court to Waltham Abbey during the late summer of 1529.[22] On being told of this conversation, Henry was interested, and summoned Cranmer to court for consultations, at the end of which he instructed him to write down his suggestions in the form of a treatise. To facilitate this process, he referred him to the household of the Earl of Wiltshire, where he was instructed to take up residence. Years later he was accused of having been a Boleyn chaplain at this time, either to Anne or to her father, but this seems to be a misunderstanding based upon his having lived for several months in the Earl's house.[23] The treatise (which does not survive) clearly pleased the King when it was written, and Cranmer was added to the team of advisers desperately seeking a way out of the impasse which continued diplomatic failure in Rome had created. At some time in 1530 he joined with his fellows Nicholas del Burgo and Edward Fox in drawing up a *consulta* for the King, usually known as the *collectanea satis copiosa*, which argued, among other things, that the King was entitled to seek a solution within his own realm, using the authority of the Archbishop of Canterbury.[24] This idea appealed to the King, but he was not yet ready for its more radical implications. Consequently his envoys in Rome were instructed to look for evidence that the ancient customs of England exempted her king from all but the doctrinal authority of Rome. Of course they found none, and this way ahead turned out to be a blind alley. Meanwhile, Henry was advancing his cause in various indirect ways. Emissaries were sent out to collect the opinions of the theological faculties, and in May of 1530 the King summoned a conference of bishops and university representatives to St Edward's chapel at Westminster. To this council he presented various English theological works, including Tyndale's New Testament, inviting their condemnation, and lectured the assembled clergy on their preaching responsibilities.[25] This was a grey area in which princes had operated before, but he was also feeling his way towards some kind of ecclesiastical authority. A proclamation issued on 22 June condemned certain named works as heretical and forbade their circulation, which was an infringement of the prerogatives of the Church as those had previously been understood.[26] By mid-1530 a total of eight universities, including Paris and Bologna, had registered favourable opinions of the King's cause, but the objective of all this activity remained unclear. It seems that at this stage Henry was mainly concerned to apply additional pressure to Clement, rather than to strike out on his own.

Embassies continued to be sent to plead and cajole. George, Lord Rochford, Anne's brother, attended the meeting of Clement and Charles at Bologna early in the year, at which Charles was belatedly crowned as Holy Roman Emperor. This was ostensibly a mission to congratulate the Emperor, but was in fact aimed mainly at the Pope. A further mission was sent in March, led by the Earl of Wiltshire in person, or, as he was disparagingly described 'the father of the king's sweetheart', the purpose of which was to declare that the King would insist upon an annulment, and that his patience was almost exhausted.[27] Absence in Italy explains the fact that when Henry called upon his council and other dignitaries to sign a final plea to the Pope for a swift and favourable judgement, Wiltshire's signature is missing. It was not until August that he returned from his fruitless embassy. The employment of the Earl in this fashion, which was not the most tactful of gestures, was almost certainly due to the urgings of Anne herself, whose will was 'law to the king', according to an Italian account of the following year.[28] 1531 was a year of Boleyn ascendancy, but it brought the King no nearer to a solution of his problem. In June, Thomas was receiving letters directly from the English ambassador in Spain, presumably on the grounds that he was 'most in credit' with the King, and in October he was granted certain lands in Kent, lately belonging to the Duke of Buckingham. These were given to himself and his heirs, with the curious proviso that if he failed of heirs male, the property was to go to his daughter Anne, again signalling the real reason behind the favour. In November a Venetian report of the councillors most influential with the King listed the Earl third after the Dukes of Norfolk and Suffolk. The same list also includes Stephen Gardiner, the King's secretary, and Thomas Cromwell.[29] Cromwell had been recruited from the service of Cardinal Wolsey at some point before the latter's death in November 1530, and had risen rapidly in Henry's confidence thereafter. Seeing the way ahead more clearly than his master, he was closely allied with the

Boleyns at this juncture, and was adding his voice to theirs in urging the King to take the law into his own hands.

As we have seen, the Earl of Ossory had given up his claim to the Ormond title in Ireland in 1529, but there was clearly still some legal dispute on going, perhaps raised by one of Ossory's Irish clients. At some stage in 1531 a challenge was mounted which required a search through the records of the Court of Common Pleas and the Petty Bag Office. There is no trace of this coming to judgement, if it was ever sued, but the expenses of the search were paid by the Crown, which indicates that it was the propriety of the King's action which was being called in question.[30] As far as we know, Thomas was not called upon to defend his position. Meanwhile, as Lord Privy Seal, the Earl was named to the majority of Commissions of the Peace in England, although it is unlikely that he sat on any of them, and at New Year 1532 the entire family received gifts from the King; not only Anne and Wiltshire, but George, Lord Rochford, his wife Jane and his sister Mary. As 1532 advanced the Boleyn/Cromwell ascendancy was expressed in a series of tracts arguing that the papal jurisdiction was a human artefact, and its claims usurped. The time had come for a long-overdue restoration of a true Christian polity in England. *The Determinations of the moste famous and mooste excellent universities of Italy and France* had appeared in 1531, initiating this wave of propaganda. There followed in the summer of 1532 *The Glasse of the Truthe*, and other works, confirming that the ancient councils of the Church, starting with Nicea, had all decreed that causes should be adjudged by the metropolitan of their province of origin.[31] In other words the issue of the King's marriage should be settled by the Archbishop of Canterbury, and any appeal beyond him was *ultra vires*. As far back as Michaelmas

1530 a select group of prelates had been charged with *praemunire*, basically for accepting Wolsey's legatine jurisdiction, which the King, of course, had approved at the time. The selection included most of Catherine's known friends, such as John Fisher, and seems to have been chosen for their obstructiveness to the King's purposes. In other words it was another expression of the Boleyn ascendancy. The charges were not proceeded with, not because of any softening in Henry's attitude, but because he was persuaded, probably by Cromwell, that such a piecemeal approach made no sense. Either the whole clerical estate was guilty, or no one was. As a result both Convocations were charged with the same offence, and towards the end of January 1531 they submitted to the King.[32] The charges were dropped, a whacking fines accepted – £100,000 in the case of the Southern province – and the submission was subsequently confirmed by statute. It looks as though Henry at this stage was treating the English Church as a hostage for papal compliance, but that is probably too simple a way of interpreting the complex signals which he was sending out. In the summer of 1531 he finally dismissed Catherine from the court, and that surely reflects another step in the painful evolution of his thinking.[33] By the summer of 1532 he was almost prepared to grasp the nettle. Unfortunately, the Archbishop of Canterbury, William Warham, was being uncooperative, and Henry was not yet sure enough of his ground to order him to act. Consequently it was the death of Warham in August which provided the final incentive to turn words into deeds. As late as March, the Earl of Wiltshire had spoken in the House of Lords in support of the ecclesiastical autonomy, which he would hardly have ventured to do without the King's consent, yet only weeks later the 'Supplication against the ordinaries' was received, and Sir Thomas More resigned the

Great Seal.[34] Perhaps the Boleyn party was trying to mend fences, but it seems a little late in day for that, and the Earl's intervention, supposing Chapuys's report to be accurate, remains something of a mystery. Probably Henry was speaking with forked tongue, hoping even at this late stage, to extract the concession which he so much needed.

Just when the King decided to install his own man at Canterbury, and proceed in defiance of the Pope, we do not know, but it must have been almost immediately after Warham's death on 22 August. On 1 September he created Anne Marquis of Pembroke, and this was the signal for a change of gear in their relationship. Overtly it was aimed at his meeting with Francis I, which had been the subject of diplomatic exchanges throughout the summer and was now fixed for October. He was determined that Anne would accompany him, and since she could not yet do so as queen, he settled on a senior peerage to give her the requisite dignity. The event took place at Windsor, and the King was accompanied by the Dukes of Norfolk and Suffolk, the Earl of Wiltshire and the French Ambassador. Anne was conducted by the Countesses of Rutland and Sussex, and Stephen Gardiner, since 1531 Bishop of Winchester, read the patent of creation. Her train was borne by her cousin Mary, the Duchess of Richmond, and she was given precedence over all other peers, the three dukes alone excepted.[35] She thus became superior in rank to her own father, who was one of the signatories to the arrangement. By a separate patent she was also granted lands worth £1,000 a year, giving her for the first time a substantial degree of financial independence. Since she had been mainly dependent upon her father for her maintenance hitherto, we can assume that this grant was as much a favour to him as to her. When Henry set off with due panoply on 10 October, the

Marquis was in his company, and in her retinue went her sister
Mary and her sister-in-law Jane Rochford. The Earl of Wiltshire
accompanied the King. When Henry first went to meet Francis at
Boulogne, he tactfully left Anne behind, having been warned that
Eleanor, Francis's second queen, would refuse to receive her, but
when Francis came to Calais, he suffered from no such inhibition,
and greeted the Marquis of Pembroke as befitted her rank.[36] In
a sense this meeting was staged with one eye on the Pope and
the Emperor, to demonstrate the 'perfect amity' which existed
between England and France, and to enlist the aid of the two newly
appointed French cardinals in promoting Henry's cause at Rome.
But in another sense it marked a parting of the ways, because
with the firm support of Francis, he was now in a position to defy
them both – or at least he thought that he was. In fact for all his
professions of friendship and support, the King of France was not
at all anxious to fall foul of the pontiff, and shortly after arranged
a marriage between his second son, Henry, and the Pope's niece,
Catherine de Medici.[37] Henry, however, now felt secure enough in
the friendship of France to believe that he could ride out any storm
which his proposed course of action would inevitably arouse. For
his part Francis, although he may have had his suspicions, did not
know what his 'good brother' would do next.

What he did in fact was to sleep with Anne, while the couple were
storm bound in Calais after the meetings. At Christmas 1532, she
kept state virtually as queen, and in contrast with the previous year,
which had been 'most miserable', this time an air of jollity seems
to have prevailed. During December the King presented her with
a vast quantity of gilt and silver gilt plate; a customary gift, but in
unusual quantities and at an unusual time. Even more exceptionally,
he appears to have shown her the royal treasure chamber, normally

a closely guarded secret.[38] Early in January, Henry sent a special messenger to bring Thomas Cranmer home from his mission in Germany, because he was to be the next Archbishop of Canterbury – a decision which must have been made several weeks earlier and which had become general knowledge by the end of January. Thomas Audley, another Boleyn supporter, was given the Great Seal on the 26th of the month, and a few days later the council was in close session over what appears to have been a draft version of the Act in Restraint of Appeals. At about the same time, Anne was discovered to be pregnant, and all the signs pointed to an early royal wedding, with all the consequences which that implied. On 7 February her father told the Earl of Rutland that the King was determined to marry her forthwith, and sounded him out about the bill of Appeals. When Rutland responded that parliament had no such power, the Earl of Wiltshire became very angry and told him to think again, bearing in mind the consequences of incurring the King's displeasure.[39] Rutland yielded to this logic, and voted for the bill when the time came. We do not know for certain when Henry and Anne were married, but the evidence points to some date between 15 and 23 February. On the latter date Chapuys, who may have been assuming a knowledge which he did not in fact possess, reported that the King had married his 'lady' in the presence of her father, mother, brother, and some other unnamed individuals.[40] The natural person to have conducted this ceremony would have been the Archbishop elect, but he did not find out about it for another fortnight, so we do not know who officiated. By early March the King was sufficiently confident to put up preachers in the court to sing Anne's praises, and to proclaim the immorality of his union with Catherine, which is a reasonably sure sign of what had happened. On 14 March Cromwell introduced the bill of Appeals into the Commons, and on the 26th Convocation was invited to pronounce on the validity of the King's two marriages.[41] Meanwhile Pope Clement had, rather surprisingly in view of his knowledge of Cranmer's track record, issued the pallium, the symbol of official approval of his appointment, and the Archbishop was duly consecrated on 30 March.

Paradoxically, there are some signs that the Earl of Wiltshire was not happy with the situation which had now been reached, and that although he supported the Act of Appeals, saw that more as a means to coerce the Pope than as a solution in itself. The evidence comes from the Duke of Norfolk, who was definitely unhappy with Henry's declaration of independence, and who claimed that Wiltshire had supported him in blocking a marriage as far back as May 1532.[42] In June the Duke had quarrelled with the French ambassador, endangering the October meeting, but he did not claim that Wiltshire had supported him on that occasion. It seems likely that the Earl would have preferred to wait for a papal decision before embarking upon a controversial matrimony, but that he was swept along by the tide of events. As late as the end of May 1533 Chapuys was reporting tensions between Anne on the one hand, and her father and uncle on the other, but since the ambassador had a constructive eye for these quarrels, it would not do to take his stories too seriously.[43] The whole narrative of events in the first three months of 1533 is bedevilled by hindsight and later recusant propaganda. Rowland Lee, later the Bishop of Lichfield, was alleged to have been the celebrant at the secret wedding, but according to another version it was George Brown, the Prior of the Austin Friars. Some had the ceremony taking place before dawn, and others alleged that the King lied to the celebrant about having obtained papal permission.[44] It was an event of such significance that these legends are inevitable, as were the scabrous stories impugning Anne's virginity, although George Cavendish, who had known her and had little reason to love her, later testified that it was so. What we can be sure about is that these events were highly controversial, and that many courtiers and councillors were opposed to the way in which Thomas Cromwell was steering events. The Duke of Suffolk was more overtly unhappy than his colleague of Norfolk, and his duchess, exercising her privilege as the King's sister, the most outspoken of them all. As these events passed into the public domain, the country became deeply divided, and the Boleyn party at court found itself riding a tiger, its only prospect of security lying in the constancy of purpose of the King. The Earl of Wiltshire could not afford to allow any doubts which he may have had about his daughter's position to be audible outside the council chamber. Meanwhile, the King's confidence was continued, and on 30 April he was commissioned along with Edward Fox, to conclude a stricter league of amity with France, Francis's support being more necessary than ever in the exposed position which Henry's actions had now created for him.[45]

On Saturday, 31 May Anne processed through the streets of London, and on 1 June was crowned as queen in Westminster Abbey. The Duke of Suffolk was constrained to appear as High Constable for the day, but the Duke of Norfolk was represented as Earl Marshall by his brother Lord William Howard, and there is curiously no mention in the published account of the Earl of Wiltshire. The Lord Privy Seal was definitely present but was given no special role. Neither was Thomas Cromwell, who more than anyone else had brought this event about, so it was presumably by the King's deliberate decision that those closest to his wife did not feature. The point of *The Noble, Triumphant Coronation* was to emphasise the attendance of those whose support could not be taken for granted, and that hardly applied to the Queen's father.[46] The Duke of Norfolk was absent on a diplomatic mission, but his Duchess positively refused to appear, although she was Anne's aunt. The ladies may have been allowed an indulgence which was not extended to their menfolk. The Queen was certainly 'well accompanied', but the ladies are not named, perhaps to disguise the absentees. However, they almost certainly included Anne's sister and sister-in-law, who were in no position to resist pressure to participate, even if they had been inclined to do so. In spite of the eulogies, it was a thoroughly controversial event and Chapuys (who did not attend) wrote a mocking report of it afterwards for the Emperor's benefit, declaring that the people stood silent and that half the nobility absented themselves.[47] It was only a week since the Archbishop's court at Dunstable had finally pronounced Henry's first marriage null and void. The Pope's reaction to these events was understandable outrage, because he had been defied on every count. On 8 August he issued a Bull calling upon Henry to restore Catherine and repudiate Anne under threat of excommunication, summoning all Christian princes to depose the schismatic if he did not yield. On the 13th, Henry responded by appealing to a general council, citing the law of God and the Pope's unreasonableness.[48] That still mattered, because in addition to the political risks involved, and in spite of the Act in Restraint of Appeals, Clement was still in some minimal sense the head of the English Church, and Henry was still seeking to have his actions confirmed in Rome. Meanwhile, one of the effects of his actions was made clear by a proclamation issued on 5 July declaring that he had 'taken to his wife after the laws of the church, the right high and excellent Princess Lady Anne, now Queen of England', and that consequently the Lady Catherine 'should not from henceforth have or use the name, style or dignity of Queen of this realm', but was to be known simply as the Princess Dowager of Wales.[49] Catherine, needless to say, repudiated the decision, and was surreptitiously supported by her household. Henry made a generous provision for her as the Dowager Princess, and was circumspect about enforcing the penalties decreed for non-observance of his proclamation. In his treatment of Catherine, he was treading on very thin ice.

Thomas was now in a sense triumphant. His extended family had played a leading role in the coronation celebrations, and in the days of festivities which had followed. His son George was absent with the Duke of Norfolk in France, but the rest had played their allotted parts well. Even the death of the King's sister Mary, the Duchess of Suffolk, on 24 June did not dampen down the hilarity. Indeed Henry, who had been seriously embarrassed by her refusal to recognise Anne, may have been secretly quite pleased. The mourning was brief, even perfunctory. More important was the delivery on the 28th of Francis I's wedding gift – a splendid litter with three mules – which had been transmitted by George Boleyn. This was taken as proof that the King of France was on Henry's side, although in fact Francis was playing a double game.[50] He was willing to intervene to get the sentence of excommunication postponed, and to continue diplomatic relations with England when it came into effect, but he was not willing to quarrel with the Pope in the process. This gesture of recognition for Henry's second marriage was as far as he was prepared to go, and Clement recognised that, so that relations between Rome and Paris continued to be amicable, to Henry's great chagrin. On Tuesday, 26 August, Anne 'took to her chamber' at Greenwich to await the birth of her hoped-for son. In view of his experiences with Catherine, the King was understandably anxious, but this time he need not have worried. After an easy labour, she was delivered of a perfect and healthy child; the only snag was that it was girl. Her parents concealed their disappointment, and named her Elizabeth after her paternal grandmother.[51] Plans for a joust were abandoned, but a magnificent christening was conducted on Wednesday, 10 September, at which all sorts of political messages were conveyed. First and foremost it was a Boleyn/Howard triumph, and of the twenty-one participants listed by Edward Hall, ten were members of one family or the other, including both the Earl of Wiltshire and his son. Thomas Cranmer was the godfather. At the same time, as many of Catherine and Mary's friends as could be persuaded or coerced also took part. Gertrude, Marchioness of Exeter was one of the godmothers, in spite of her obvious reluctance, while her husband, the Marquis, bore the taper of 'virgin wax'. The Dowager Duchess of Norfolk, who was the other godmother, carried the child, her train borne by the Earl of Wiltshire and the Earl of Derby. Lord Hussey, the Lady Mary's Chamberlain, was constrained to help bear the canopy, while the Duke of Suffolk escorted the child.[52] They must have felt that they were assisting at a Roman triumph. Nevertheless Elizabeth's sex was a set back for the whole clan, and Anne, who had manoeuvred herself into what had seemed in June to be an impregnable position, was now again acutely vulnerable. Chapuys's despatches continue to breathe venom against 'the concubine', and now against the 'little bastard' also, while emphasising the love which 'all the people' have for the Queen and Princess (Catherine and Mary). He overstated his case, but the support was there, and Henry knew it.[53] While the courts of Europe amused themselves with thoughts of his discomfort, the King still knew that he had an uphill battle to win hearts and minds to a cause to which he was totally committed.

Part of that battle was fought in parliament where, early in 1534, the Act of Succession described the 'lawful matrimony had and solemnised between your Highness and your most dear and entirely beloved wife Queen Anne', and decreed the succession to lie in the offspring of that union. This was followed by a Treasons Act later in the year, which declared it to be high treason to deny the King any of his titles, notably that of Supreme Head of the Church.[54] Both these Acts were drafted by Thomas Cromwell, and it is not clear that the Earl of Wiltshire played any part other than that of a councillor, who would have been expected to approve the draft before it was submitted to parliament, and to speak in its support in the House of Lords. It was under the terms of this Act of Treasons that John Fisher, Thomas More and the Carthusian priors were arraigned in 1535. The Earl of Wiltshire was a member of each of the Commissions of Oyer and Terminer which tried these offenders, and was certainly present at the execution of the priors. As a councillor it was a duty which he could not have avoided. Perhaps it had been in anticipation of such a responsibility that he had in November 1533 asked the great Erasmus to write a treatise 'how everyone should prepare for death', although at the age of fifty-seven his concern was probably more personal.[55] Whereas Anne's fingerprints are all over the public policy of the period 1533–36, and her role and importance are well attested by correspondents both foreign and domestic, her father is a shadowy figure. That she was the real leader of the family-based faction seems beyond all reasonable doubt, and Lord Wiltshire may well have found this hard to stomach. Most of the records of his activity refer to his official functions as councillor and Lord Privy Seal. Even his diplomatic role seems to have been taken over by his son George. We catch glimpses of him from time to time. He apparently joined with the Duke of Norfolk to browbeat his kinswoman Anne Shelton for being too lenient with the Lady Mary, whose outspoken defiance was a source of great irritation to Anne.[56] In June 1535 he wrote to Cromwell asking for the Secretary's favour over a bill of complaint which had been brought against himself and his brother James by one Leonard Spencer of Norwich. He obviously thought that Spencer was acting out of mere malice. The rights and wrongs of the case are obscure, but it is significant that the favour was sought that way around.[57] In August 1535 he apparently asked for a bill in the Irish parliament concerning the legitimacy of the Earl of Ossory's siblings to be deferred while he and his 'copartner sentleger' searched their own evidences. In this case it would appear that he was not successful, because a week later he signed an instruction to the Lord Chancellor to process certain acts for that parliament, including one of repeal for a previous act which had legitimated the Earl's bastard brethren. The Earl himself had sought this bill so presumably it was a safeguard against co-lateral claims on his estate.[58] Cromwell instructed the Chancellor to ensure that neither the Earl of Ormond's interests nor the King's were adversely affected. It may also be that the search of his own 'evidences' produced nothing relevant. As late as March 1536 the Earl of Wiltshire secured a beneficial extension of his lease on the Crown honour of Rayleigh, including his son George in the terms and reducing the rent. All the evidence suggests that Thomas Boleyn remained a favoured courtier right up to the last minute, and that when the crash came in the King's relations with Anne, he was not directly involved.

There are, however, signs of tensions within the Boleyn 'camp'. The whole logic of their position suggested that they should support the evangelical party – those seeking reform of the Church – which the Royal Supremacy was ostensibly designed to facilitate. Anne was certainly of that opinion, and so was Thomas Cromwell. John Foxe was right when years later he described her as a 'great promoter' of the Gospel.[59] That did not make her a Lutheran, but it did make the infiltration of Protestantism easier, and to that extent she was a promoter of heresy. This the Duke of Norfolk found totally unacceptable, and his acceptance of the Supremacy was conditional upon its being used for the suppression of heresy, which was Henry's first expressed intention. The Earl of Wiltshire's position seems to have been rather similar. He supported a fact finding mission in 1535 and 1536 by one of Cromwell's agents named Thomas Trebold, who reported on the arrest of William Tyndale and the affair of the placards in France. Trebold's surviving reports are directed partly to Cromwell, but also to Cranmer, and to Lord Wiltshire. His cover was scholarship, and he travelled widely in Germany, meeting Luther in Wittenburg and Martin Bucer in Strasburg. Part of his mission seems to have been to convince the continental reformers, not only of the merits of Henry's position, but also of the potential of the Earl of Wiltshire as a patron.[60] At one point he sent to the latter a work published by the French reformer Clement Marot. Anne's affinities were with the Christian humanists of France, and Trebold may have assumed that her father's were the same, but in fact he seems to have sat on the conservative wing of the King's affinity, and to have followed his daughter's lead only reluctantly. He patronised the scholar Robert Wakefield, but that was in the context of annulling the King's first marriage rather than of evangelical reform, and, unlike

Anne, his promotion of reforming clergy is hard to be discerned.[61] It would be wrong to suggest that the Boleyns as a political party were divided by these differences, but whereas Anne and her brother were undoubtedly in the evangelical camp, their father did not go much beyond the ecclesiastical supremacy which was the fundamental underpinning of their whole position. Time was to show that his position was closer to that of the King than theirs was.

# 6

# THE BOLEYNS AS A POLITICAL FACTION – THE WHITEHALL YEARS

Viscount Rochford became a member of a recognisable group within the council as the result of two developments of the summer of 1527. The first was the emergence of his daughter Anne as a realistic queen in waiting, and the second was a serious wobble in the confidential relationship between the King and Cardinal Wolsey. Because of the importance of Anne's personal and political ties to Henry this is normally known as the 'Boleyn faction', but its acknowledged leader was not her father but her uncle, the Duke of Norfolk. It was a group primarily defined by its negative purpose – to get rid of Wolsey – and for that reason included among its members both the Duke of Suffolk and Lord Darcy, neither of whom was particularly sympathetic to Anne's ambitions.[1] According to Inigo de Mendoza, the Imperial ambassador, this group had coalesced during the Cardinal's absence in France, for the express purpose of exploiting the apparent fact that the King no longer trusted him as fully as he had once done. He suspected that Wolsey feared Anne's advance, and would retire from active politics if she became queen. Because the Cardinal had no desire to be forced out in this manner, he was doing his best to sabotage Henry's plans and would try to convince the King that he was in error.[2] The French ambassador came to the same conclusion, and expressed the view that Rochford's hostility was grounded on the fact that Wolsey had forced him out of the treasurership of the Household when he was created a viscount. There is no evidence for the latter conclusion, and in any case Wolsey reasserted his supremacy after his return from France, particularly through the organisation of various set pieces, notably on 1 November when a French delegation invested the King with the Order of St Michael. At about the same time, news was received of the failure of Henry's latest bid in Rome, and both the King and Anne seem to have come to the conclusion that the Cardinal was even more indispensable.[3] His credit was fully restored, and his enemies, both within the council and outside it, controlled their fury and awaited another opportunity. Throughout the first half of 1528 Anne was studiously polite to Wolsey and his agents, and he returned the compliment, sending her fish for Lent from his famous ponds, and solicitously enquiring after her health when she was indisposed in June. Whatever his private thoughts may have been, when she was recovering from the dreaded sweat in July, he was even more fulsome, and sent her a 'rich and goodly' present into the bargain. She responded in kind, professing herself 'most bound of all creatures, next to the king's Grace, to love and serve your grace' and concluding that she will do everything possible to further Wolsey's favour when the King's great matter was at 'a good end'.[4] There is no sign of the lurking grudge which Cavendish attributes to her, although the conditional element in her professions of love and service might well have given him pause for thought.

Anne may have been dissimulating, but then so may Wolsey; except that neither of them had any obvious cause to deceive the other. The granting of the Legatine commission, and Campeggio's arrival in October appeared to signify important progress, and Wolsey's stock was riding high. However, trouble was lurking just below the surface. Anne was understandably suspicious that she was being kept out of Campeggio's way, and a month after his arrival nothing had happened. Wolsey became increasingly exasperated, and warned the Pope that 'many people' were pressing the King to solve his problem at home, which would be disastrous for the papal authority.[5] There is no doubt as to who these people were, and at the end of November Henry sent Anne's cousin, Francis Bryan, to Clement with a virtual ultimatum, threatening the withdrawal of obedience. At the same time the Boleyns were beginning to press for another policy involving a great petition from the elite of England, seeking an annulment in the national interest. This was not aimed specifically against Wolsey, but he was no party to it because it would have meant bypassing his efforts altogether, and that was something which he could not contemplate.[6] By the third week of January 1529 the French ambassador noticed that Norfolk and his allies were talking themselves up, and Mendoza had picked up a story to the effect that Anne had concluded that the cardinals were out to frustrate her, and had formed an alliance against them with her father and the Dukes of Norfolk and Suffolk. This was the first time that the latter had featured so prominently in these rumours, and the first time that Anne had been recognised as the political equal of the King's councillors.[7] Nevertheless, for the time being the anti-Wolsey coalition made no progress because Henry was not to be persuaded, and throughout the spring the King and the Cardinal worked in apparent harmony to apply increased pressure in Rome. The opening of the Blackfriars court on 18 June was a fruit of that collaboration. Anne, however, was not convinced, possibly because her supporters in Italy, notably Francis Bryan, were warning her of the papal intransigence, and representing Wolsey as (at best) a dupe, which turned out to be pretty near the mark.[8] It was a bad sign when the Cardinal's representative, Sir

John Russell, was due to go to France in June, that his mission was countermanded and the Duke of Suffolk sent instead. Suffolk achieved nothing, but that is not the point; when he returned in July he found Wolsey bogged down in the Legatine court, and the Boleyn faction geared up for a showdown. Lord Darcy, who had his own reasons for hating the Cardinal, had drawn up an action plan, which ambitiously proposed the immediate arrest of Wolsey and his agents, the impounding of their papers and a thorough investigation of their administration.[9] When the Legatine court was adjourned, many thought that the moment to strike had come. Anne had apparently convinced Henry that he had been double-crossed, and a document detailing thirty-four charges against the Chancellor was presented to the King before he left for his summer progress, that is not later than 4 August.

> When the nobles and prelates perceived that the king's favour was from the Cardinal sore minished, every man of the king's council began to lay to him such offences as they knew by him, and all their accusations were written in a book …[10]

Yet for the time being, nothing happened. This may have been partly because when he had exchanged the see of Durham for that of Winchester, that had left the revenues of the former office in the King's hands, and at the end of July Wolsey had used his influence to secure the grant of those revenues (which amounted to nearly £3,000 a year) pro tempore to Lord Rochford.[11] It was also partly due to the fact that Henry simply could not make up his mind. The progress went on for nearly six weeks, and during that time Wolsey continued to run affairs as usual. Nevertheless, Anne was not prepared to give up. As a result of the failure of the Legatine court, she had decided that the Cardinal was a broken reed, and with his papal allegiance actually an obstacle to the course which now appeared to be increasingly necessary – some kind of a unilateral declaration by the King. Her professions of goodwill evaporated and she began to exercise her considerable powers of persuasion to bring about his overthrow. However, when it came to the point, her persuasions were less important than the fact that Wolsey made mistakes. The Legatine court fiasco was not his fault, but the mess over the treaty of Cambrai was, and he also misread the King's mood during the latter part of August. Wolsey was well aware of the peace negotiations planned for Cambrai, but was in ignorance when they would begin, and how seriously they were intended. He asked that they be postponed until the Legatine court had finished its deliberations, but he had no leverage, and his request was ignored.[12] When he learned that they were due to commence on 5 July, he wanted to go, but the King insisted that the Blackfriars court took priority, and he sent Cuthbert Tunstall and Thomas More instead. In the event they wasted their time, being kept on the sidelines and largely in ignorance of the proceedings. The treaty of Cambrai was signed on 3 August, and although Tunstall and More were signatories, English interests were virtually ignored.[13] Not only was this a humiliation for Henry, it also meant that his diplomatic leverage against the Emperor had disappeared. A series of meetings with du Bellay, the French ambassador, failed to produce a text of the treaty, and Henry became increasingly suspicious, not only of the French but also of Wolsey, whom he believed to have been duped. A detailed examination of the treaty, when it became available, convinced him that he was wrong to doubt the French, but not Wolsey. On 1 September du Bellay reported that Norfolk, Suffolk and Rochford were in high favour, and that Wolsey was on the way out.[14]

The Cardinal knew that the only way to redeem this situation was through a face to face interview with Henry, and that Anne now set herself to prevent. His attempt to go to Cambrai in July was represented as an attempt to sabotage the Legatine court and thus delay any annulment of the King's marriage in the interests of his own position. He was accused of having been for years in the pocket of Louise of Savoy, the Queen Mother of France, from whom he had undoubtedly received large payments, but not larger than his position in England merited. The charges of pride and vainglory, levied in the earlier 'book' were revived. On 12 September he was instructed to write to the King outlining the topics to be discussed. This was an unprecedented request and probably indicates Anne's determination not to be surprised, because the letter was sent in the name of a council now dominated by her allies.[15] Accounts of the interview, when it came, were much embroidered by contemporaries anxious to show Anne's malice towards the Cardinal, and her influence over Henry. However, other observers noted nothing unusual in the fact that the two men were closeted together for many hours, nor in the demeanour of Rochford, Tuke and Gardiner, the latter two having supposedly deserted Wolsey as a sinking ship. They had showed 'as much observance and humility to my Lord's Grace as ever I saw them do …'. If they were inwardly fuming, they did not show it.[16] So if Anne was victorious over this interview, it was by no means obvious to a well positioned observer. Nevertheless, some one, or something, convinced Henry that he was not being well served, because about a fortnight later, on 9 October, the Cardinal was dramatically charged with *praemunire* in King's Bench, and about a week later deprived of the Great Seal.[17] The King's change of mind is not visible to the naked eye, but it is reasonable to suppose that the Boleyns and their allies, working both in council and through Anne's unique personal access, succeeded at last in persuading him that Wolsey had a case (or several cases) to answer. According to Cavendish his enemies prepared an attack against him in the parliament, but abandoned it in favour of a *praemunire*, presumably on the grounds that it would enjoy a better chance of success. The stories about the interviews at Grafton may not have been literally true, but they were a convenient and persuasive metaphor for a victory gained somewhere behind the scenes.

It is quite possible that, although the King's decision appears to have been sudden, it was based upon accumulating doubts over a number of years. As we have seen, there is evidence of uncertainty in their relationship going back at least to the failure of the Amicable Grant in 1525, and becoming noticeable to hostile observers in the summer of 1527. There was also the little matter of the nunnery of Wilton.[18] When Cecily Willoughby, the abbess died in April 1528, there had been competition over the appointment of her successor. The obvious choice was the prioress, Isabel Jordayn, but William Carey was anxious to promote his sister Eleanor, who was nun at Wilton. He apparently secured the support of both Wolsey and the King, the latter as a favour to Carey's sister-in-law, Anne, in what was clearly a little bit of Boleyn networking. It transpired, however, that Eleanor was a most unsuitable candidate, having produced illegitimate children by at least two priests, although whether before or after taking the veil is not clear. Henry withdrew his support, and asked Anne to do the same, which she did. In order to preserve her credibility, however, he also instructed that Jordayn was not to be appointed either, 'but that some other good and well disposed woman should have it'.[19] Meanwhile Wolsey, apparently ignorant of the King's order, had nominated Isabel, which provoked a terrifying letter of rebuke from Henry, and grovelling apology from the minister. At that time Anne had continued her professions of good will, but it had been demonstrated that even the Lord Chancellor could not cross the Boleyn party with impunity. A year later the memory of that mistake could well have contributed to the decision to oust Wolsey, because it was another demonstration of his fallibility. By that time William Carey was dead, and the Wilton controversy long since resolved, but Anne's influence in the patronage market was as strong as ever, and may well have contributed to Henry's decision to promote her father to the earldom of Wiltshire in December.

Wolsey was down, but not yet out. For the first few weeks after his fall he remained at Esher, borrowing money to keep body and soul together while the King plundered his possessions.[20] He was deprived of the bishopric of Winchester and the Abbey of St Albans, while Henry sought for (and found) a legal pretext to lay hands on York Place, which belonged to the province of York rather than to the Cardinal. Wolsey, rightly it would seem, blamed these depredations on the Boleyn party in the council, and protested vigorously that they should 'put no more into his head than ... may stand with a good conscience'. Cavendish was of the opinion that 'the Council' was out to torment and humiliate the fallen minister, and indeed there seems to have been an inconsistency in Henry's own actions which suggests as much.[21] In spite of the plunder, more than once he sent Wolsey a ring as a gesture of his continued favour, and even persuaded Anne to send him a similar token. He sent his physicians to him at Christmas when he was unwell, and in February 1530 sanctioned his move from Esher to Richmond. This last without the knowledge of his council.[22] Then in April Wolsey was given leave to retire to his diocese in the north, which may have been the King's idea of favour, or it may have been the Duke of Norfolk who was anxious to have him out of the way. Henry gave him £1,000 towards his removal expenses, which would be consistent with either interpretation. By that time, however, the Cardinal was embarked upon a dangerous course. He decided to mobilise his European contacts and prestige in an effort to recover the King's favour, and apparently entered into a secret negotiation with Clement VII. Inevitably his messages were intercepted, and although not very explicit, were sufficient to tip the balance in the King's mind in favour of his enemies. On 1 November 1530, just a few days before his planned enthronement in York Minster, his arrest was ordered on a charge of treason. He had, it was alleged, 'intrigued ... both in and out of the kingdom' and had entered into 'sinister practices made to the court of Rome for reducing him to his former estates and dignity'.[23] Apprehended on 4 November, he began a slow and painful journey south, but at Leicester Abbey on the 29th he died, and so deprived his enemies of the satisfaction of seeing him tried and executed.

This was, in a sense, a victory for Anne, her family and friends. It had been demonstrated more than two years before the Act in Restraint of Appeals that any negotiation with Rome not conducted through the King would be deemed high treason. That was sufficient warning to the prelates of England to curtail their normal business relationship, and was an act of Supremacy well ahead of the game. However, with Wolsey gone, the coalition of hostile interests which he had held together, fell apart. The Duke of Norfolk, swallowing his increasing dislike of Anne and her ways, continued to back her in his own interest, but Lord Darcy fell away, and so did the Duke of Suffolk, taking his clients with him. Significantly, as early as 29 October 1529 Sir Thomas More was named as the new Lord Chancellor. More was not only not a client of the Boleyns, he was fundamentally opposed to Anne and her ambitions, and his appointment represents a gesture of independence on Henry's part which should not be overlooked. The King was determined to have no more clerical chancellors, and his choice fell upon a prestigious lawyer, whom he wrongly supposed would be amenable to his wishes when the time came. Wolsey had clients, but few friends when it came to an issue, and even many of his clients proved unreliable, witness the career of Stephen Gardiner, but the Queen was an altogether different proposition.[24] With the Cardinal's confusing presence removed, the Boleyns found themselves confronting Catherine and her supporters in undisguised hostility. The court and the council both became divided, with the King apparently undecided what to do next. The pardon of the clergy, which they purchased at the beginning of 1531 was a victory for the annulment party, but only a partial one, because Henry did not follow it up with any decisive action. Meanwhile, Francis I was trying to use diplomatic means to bring England and the papacy together, because he did not want to sacrifice the alliance of either, and Henry, in spite of his bluffings, had not given up on the papacy. Consequently a strong conservative party rallied to the Queen, pointing out the dangers of the course which the King was apparently proposing to take. These included the Duke of Suffolk (not without prompting from his wife), the Marquis of Exeter, the Earl of Shrewsbury, and the King's intimate friend, Nicholas Carew.[25] Rather more surprising, they were joined by Elizabeth Howard, Duchess of Norfolk, who was bitterly at odds with her husband over his affair with Bess Holland, and for that reason was deeply suspicious of Anne and her pretensions. Most effective of all in thwarting Henry's wishes was his Archbishop of Canterbury, William Warham. Warham was too old a royal servant to defy his master openly, but his obstructiveness became more and more apparent as the King began to move towards finding a domestic solution to his problem.[26] Against this formidable line up there stood in the Boleyn camp, not only Anne, her father and brother, but the earls of Huntingdon and Sussex, the veteran diplomat Sir Thomas Wyatt, and the rapidly rising Thomas Cromwell. Eustace Chapuys who is our main source of information, may have exaggerated the strength of the conservative position, because his whole sympathy was that way inclined, but he gives the impression of an aristocracy on the verge of revolt, and of a population entirely supportive of their concerns.[27] Nevertheless, at the centre it was an uneven battle, because Catherine's friends relied for success on either the Pope giving a definitive sentence against Henry, and his accepting it, or else upon his becoming weary of his never-ending quest, and simply giving up. With Anne on the war path, however, neither of those things was likely to happen. She might rely on her supporters for decisions which had to be made in council, but when it came to the vital task of influencing the King, her own combination of sexuality and intelligence was invincible. Henry might waver from time to time, but when it came to the point, he wanted her as he had never wanted any woman before – and she knew it.

From the autumn of 1532 to the summer of 1533, the Boleyns were riding a high tide of success. This was partly political, Warham's death, the creation of Anne as Marquis of Pembroke, the success of Henry's meeting with Francis I at Calais, and partly sexual. Anne slept with Henry and became pregnant; he married her and appointed Thomas Cranmer to the archbishopric to regularise that position. None of this had much to do with her family or supporters, it was all down to Anne herself. The most that her party could do was to organise the propaganda campaign which backed the King's decisions.[28] Her coronation was fair trial of strength, and all the honours went to the Boleyns, who turned out in force, male and female, and shanghied all but the most determined of Catherine's following into taking part. It may have been a distasteful spectacle as far as the onlookers were concerned, but that is by no means certain, and all the honours of the occasion went to Anne. The same was true, as we have seen, of Elizabeth's christening in September. Meanwhile, she had secured another tactical success in the affair of Elizabeth Barton.[29] Elizabeth had been around for a while. Originally a servant girl, in about 1525 she had begun to see visions and to utter prophecies, and at that point her vocation had been recognised and she had retired to a convent in Canterbury. This was unusual, and earned her a reputation for sanctity, but it was politically harmless. However, towards the end of 1527, when rumours of the King's search for an end to his marriage were circulating, she began to make pronouncements on that issue. Summoned to the royal presence, she warned Henry to his face that disaster would befall him if he persisted in his plans, and is alleged to have had considerable influence over both Warham and Wolsey. She also publicly warned the Pope of the dangers of yielding to the King's petition.[30] All this was sufficiently irritating, but Anne Boleyn was not yet a public factor in this equation, and the King apparently shrugged off the warnings as the fruits of 'hysteria', an ailment to which women were particularly prone. Elizabeth, however, persisted in her prophecies, and once Anne was identified as the Queen's rival, began to warn Henry specifically of the dangers of marrying her, predicting that he would not survive a month thereafter and would die a villain's death. These prophecies may have been spontaneous, or they may have been inspired by a group of clerical 'managers' led by Dr Edward Bocking, a monk of Christ Church, who appears to have been manipulating her in the interests of the Queen's party. By 1531 the Boleyns were mobilised against her, and she began to feature in the front line of the political battle. Prominent people were associated with her, not only the Friars Observant and the London Carthusians, but John Fisher, Thomas More, and even Catherine herself.[31] Henry waited until a month was past from Anne's coronation, and the more lurid of the nun's predictions were discredited, and then struck against what was becoming by then a serious nuisance. In mid-July Cromwell and Cranmer were ordered to act. Elizabeth was arrested, taken to the Tower and interrogated. Her associates were rounded up and her writings suppressed. According to Richard Grafton 'the juggling and crafty deceit of this maid was manifest and brought to light', and she and Bocking, together with two other priests and sundry Kentish gentlemen, were made to confess their fraud at Paul's Cross.[32] The council, we are told, was much exercised against her, and debated the case for three days. The Earl of Wiltshire was of the opinion that they should be condemned as heretics and burned, in which he was no doubt voicing the desire of his daughter for revenge against this dangerous group. Heresy, however, was a tricky issue in the embryonic state of the Royal Supremacy, and they were eventually condemned as traitors by Act of Attainder in the parliament which met from 15 January to 30 March 1534. The King personally drove the case on, using it as a means to purge some of his ex-wife's more recalcitrant followers, and to frighten other more substantial figures.[33] Catherine and More were too clever to be caught, but Fisher was convicted of misprision. He was not proceeded against, but his case was clearly intended as a warning to others who might be similarly tempted. Elizabeth Barton, Edward Bocking and five others were hanged at Tyburn in April. It was clear thereby that open support for Catherine would henceforth be classed as treason, and her remaining friends in the council were forced to draw in their horns. Queen Anne and her friends were triumphant, but it had become more obvious than ever that their continued enjoyment of that success was dependant upon the Queen herself, and upon her influence over her husband. As long as Catherine lurked in the background, there seemed little danger that that would diminish. Henry had burned his boats, and the beneficiaries of the fire were the Boleyns.

There were, however, issues which threatened the unity of that party. Anne was by taste and political logic strongly pro-French, but Francis was determined to maintain amicable relations with Rome, and Thomas Cromwell did not trust the French. When Clement pronounced his sentence of excommunication against Henry in September 1533, the King took umbrage with his colleague, and withdrew the Duke of Norfolk and Lord Rochford, who were then on embassy in France.[34] In fact Henry's display of bad temper at the thought of a meeting between Francis and Clement in October was seriously counterproductive. The French king had done his best for Henry, securing the postponement of the sentence for two months, but he got little thanks for his efforts. It was not Anne who was behind this outburst, because she knew well enough that as long as Catherine was being backed by the Emperor, the only diplomatic support that her husband was likely to get would come from Francis, who it would be folly to annoy. The Duke of Norfolk and the Earl of Wiltshire apparently felt the same, but Cromwell did not agree. Towards the end of 1533 he arranged the publication of *The Articles Devised by the Whole Consent of the King's Council*, a strongly anti-papal justification of Henry's policy in which the King of France's new friend was denounced as a bastard and a heretic, and Francis became even more annoyed.[35] Early in 1534 Cromwell, who 'ruled everything about the king' persuaded Henry to send a mission to the Lutheran princes of Germany, because they were also committed to oppose the Emperor. What Anne thought of this effort we do not know, but her father was not a little put out at this evidence of dabbling in heresy. Nothing came of the embassy at this time, and when Clement died in September 1534 Henry appears to have contemplated re-opening negotiations with Rome. He sent Gregory Casale in an attempt to influence the conclave, and was pleased by the election of Cardinal Farnese as Paul III. Paul would, he hoped, be amenable to seeing things Henry's way, but since he was not prepared to moderate his position in the slightest, this was forlorn hope. Although he may have been personally sympathetic to the King's dilemma, Paul was not prepared to surrender the principles upon which his predecessor had acted.[36] It is fairly safe to conclude that the King's intransigence on this issue owed not a little to the combined influence of his Queen and Thomas Cromwell.

The other issue generating tension within the Boleyn party was religion. There is no reason to suppose that Sir Thomas's children were brought up to question any of the teachings of the Church, and in later years both the Earl of Wiltshire and his wife were strictly orthodox in their beliefs. Anne, however, picked up evangelical ideas in France, perhaps from Margaret of Angouleme, but more likely from other members of her circle. Such ideas, which might be broadly classed as Christian humanist, are associated particularly with Jacques Lefevre d'Etaples, and were very widespread among the French aristocracy of that period (1515–1525).[37] Women were particularly likely to be influenced, and both Queen Claude and her sister Renee were sympathetic, so it would have been difficult for Anne to have avoided such an 'infection'. Indeed it is quite possible that she underwent some kind of spiritual awakening, because she was highly intelligent and the burning issue of the day was the nature of religious experience. Margaret seems to have been something of a role model for her, and their tastes in piety bear a strong resemblance. One of the habits which she certainly acquired was that of reading the scriptures in French, particularly the epistles of St Paul, and this was a habit which she retained after her return to England.[38] During her years as queen she was to be a keen supporter of the bible in English, and may well have influenced the King in that direction in 1535. None of this made her a Lutheran, or any other kind of heretic, and the evidence suggests that her beliefs on such key issues as justification remained strictly orthodox. What it does suggest, however, is that her personal faith was quite compatible with that support for the Royal Supremacy which her political position dictated. Years later William Latymer, writing for the benefit of Queen Elizabeth, represents her as saying:

> the royal estate of princes, for the excellency thereof doth far pass and excel all other estates and degrees of life, which doth represent and outwardly shadow unto us the glorious and celestial monarchy which God, the governor of all things, doth exercise in the firmament ...[39]

This reflected accurately Henry's own sense of his exalted position, which owed nothing to Martin Luther's concept of princely power

*Above*: 1. Blickling Hall,
Norfolk. A seventeenth
century rebuilding of
the 'fair brick house'
constructed by Sir Geoffrey
Boleyn.

*Right*: 2. Blickling church
contains many Boleyn
memorials, starting with Sir
Geoffrey in a stained glass
window.

3. The tomb of Thomas Howard, 3rd Duke of Norfolk, Anne Boleyn's uncle. He was originally interred at Thetford Abbey, then moved to Framlingham, where this memorial was erected. 4. Henry Howard, Earl of Surrey, who took part along with his father, the 3rd Duke of Norfolk, in the trials of Anne and George Boleyn. He was executed for treason in January 1547.

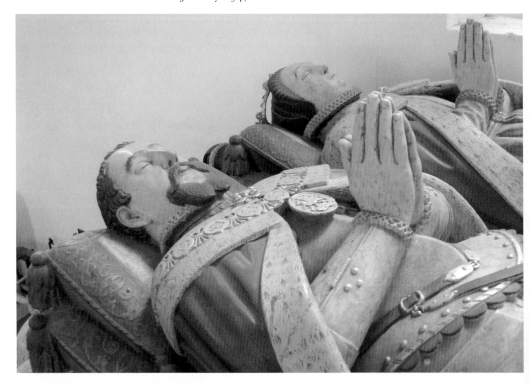

*Right*: 5. Thomas Boleyn, Earl of Wiltshire, who died at Hever Castle in Kent in 1539. From a monumental brass in St Peter's church at Hever.

*Below left*: 6. Isabella Boleyn, Sir Geoffrey's daughter, and Anne's great aunt. She married Sir John Cheyney, and her memorial brass remains in Blickling church.

*Below Right*: 7. Lady Anne Shelton, daughter of Sir William Boleyn of Blickling, and sister to Sir Thomas. She died in December 1555, and was buried at Shelton, ten miles south of Norwich.

8. Hever Castle, Kent. After the Earl of Wiltshire's death, Henry VIII purchased the castle from his heirs, and bestowed it on Anne of Cleves. When it reverted to the Crown on her death in 1557, Mary sold it to Sir Edward Waldegrave.

*Above*: 9. The 'Henry VIII bedroom' at Hever Castle.
*Below*: 10. The gardens at Hever.
*Following page spread, left*: 11. A portrait of Anne Boleyn at Ripon Cathedral, artist unknown; probably a seventeenth century copy.
*Following page spread, right*: 12. A lady, thought to be Mary Boleyn. Artist unknown. At Hever Castle.

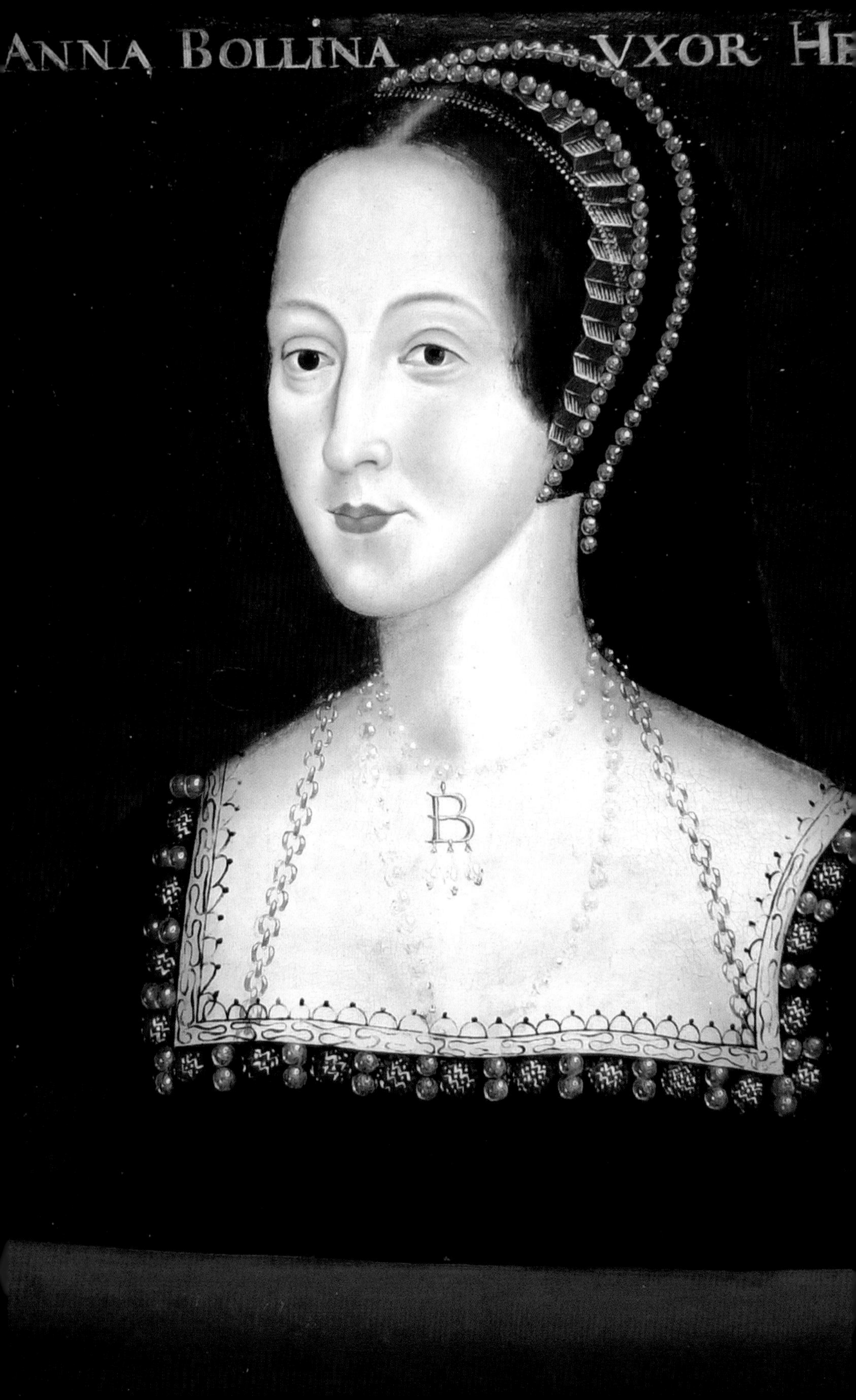
ANNA BOLLINA VXOR HE

*Top*: 15. From a bas relief depicting the Field of Cloth of Gold, 1520, which was something of a 'family reunion' for the Boleyns.
*Centre*: 16. The meeting of the two kings, Henry VIII and Francis I, from the same bas relief.
*Bottom of page*: 17. Another depiction of the Field of Cloth of Gold, showing the temporary English palace which was built for the occasion.
*Previous page spread, left*: 13. Henry VIII, *c*. 1540. From the Great Gate at Trinity College, Cambridge.
*Previous page spread, right*: 14. Henry VIII, from the cartoon by Hans Holbein in the National Portrait Gallery.

*Above left:* 18. Thomas Wolsey from a drawing attributed to Jacques Le Boucq.
*Above right:* 19. Sir Thomas More by Hans Holbein.

*Above left:* 20. Thomas Cranmer, Archbishop of Canterbury, by Gerhard Flicke.
*Above right:* 21. William Warham, Archbishop of Canterbury, *c.*1528. By Hans Holbein.

*Top left:* 22. Henry VIII and Anne Boleyn's initials entwined at King's College Chapel, Cambridge. *Top right:* 23. Detail from Holbein's design for a coronation pageant. It was staged on the eve of Anne's coronation, 31 May 1533.

24. Anne Boleyn's coronation procession approaches Westminster Abbey, 1 June 1533. This was an event boycotted by Catherine's supporters.

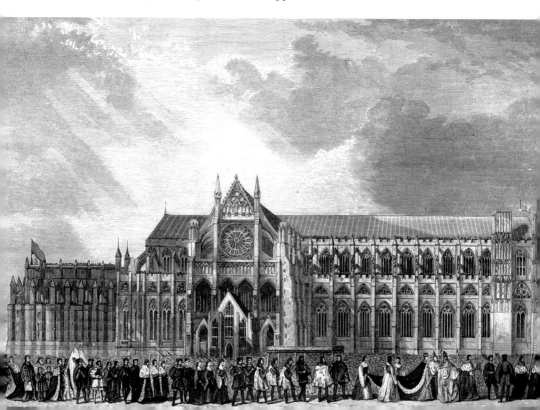

25. A view of London, showing the Tower, where Anne was taken following her arrest. By Claes Visscher, 1616.

*Above right:* 26. The execution of Anne Boleyn, 19 May 1536. A nineteenth century reconstruction. *Above left:* 27. Princess Elizabeth, later Queen Elizabeth I, aged about twelve in 1545.

*Top left*: 28. Catherine Parr, Henry VIII's last Queen and Elizabeth's stepmother, from her memorial at Sudeley.

*Bottom Left*: 29. Elizabeth I at prayer from the frontispiece to *Christian Prayers* (1569).

*Top right*: 30. Great Seal of Elizabeth I.

*Centre*: 31. Signature of Elizabeth I.

*Final page*: 33. Engraved portrait of Elizabeth I by William Rogers *c*. 1595.

*Below*: 34. Thomas Seymour. Catherine Parr's fourth husband. While Catherine was unavailable to him through pregnancy, Thomas began to make passes at Princess Elizabeth.

32. Robert Dudley, Earl of Leicester, in old age. He was Elizabeth's favourite from the beginning of her reign until his death in 1588. A copy of a portrait, probably by William Segar.

Th'admired Empresse through the worlde applauded
For supreme vertues, rarest Imitation
Whose Scepters rule fames lowde-voyc'd trumpet laudeth
Vnto the eares of euery forraigne Nation
Canapey'd vnder powrefull Angells winges
To her Immortall praise sweete Science singes.

Willms                    Rogers sculp.

and responsibility, but a great deal to what might be called the '*praemunire* tradition' of the English monarchy.

The difficulty in attempting to assess Anne's religious position is that it is bedevilled by hindsight. To Cavendish she was arrogant and a serial temptress, neither of which attitudes would be compatible with sincere piety, yet her own words do not suggest a lack in that direction:

> There is nothing better than by true faith to take Jesus Christ of our side for mediator, advocate and intercessor. For who that believeth in him and doth come with him to this judgement, shall not be confused.[40]

To Nicholas Harpesfield she was an arch-heretic, who seduced Henry from the true path of the Church, while to John Foxe and William Latymer she was an heroic champion of the gospel, who paved the way for the introduction of Protestantism, and died partly for that reason.[41] The truth seems to have been that she was an evangelical by conviction, and that her political influence was exercised on behalf of Thomas Cranmer and Thomas Cromwell, both of whom were concerned to pursue an evangelical policy. Her possession of an English translation of Lefevre d'Etaples' *Epistres et Evangiles*, which was dedicated to her, and may have been commissioned specially, points in the same direction. Lefevre was very insistent upon the dependence of the believer on Christ alone for salvation, a position which left him at loggerheads with the ecclesiastical establishment, which emphasised the intercession both of the saints and of the Church, but was entirely consistent with what we know of Anne's faith.[42] We know that she was contemptuous of the cults of saints, of their shrines and of the pilgrimages which they attracted, all of which attitudes found reflection in royal policy both before and after her death. Significantly, she received the dedications of a number of evangelical works, and patronised clergy of that persuasion. Mathew Parker, later Elizabeth's first Archbishop of Canterbury, was one of her chaplains, and Hugh Latimer is alleged to have owed his promotion to the see of Worcester to her intervention.[43] She was close to Thomas Cranmer, who was godfather to her daughter, and supported Richard Tracy, whose father had been posthumously condemned for denying the validity of prayers for the dead. She was also generous with her charitable giving, the estimates of which vary from £1,500 a year to 'xiiii or xv thousand pounds', both of which are exaggerations (and the latter grossly so), but the truth was substantial enough to earn the gratitude and respect of contemporaries.[44] Altogether her piety was practical and bibliocentric, devoted to the idea of reform in the Church, and critical of its more popular practices, but not stepping outside the parameters which Henry himself laid down. Unlike Thomas Cromwell later, she was not suspected or accused of sacramentarianism, and all the evidence suggests that her belief in the mass was strictly orthodox. She received the sacrament devoutly before she died, and Henry (who was prepared to believe almost any charge against her at the end) never accused her of heresy.

Nevertheless she and her brother both fell out with their parents over their evangelical programme. The Earl, like the Duke of Norfolk, was as ambivalent as he could afford to be about the Royal Supremacy. Even after the failure of the Legatine court he would have preferred (as we have seen) to wait for a papal decision before deciding upon a course of action, and was deeply unhappy about his daughter's pregnancy which forced the issue in the spring of 1533.[45] Insofar as there was a shaper of policy in the years 1532–1536, that person was the King, which helps to explain its erratic progress and apparent inconsistencies. Thomas Cromwell was his 'man of affairs', who devised the ways and means to achieve what his master wanted, and insofar as he ran his own programme, that depended upon the limits of Henry's tolerance. The Duke of Norfolk and the Earl of Wiltshire fade from the picture after 1533, and that may well be due to their lack of sympathy with the approaches which Cromwell was making to the Schmalkaldic League, and the uncertain state of relations with France. They were both great officers of State, because Thomas Howard had been Lord Treasurer since 1522, so they continued to sit in the council, but after 1532 are no longer described as 'ruling all' under the King. Both were hopeful of a rapprochement with the papacy after Clement's death, but the King overruled them. The court observers concentrated their attention on Henry's relationship with Anne, both charting and exaggerating its ups and downs, but there are distinct signs that the Earl of Wiltshire thought that his daughter was overplaying her hand, and was even overheard muttering at one point that she would be the ruin of her family.[46] Having come to power (in a sense) on the back of her sexual prowess, he found himself increasingly out of sympathy with her tactics, and out of sympathy with the evangelical programme which she shared with Thomas Cromwell. Wiltshire was a religious conservative, who went along with the King's policy because he had to, but was deeply suspicious of Cranmer, and of the other reforming bishops whom Anne had helped to promote. So a fault line ran through the Boleyn party, even at the height of their apparent success, with Anne, Lord Rochford and Thomas Cromwell on one side, and her father, her uncle, and other conservative peers such as the Earl of Shrewsbury on the other.

They could not, however, afford to fall out publicly, because behind them continued to lurk the shadow of Catherine and her friends. Anne had in a sense seen off her principle rival in June 1531, when the King had brought an end to the *ménage a trois* which had prevailed since 1528 by dismissing Catherine from the court with the curt observation that he never wished to see her again. She retired, first to Ampthill, before being moved to Buckden, and then to Kimbolton, but she was well provided for and continued to be an embarrassingly popular figure.[47] Politically, her friends were in limbo, but were kept in touch with her and with each other, by the Imperial ambassador Eustace Chapuys. Those who made their allegiance too obvious were at best out of favour at court, like the Marquis and Marchioness of Exeter, or at worst in prison, like Lady Hussey, or even on the block, a fate which befell Sir Thomas More and Bishop John Fisher in the summer of 1535. Some went into exile, as Reginald Pole did in 1532, when he could no longer stomach Henry's pursuit of an annulment. Pole was a formidable scholar and polemicist, who became a cardinal in 1535, and who was to 'carpet bomb' the King's position in *Pro Ecclesiasticae Unitatis Defensione* in 1536.[48] Henry was perfectly well aware of Catherine's popularity, and feared at one point that she might raise a rebellion against him. That, however, was not her way. Her claim was always to be the King's lawful and dutiful spouse, and armed insurrection would have been quite inconsistent with that position. For the same reason she refused to countenance Chapuys's ambitious plans for an Imperial intervention. She was always grateful for the ambassador's support, but probably realised perfectly well that her nephew was not prepared to commit men and money to what was, in effect, a personal quarrel.[49] Catherine's most determined, and most politically significant supporter, was her daughter Mary. Mary was seventeen in 1533, and full of her mother's obstinacy. She refused to accept either Catherine's demotion to the status of dowager princess, nor her own designation as 'The lady Mary', decreed by proclamation in July 1533. As a result the Countess of Salisbury was dismissed from her position as her Lady Governess, and her household was dissolved.[50] Instead she was placed in the household being created for the Princess Elizabeth, and run by Anne Shelton, who was Anne Boleyn's aunt. This household was something of a Boleyn family institution, and was deliberately designed to be as uncomfortable as possible for Mary. Mary lacked her mother's restraint, and the 'Aragon' party began increasingly to look to her for a political lead, because her position as her father's daughter made her a possible replacement for him if any insurrection were to take place. For this reason, Queen Anne and her whole political backing, were apprehensive of Mary, and extremely hostile to her. Mary made this situation worse by deliberately insulting Anne whenever she came to visit Elizabeth, and by throwing tantrums whenever she was not addressed as 'Princess', a practice which Elizabeth's servants carefully avoided.[51] Henry, however, remained attached to his daughter, difficult as she was, and that prevented any drastic action from being taken against her – a situation which drove Anne's father to an indiscreet fury. Communication between Catherine and her daughter was supposed to be forbidden, and they were certainly not allowed to meet, even when one or the other of them was ill, but in practice messages continued to be passed. Some of these were apparently written in Spanish, with which Mary must have been familiar, and they were conveyed by loyal servants, of whom Catherine had a good supply, and Mary a handful.[52] It may well be that Henry unofficially instructed that these be allowed to pass, because otherwise it is hard to see why Elizabeth's servants did not detect the practice and put a stop to it.

The Boleyn ascendancy depended ultimately on Anne's hold over Henry VIII's affections, and that relationship continued to be the subject of anxious scrutiny by friend and foe alike. In this connection there were two problems. The first and most obvious was Anne's failure to bear a son. Elizabeth's birth was a setback, but the fertility omens were good, and she fell pregnant again early in 1534. The second was her failure to adjust to the status of wife. The conventional view of a wife was that she should be chaste, humble and obedient. She ought also to be pious and silent, the nagging wife being a stock figure of ridicule for husbands. Anne however, was a woman with a mind of her own, and her own political agenda, more suitable in many ways for the council chamber than for the boudoir. She had held her lover's attention through the interminable years of their courtship by her intelligence and her temper. She had steered Henry's policies when he had seemed uncertain which way to go, she had led her family based faction, often in spite of her father, and she had not hesitated to tell her lover what she thought of him when he attempted to stray. Henry had found this fascinating, and although her behaviour had resulted in flaming rows, these were always followed by passionate reconciliations. Observers were baffled and intrigued by his reactions, but Anne always appeared to know what she was doing. However, what she failed to realise was that what was acceptable behaviour in a mistress, was not acceptable in a wife. Henry was nothing if not conventional in his expectations, and he began to find her tantrums and her political interference intolerable. After becoming queen, she should have left the politics to her father and her brother, to say nothing of Thomas Cromwell. Her piety, and the use of her patronage, were appropriate, but that she should be receiving the French ambassador and briefing the envoys whom the King was sending abroad was not. Then in the summer of 1534 she miscarried. It is not known whether the foetus was male or female, and may not have been known at the time, but this was a serious setback which aroused the demons of doubt in the King's mind.[53] Had he made another mistake?

As with most strongly physical relationships, theirs blew hot and cold. Chapuys alternately rejoiced that 'the concubine' appeared to be losing favour, and lamented that Henry's affection was as strong as ever. They quarrelled, danced, hunted and copulated with all the enthusiasm of a couple in love. But she reacted very badly when he was rumoured to be pursuing another damsel at the court, and that quarrel did not go away quite so easily. Nevertheless, she was pregnant again at Christmas 1535, and expectations were rising for the third time. Then, in January 1536, Catherine of Aragon died at Kimbolton. The Earl of Wiltshire was heard to mutter that it was pity that Mary had not gone the same way, but in the politics of marriage it was Catherine who mattered, and the landscape would never be quite the same again. Anne's shield had been removed.

# 7

# GEORGE & JANE – THE GRIMSTON YEARS

As with his sisters, there is controversy over George's date of birth, but the prevailing view is that he was born about 1504, and was thus the youngest of the three siblings. Nothing is known for certain about his education, except that it appears to have been in the best humanist tradition, and may have taken him to Oxford as an adolescent.[1] He appears at court for the first time when he took part in the christmas revels in 1514–15, an introduction which he certainly owed to his parents, both of whom were active courtiers. By 1516 he was a page in the King's chamber, and in April 1522 received along with his father a grant in survivorship of various minor offices in Kent, formerly in the possession of the Duke of Buckingham.[2] If he did put in any time in Oxford, it would have been between the years 1518 and 1522, but he certainly never graduated. That would have been normal for a young man of his status, but the lack of any subsequent reference to such a time makes it highly uncertain. In July 1524, probably when he achieved his majority, he was granted the manor of Grimston in Norfolk, where he may have taken up residence when his duties at court permitted. By 1525 he was a member of the Privy Chamber, a position which he lost when Wolsey re-shuffled the personnel in 1526. This was not due to any loss of favour on George's part, because he was shortly after installed as an Esquire of the Body, and in September 1528 received a modest annuity of 50 marks (£33 6s 8d), presumably over and above his regular fee.[3] As was appropriate for the brother of the King's leading lady, he was created Keeper of the Palace of Beaulieu (al. Newhall) in Essex with all the various privileges attached to that office, and in July 1529 he was appointed to the lucrative and not very onerous post of Keeper of St Mary's hospital in London – better known as Bedlam. At some point during September 1529 he was knighted, not for any military service which he had performed, but simply in recognition of his status as the son of Viscount Rochford. This was about the time of Wolsey's fall from grace, but not being a member of the council, George, unlike his father, was not involved in those events as far as we know.[4]

George was modest about his linguistic accomplishments. In July 1530 he confided to William Bennet that he was reluctant to write directly to either Geronimo de' Ghinucci or Gregory Casales because neither his Latin nor his Italian was up to it.[5] Like the rest of his family, however, he had excellent French, and that may have prompted Henry to send him on his first diplomatic mission to Francis I, almost before the honour of knighthood had settled upon him. On 18 September Du Bellay wrote to Anne de Montmorency that the Grand Esquire (George), accompanied by the Dean of the Chapel (John Stokesley) were shortly to depart, as he thought to the Emperor. He was mistaken, and on 8 October the King himself wrote to Montmorency accrediting Sir George Boleyn and Dr Stokesley to the court of France in place of Sir Francis Bryan who was recalled. They were instructed to confer about the Duke of Albany's activities in Scotland, to which Henry took exception, and about the possibility of convening a General Council of the Church, to which the King was presumably thinking of referring his matrimonial problem.[6] The documentation of their mission is scanty, and they were back in England shortly after Christmas. Henry, however, seems to have been well pleased with the efforts of this tyro diplomat and early in 1530 despatched him again, this time to attend the meeting between the Pope and the Emperor, and to offer congratulation to the latter on his coronation. In addition he was briefed to try, once again, to secure a favourable verdict from the Pope in his Great Matter, and in this, once again, he was completely unsuccessful. It may, indeed have been an error of taste to send the brother of so interested a party as Anne Boleyn upon such a mission, but that was not made apparent. Instead the Emperor and the Pope were upon the best of terms, and regarded the English intrusion as nuisance.[7] By the end of March, George was back in England. After the creation of his father as Earl of Wiltshire in December 1529, he was styled by the honorific title of Viscount Rochford, and, like his father, benefited from the self interested generosity of Cardinal Wolsey. In the same month, while he was in France, he received an annuity of £200 out of the revenues of the bishopric of Winchester, and 200 marks (£133 6s 8d) from those of the Abbey of St Albans. Since such temporalities were, or were about to be, in the hands of the King following Wolsey's surrender, it is uncertain how real these grants were, but the King apparently chose to honour them.[8] On 13 July 1530 he signed (as a baron) that letter from the nobility of England to Clement VII, petitioning him to find in favour of the King. The security of the English succession, they pointed out, depended upon a favourable verdict, and if it were not accorded, 'other means' might be found necessary. It had no effect.

Meanwhile, in 1526, he had married. His bride was the eminently suitable Jane Parker, the daughter of Henry Parker, 10th baron Mountjoy. She was about the same age as himself, and had been introduced at court at about the same time, surfacing in

1522 when she played the part of *Constancy* in the siege of the
Chateau Verte. It was probably an arranged marriage, because
the King gave them £20 a year as a marriage gift, and there are
no great signs of affection between them. They had no children.
Indeed George may well have taken himself to other beds, because
that George Boleyn who matriculated as a sizar at Trinity Hall,
Cambridge in November 1544, and was therefore born in about
1529, is supposed to have been his son.[9] The name of his mother
is not known, and the speculation that it might have been Jane in
a prenuptial fling is unsubstantiated and unlikely. He took a series
of degrees, culminating in a D.Th. in 1576, in which year he was
appointed Dean of Lichfield. The only signs that he may have been
considered (in a sense) royal kindred came with his appointment to
a prebend in York Minster on 29 September 1559, and to another
at Canterbury in plurality in December 1566. If he was George's
bastard, he outlived his royal kinswoman, dying in London in
1609.[10] Jane was inevitably expected to attend upon the dominant
Boleyn lady, who was Anne, and was in her entourage when she
accompanied Henry to his rendezvous with Francis I in October
1532. She also attended her coronation on 1 June 1533, and her
lying-in in September. She was probably present when Anne was
created Marquis of Pembroke in September 1532, but the records
are silent in that respect. However, she appears thereafter to have
fallen out with her husband's family, being banished from the
court in December 1534, and spending some days in the Tower
in 1535 as a result of taking part in a female demonstration
against the Queen.[11] Life at Grimston must have become distinctly
uncomfortable, as Jane became increasingly suspicious of George's
relations with other women, including his sister Anne. By 1536 she
was far from being either loyal or supportive.

It may also have been that a part of the shadow which had fallen between them was caused by religion. There is no sign that Jane was anything other than strictly orthodox in her faith, and she had no patronage of any significance to indicate otherwise, while George was clearly in the evangelical camp.[12] John Foxe later listed Lord Rochford along with Cromwell and Anne herself as favourers of the Gospel in these years.[13] Chapuys thought him a perfect Lutheran, and disliked talking to him because of his propensity to start religious arguments. He appears to have been personally responsible for the translation into English of Le Fevre's *Epistres et Evangiles*, the original edition of which had been published at Alencon in 1532, and also of *L'Ecclesiaste*, published in 1531. Both these manuscripts now survive in the British Library, and both are dedicated to Anne. However, they cannot have been for her exclusive use, because her French was every bit as good as his, and it is natural to suppose that they were intended as a contribution to that evangelical propaganda campaign which did not eventually come about because of the King's hostility.[14] They probably circulated among the Queen's ladies, and may well have been partly responsible for the hostility which Jane Rochford was showing by 1535. The translation was undertaken at Anne's request, and the dedication indicates the degree of closeness which existed between them:

To the right honourable lady, the Lady Marquis of Pembroke, her most loving and friendly brother sends greetings.

Our friendly dealings, with so divers and sundry benefits, besides the perpetual bond of blood, have so often bound me, Madam, inwardly to love you, daily to praise you, and continually to serve you, that in every of them I must perforce become your debtor for want of power … considering that by your commandment I have adventured to do this, without the which it would not have been in me to have performed it … I shall be ready to obey, praying him on whom this book treats to grant you many good years …[15]

George was certainly one of these courtiers who was committed to the idea of printing the bible in English, and may well have been responsible for keeping Anne in touch with the French reformers through his frequent diplomatic sorties across the Channel. Ironically, the most unequivocal expression of that commitment came in the scaffold speech which he made in May 1536, when, with his life on the line, there is no reason to doubt the truth of what he said:

Truly so that the word should be among the people of the realm I took upon myself great labour to urge the king to permit the printing of the scriptures to go unimpeded among the commons of the realm in their own language …[16]

This enthusiasm helped to set him at odds with his own father, but it did not make him a Lutheran, or a heretic of any kind. He did indeed advocate an invitation to Philip Melanchthon in 1535 'considering the conformity of his doctrines here', but that was in association with the Duke of Norfolk, and clearly reflects a misunderstanding of Philip's theology.[17] As the King was well aware, Archbishop Arundel's early fifteenth-century prohibition of translations referred only to unauthorised copy, and for that the Royal Supremacy offered the perfect answer. Let the King authorise it himself! George, like Anne, was an active evangelical, but he never transcended the boundaries which the King laid down for his subjects, and was never accused of heresy. In 1531 he was deputed to argue the King's case in convocation, and that indicates a high degree of trust. His death, like that of his sister, was a victory for conservative forces within the court, but it was not a victory over the King.

That Jane was to some extent involved in the charges against her husband in May 1536 seems reasonably well established. The lost journal of Anthony Anthony, which was used by Gilbert Burnet in the late seventeenth century was explicit that 'the wife of Lord Rochford was a particular instrument in the death of Queen Anne', apparently by carrying stories about Anne's infidelities to the King. These stories related to her brother as well as to Mark Smeaton and others, and Burnet speculated that they may well have been provoked by jealousy of 'a familiarity between the Queen and her brother beyond what so near a relationship would justify'.[18] These stories must relate back to 1534, because that was when Jane's intimate association with Anne came to an end, but they could well have been remembered against him, or brought up afresh at the time of his trial. That she actually gave evidence at his trial is unlikely because the close relationship between them would have precluded that, but in a case that was largely circumstantial, such stories may well have carried considerable weight, especially if skilfully deployed, as they would have been by Cromwell. Jane in any case seems to have felt that Cromwell owed her a favour because before the month was out, she was writing to him, asking that the King should grant her the moveable property of her late husband, which was in his hands by virtue of George's attainder. Her only income, she alleged, was an annuity of 100 marks (£66 13s 4d) which had been settled on her by the Earl of Wiltshire for the term of his life.[19] That this had not been cancelled probably indicates that she was less estranged from Thomas than she was from George, and indicates a religious element in their relationship.

Jane's exclusion from the court seems to have been explicitly Boleyn related, because within a few weeks she was back as a Lady of the Chamber to Jane Seymour, who married Henry as his third wife on 30 May. She probably needed the income which such a post conferred. It is by no means certain where she was living when not at court, unless she was given the use of Grimston, which would have been in the hands of the King. After Jane Seymour's death, and a period in limbo, she was appointed to a similar position in the English household of Anne of Cleves, a place which she may well have owed to Cromwell's continuing favour. By that time the Earl of Wiltshire was dead, and her annuity presumably expired with him. It was while serving in this capacity that she uttered the famous words about 'it being a long time before we shall see a Duke of York' in reaction to Anne's account of her wedding night.[20] By this time, although she did not remarry, she was thoroughly experienced in the ways of the bedchamber, and it may well have been for that reason that she was promptly transferred to the service of Henry's fifth queen, Catherine Howard soon after they married at Oatlands on 28 July 1540. This promotion she certainly did not owe to Cromwell who had been executed on the day of the King's marriage, but probably to the Duke of Norfolk, who was instrumental in arranging the match.[21] Aged about thirty-six, she must have seemed a motherly figure to the nineteen-year-old queen, and it may have been for that reason that Catherine chose to confide in her. How much she told her about her pre-nuptial adventures we do not know, but Jane can have had few illusions as to what kind of girl she was dealing with. She was thus caught in a trap partly of her own making, because she could not resign her position without explaining why, and thus betraying the confidence with which she had been entrusted. She may also have felt a good deal of affection for her wayward mistress. Whether she acted as agent provocateur (Catherine's story) or on the Queen's explicit instructions (her own version) she found herself in the position of pander between the Queen and two putative lovers, Francis Dereham and Thomas Culpepper.[22] These antics came to a climax during the royal progress to the north in the summer of 1541, when at each stopping place, she arranged backstairs access to Catherine's apartments, and presumably made sure that other servants were not around. She did not actually witness any sexual activity, but later claimed (with good reason) that she believed it to have taken place. By the time that she made that statement she was trying desperately to dig herself out of the pit into which she had fallen when the story came out. However, Thomas Culpepper at his trial alleged that she had 'provoked him much' to intercourse with the Queen, and that was probably close to the truth.[23] Both women were thoroughly interrogated, and Catherine broke down in hysterics, but the violation of a queen was ancient treason, and both Dereham and Culpepper were tried and executed. That left the women with nowhere to go, and both were condemned by Act of Attainder in January 1542. In aiding and abetting the actual bodily harm of the King's consort, Jane was also judged guilty of high treason, and she was executed along with Catherine on 13 February. After her death she was described as a 'meddlesome female' and as 'that bawd, the lady Jane Rochford'.[24] Perhaps her own sexual frustrations lay behind her actions, and she welcomed the chance of vicarious experience. She seems to have died unlamented, because her actions had done irreparable harm to the Howard political interest, and thoroughly alienated the Duke of

Norfolk to whom Catherine had originally owed her opportunity.

Chapuys heard that George was among that select band who attended Henry's secret wedding to Anne, and that is likely enough, although the ambassador also heard that the celebrant had been 'the elect of Canterbury' whereas Cranmer appear to have been in ignorance of the event until some time later.[25] Apart from that, various references to George in the records present merely a picture of a courtier and royal servant in favour. He was summoned to parliament in February 1533 as Viscount Rochford, which was an indication that he was expected to support the King in the House of Lords, since it was by no means automatic that the holder of such a title of honour would be summoned in his father's lifetime. It was matter for the royal discretion, so it can be assumed that Henry had a good reason for wishing him to be included. The parliament sat until 7 April, and passed the Act in Restraint of Appeals, for which George dutifully voted. However, before the parliament was through, on 11 March, he was briefed to accompany the Duke of Norfolk in embassy to Henry's 'perpetual ally the French king', and set off soon after for the express purpose of preventing another meeting between Francis and Clement which he knew was under consideration.[26] Disconcerted by the news of Henry's excommunication in June, Norfolk sent his colleague back to England for instructions between 8 and 27 August, with the result that both of them were recalled, and George was paid his expenses amounting to £100. They arrived back in time to perform their allotted offices at Elizabeth's christening on 10 September. Francis was apparently considerably put out by their withdrawal, and Henry very annoyed at failing to prevent the meeting, so the alliance was under considerable strain as 1533 came to an end.

On 15 January 1534 it was again noted that Lord Rochford had been summoned to parliament, and in this session were passed the Act in Restraint of Annates and the first Succession Act.[27] Once more the Boleyns did their duty, and on 30 March, the day the session ended, both were noted as being present in the House. No sooner was the parliament over, on 12 April, than Rochford and Sir William Fitzwilliam were briefed again for France, apparently to mend fences and carry out the more or less honorific task of conveying 'a book' from Henry VIII to Francis I. What this may have been is not apparent, but it was presumably a French version of the King's case against the Pope. On 14 May, Chapuys noted their return, but made no comment upon their errand.[28] By the summer of 1534 there are some signs that George's favour was outstripping that of his father, which may well have been due to his close relations with Anne, and the fact that her father was becoming grumpy about her evangelical agenda, of which George was fully supportive, and towards which the King was at this stage indulgent. In June the related offices of Constable of Dover Castle and Lord Warden of the Cinque Ports were conferred on him.[29] This may indicate that he was transferring his main operations from Norfolk to Kent, possibly to avoid Jane who seems to have remained at Grimston. Being no longer welcome at court, she no doubt had a good deal of time on her hands. In April 1535 he was granted the manor of Southe in Kent, which had belonged to Sir Thomas More, but it is doubtful whether he ever lived there. As Constable of Dover Castle adequate accommodation was provided, and in any case as a Gentleman of the Privy Chamber he would have been spending most of his time in London. In May of the same year he was granted to manor of Oteham, but he did not live there either.[30] He served on the Commissions of Oyer and Terminer against the Carthusian Priors in April, and against More in May. Fisher, as a bishop and a lord of the parliament, was condemned by Act of Attainder.[31] On 11 April George was reported as preparing 'in all haste' to return to France, but the order was apparently countermanded because on 8 May John Husee wrote to Lord Lisle, 'My Lord of Rochford goes not', Sir William Paulet having been appointed in his place.[32] The work of the Commissions clearly took precedence. He did, however, go to Calais at the end of May, as one of the team intended to negotiate for a marriage between Princess Elizabeth and the infant Duke of Angouleme, going in place of Thomas Cromwell, who pleaded sickness. The negotiation failed, and Rochford was later claimed to have spent eight days at Calais 'and done nothing'.[33]

All the evidence suggests that he continued to be close to the King and in high favour as 1535 turned to 1536. In January the ever-partial Chapuys reported:

> You could not conceive the joy that the king and those who form this confederacy have shown at the death of the good Queen (Catherine), especially the Earl of Wiltshire and his son, who said it was pity that the Princess (Mary) did not keep company with her ...[34]

If they ever said any such thing, it was to reflect the King's mood, because it would not have been lost upon such shrewd politicians as the Boleyns that Catherine's death had removed an important safeguard of Anne's position, and left her exposed to the fluctuations of Henry's conscience in a way which she had not been exposed before. As we have seen, George was included with his father in the favourable lease of the Crown manor of Rayleigh in March 1536, and was writing to Lord Lisle about matters of routine business as late as 17 April. There is no reason to suppose that he had any indication of the disaster which was about to engulf his family, and may well have been on his way to intercede for his sister when he was arrested and taken to the Tower on 2 May. The surprise appears to have been complete.[35] In spite of his success, Lord Rochford was not a wealthy man, and a desire to seize on his assets can have played no part in his downfall. At the time of his attainder his lands were valued at £441 10s 9d. He was of course the heir to the earldom of Wiltshire, but that was another prospect which was cut off by his death at the hands of the executioner on 19 May.[36] He left no lawful children, and the legitimate Boleyn line became extinct with the death of his uncle James in 1561.

George is not an easy man to get to know. In his youth he was overshadowed by his father, and in later years by his sister. He was only thirty-two when he died. Most of the intimate record which we have of him derives from his trial, when he showed himself to be intelligent and resourceful. His enthusiasm for the Gospel is well attested, but appears more in the support which he gave to Anne than in any independent action of his own. Apart from a certain skill in translating evangelical treatises into English, his only well attested talent was for diplomacy. But owing to the difficult circumstances in which he was operating, he was denied the kind of triumph which his father had enjoyed at Mechelen. Even his poor relations with his wife, which could explain some of his conduct after 1529, is largely a matter of deduction and supposition. He was later alleged to have been a covert homosexual, and his childless marriage explained in those terms, but there is no contemporary evidence for any such orientation.[37]

If anything the indications are that he was a 'ladies man', with a certain charm of manner and a gift for versifying. It was that which his wife resented, but her own sexuality is questionable, and she may well not have offered him a very attractive option. In terms of family politics, he was from about 1525 onward an ever present factor, and enjoyed a good deal of favour, but nothing is known of his relationship with the King. As a member of the Privy Chamber he is shadowy by comparison with, say Henry Norris or William Compton. Inevitably he has gone down in history as Anne Boleyn's brother, who was executed for having sex with her, a charge implausible enough to have cast doubt upon the whole case against her – perhaps more than is justified.

# 8

# THE FALL OF THE BOLEYNS –
# THE TOWER DAYS

On the morning of Tuesday, 2 May 1536, Anne Boleyn was arrested and taken to the Tower. Later that same day, her brother George was also apprehended, and less than three weeks later, on 17 and 19 May, they were executed. The background to these seismic events has been much written about and speculated upon.[1] Chapuys was writing of quarrels between the royal couple as far back as 1534, when Henry was alleged to have been enamoured of another damsel, a development which Anne had taken badly. Given the ambassador's hostility to 'the Concubine', it is wise not to take these stories too seriously, but that there should have been tiffs and reconciliations would be entirely consistent with the relationship which existed between them. It is likely that Henry went on playing games of courtly love with a variety of ladies, and that his queen took exception to such antics, but that did not mean that his marriage was breaking down. It was not until January 1536 that the King began to show a serious interest in Jane Seymour, and by then the political circumstances had changed. Jane was twenty-seven, and an experienced courtier, having been a lady-in-waiting to both Catherine of Aragon and Anne herself. She was no great beauty, but she was a daughter of Sir John Seymour of Wolf Hall, near Marlborough, and therefore came of a good breeding stock.[2] Henry and Anne had actually visited Wolf Hall in the course of the summer progress, and had stayed for nearly a week in September

1535, but it is by no means certain that Jane was actually there at the time. In any case, the King would hardly have needed such an opportunity to get to know her. The visit to Wolf Hall was more about the career of Jane's elder brother Edward than it was about her own. Antoine de Castelnau, the French ambassador, picked up a story in October 1535 about the King having 'new amours', but this belongs in the same category as Chapuys's tales, and is contradicted by direct evidence from the English court.[3] Besides it would have been at about that time that Anne became pregnant for the third time. However, by 29 January 1536 Chapuys was reporting that the King was contemplating a third marriage, and that was an altogether a more serious business.[4]

Henry was well aware that his second marriage was as unpopular as ever. While the court was in Hampshire on the summer progress, there had been hostile demonstrations in London, and support for Mary in particular appeared to be growing. Cromwell's commissioners were compiling the *Valor Ecclesiasticus*, confiscating relics and closing down shrines. The threat of religious change was in the air, and people, including many of the nobility, did not like it. The Queen's condition therefore became doubly important. If her pregnancy should fail, as had happened before, and with Catherine dead, the King would be free to repudiate Anne and take a third wife. It was no doubt some such speculation that Chapuys had picked up. This does not mean that Henry had given up on Anne, but merely that the way was open for him to do so if he chose, and the modest figure of Jane Seymour lurked in the background ready to give him an additional incentive. Meanwhile, the complex international situation added another dimension to the equation. Paul III had responded to the news of John Fisher's execution by excommunicating Henry (again), and by seeking to persuade the

Emperor and the King of France to sink their differences in an attack on schismatic England.[5] Fortunately for Henry, the Duke of Milan died without heirs on 1 November 1535, and that re-opened a long festering controversy between the two major powers. It also persuaded the Boleyns and their allies to press the King for closer ties with France, which explains why Anne was trying (without success) to arrange a French marriage for her two-year-old daughter Elizabeth, and also why she was plying a renewed correspondence with Margaret of Angouleme during November and December.[6] Thomas Cromwell, meanwhile, was eyeing a different prospect. Picking up on some positive signs from Charles, he was coming round to the view that England's security would be best served by doing a deal with the Emperor. The main obstacle in the way of such a policy was Catherine, but with her death the whole scene changed, and Cromwell's policy suddenly seemed to the King to be a viable option.

January was an eventful month. Catherine died on the 7th, and on the 24th Henry fell heavily from his horse in the tiltyard at Greenwich, where he was celebrating his freedom with a little jousting. The fall left him unconscious for two hours, causing something like panic among those close to him, and five days later, Anne miscarried. She alleged that this was due to anxiety at the news of his accident, but the truth seems to have been that she had had a difficult pregnancy, possibly because of her age.[7] This event was controversial from the start. One not particularly well informed contemporary did not believe that it had happened at all, and the whole pregnancy was a figment of Anne's imagination, driven on by her intense desire for a son. The Emperor was also apparently sceptical at first because he had convinced himself that Anne's childbearing days were over, a perception fuelled by his desire to bring the marriage to an end. However, there is no reason to doubt the truth of Chapuys's despatch of 10 February, which carried the details as far as he had been able to discover them. He reported that the foetus had 'the appearance of a male about three and half months old', information which he must have derived from one of the women in attendance upon her, and which is confirmed independently from other sources.[8] Many years later Nicholas Sander retailed a story to the effect that the foetus was deformed, but there is no contemporary evidence to that effect, and if it had been true, Chapuys would surely have reported it. When he heard the news, Henry was bitterly disappointed, and declared that there must surely be some reason why God was denying him a son. His reaction was typically self-serving, and he seems not to have given a thought to his equally distressed wife, but that is not a reason to suppose that he had already decided to repudiate her. The only merit of the deformed foetus theory is that it provides a tidy explanation for that decision, because it was a contemporary belief that deformity in a child was a sign that it was misbegotten. In other words that Anne had been playing away from home, and the conception was not by the King.[9] If Anne was guilty of adultery, however, some explanation was needed as to why Henry had never noticed until his face was, so to speak, rubbed in it. Witchcraft could of course provide a convenient excuse, and there is some evidence that as early as 1533 the King had been speaking of his infatuation in those terms. Then, however, he had spoken in a moment of casual anger; now he returned to that theme in a more considered fashion. Deformed foetus or not, there must be some explanation as to why this woman had held him in thrall for nearly a decade. The obvious reason lay in his own weakness and susceptibility, but that is hardly likely to have appealed to such an egotist as Henry was. She had cast a spell over him, which in a sense was nothing but the truth, however her weapons had been her own sexuality and wit, weapons which he could have resisted had his own personality been more robust. His pride demanded some more tangible cause for his own vulnerability, and witchcraft provided the ideal explanation.[10] Shrovetide came at the end of February in that year, and Chapuys noted that Henry spent the feast alone at Whitehall. That may have been significant, but there were perfectly good business reasons why Henry needed to be at Westminster at that time, and Anne was, in all probability, still convalescent after her miscarriage. So it does not follow that the King had already made up his mind about her. What the evidence does suggest is that Henry was in a very uncertain state, and prone to quarrel with his wife for no very obvious reason. Only this time there was no passionate reconciliation. Anne's natural magic was ceasing to be effective.

There was, moreover, another very important piece in this jigsaw puzzle, and that was Thomas Cromwell. Cromwell had never liked the pro-French orientation which the logic of Henry's policies had demanded over the last few years, and the death of Catherine offered an opportunity to mend fences with the Empire. For his part, Charles was anxious to detach the King of England from Francis for reasons quite unconnected to his marriage, and early in 1536 had blocked a papal decree depriving Henry of his throne.[11] Such a decree, as he well realised, would be so much hot air unless he was prepared to enforce it, which he had not the slightest intention of doing. In an ideal world, he would like to see Anne removed, and Mary recognised as the heir to the throne. However, the world was not ideal, and he was prepared to do a deal which would leave 'the Concubine' in place, provided some sort of an arrangement could be made over Mary. He therefore instructed Chapuys to swallow his distaste and make a friendly approach to Cromwell to see if this was possible. The ambassador was even prepared to make a gesture of recognition towards Anne as queen, which he had hitherto studiously avoided.[12] However. the obstacle to this promising line of negotiation was the Queen herself. She had no objection to the negotiations themselves, and George greeted Chapuys effusively when he came to court. There were obvious advantages in a rapprochement with the Emperor, but she had no intention of allowing any deal which hindered Elizabeth's title to the throne, and consequently was firmly opposed to any suggestion that Mary should be restored.[13] This presented Cromwell with a dilemma. Either he could leave Anne alone, and hope to do a deal which made no mention of Mary, or he could take the risk of seeking to remove her in the hope that the King would then become amenable to a fuller agreement. Perhaps if the biddable Jane Seymour could be elevated in her place, both Mary and Elizabeth would cease to be issues. It was at this stage that he realised that Henry was having serious doubts about his wife.

Anne was a politician as well as a queen, and there were more issues in train than Mary's status. Henry had decided to confiscate the property of the smaller religious houses, and a statute for that purpose was going through parliament at the time. Cromwell had invested a good deal of time and energy in this proposal, but Anne was opposed to it.[14] This seems to have been not out of any affection for monks or nuns, but because she believed that the revenues so released should have been recycled to other religious purposes. This was a view which she shared with Thomas Cranmer, but whereas the Archbishop had made his objections known privately to the King, Anne had spoken out publicly against the bill, and thereby endangered its passage. In spite of the congruence of so many of their ideas, and the fact that he owed some part of his career in the royal service to her support, in the course of April 1536 Cromwell shifted his allegiance from Anne to Jane Seymour. This involved a suspension of hostilities with the conservative elements in the court, because it was they rather than Jane's family which provided her substantial backing, and a high level of risk.[15] Because the Queen was such a formidable figure, she could not simply be shunted aside, as Catherine had been. A capital charge would be necessary, and that would involve converting the King's suspicions into an absolute conviction that she had been guilty of adultery, and not merely of adultery but of a conspiracy to destroy him. What the indictments found against her eventually said was that she had been, on various specified dates, guilty of adultery with no less that five men, including her brother George, and that she had 'compassed and imagined' the King's death, mainly in a conversation with Henry Norris in which she had claimed that 'he looked to have her if ought came to the king but well'.[16] Adultery was an ecclesiastical offence, not a criminal one, so a lot hinged on this somewhat problematic charge, but first it was necessary to convince the King that these crimes had been committed. With that conviction in place, a capital sentence could be expected, and that was what the circumstances required.

Both Henry's and Cromwell's actions during April 1536 have been subjected to a variety of interpretations. On the 25th the King wrote to Richard Pate, his ambassador in Rome, alluding to his 'entirely beloved' wife and to the likelihood of her giving him a son. It was a routine communication, instructing Pate to keep up his pressure for a reversal of papal policy, and gives no indication that Henry was in any way dissatisfied with Anne, indeed the impression is quite the reverse.[17] Meanwhile, on the 24th an open-ended commission of Oyer and Terminer had been issued for the trial of high treasons, and it has been suggested that this indicates that Cromwell already had his evidence against the Queen's lovers, and was intending to proceed against them. However, the normal practice was for suspects to be arrested and interrogated before any such commission was issued, so unless this Oyer and Terminer was issued speculatively, the probability is that it had nothing to do with Anne or her lovers.[18] Similarly on the 27th, writs were issued for a new parliament, and this was unusual in that it was only a fortnight since the last session had been dissolved. Perhaps the Secretary was laying careful plans, because in the event one of the pieces of business which this parliament was to discharge was to fix the succession in the King's offspring by Jane Seymour, and to bastardise Elizabeth. Or perhaps not. The parliament discharged a variety of other business, including the Franchises Act, which may well have been uppermost in his mind.[19] The evidence is not clear cut, but it suggests that as late as 28 April Henry had still not made up his mind about Anne. Indeed a betting man would probably have wagered, not only on her survival, but even on her eventual triumph.

However, it was not to be, because between the 28th and the 30th the King was 'bounced' into a judgement which was not merely hostile to Anne, but positively paranoid in its intensity. The most plausible account of what happened is given by Lancelot de Carles, at the time serving as secretary to the French ambassador, in a piece which he wrote early in June. De Carles was not exactly an eye-witness, but he was close enough to events to have credibility. According to him a lady of the Queen's Privy Chamber had fallen pregnant, and for reasons best known to himself her brother, who was member of the council, suspected that the child was not her husband's. She responded by confessing her fault, but claiming that she was not the only guilty one, because her mistress had been similarly adventurous, not once but many times.[20] The lady in question has been identified as Elizabeth, Countess of Worcester, and her brother as Sir Anthony Browne. Sir Anthony did not know what to do about this revelation, for fear of being accused of defaming the Queen, so he confided in two of his friends, who were also councillors, and they informed the King. One of those whom the countess had accused (with circumstantial details) was Mark Smeaton, a musician of the chamber who had often been in attendance upon the Queen. Smeaton was vulnerable, partly because he was a man of humble origins, and partly because he appears to have had a genuine feeling for Anne. On the 30th, Cromwell had him arrested and taken to his own house, where he was interrogated. Under intense pressure which may have included the threat of torture, Smeaton confessed to having had sexual intercourse with Anne. He was remitted to the Tower, and the Secretary took this confirmation of the Countess's story to Henry.[21] Several other members of the Privy Chamber were also named, including Sir Henry Norris, and that gave a sinister twist to that otherwise harmless conversation which appears to have taken place between Norris and the Queen on the 29th. Irritated by his failure to 'come on' to the girl whom Anne had looked out for him, she jestingly made the remark quoted above, that Norris was waiting for herself in the event of the King's death. This story was soon all over the court, and Henry heard it almost immediately.[22] In the circumstances it confirmed his worst suspicions, and he became convinced that all the stories told of his wife's infidelities were true.

This fairly straightforward account, however, creates some difficulties. Why did Henry postpone a trip which he was apparently planning to make to Calais, and why did he allow a public tournament to go ahead on 1 May, a tournament in which both Norris and George Boleyn were taking part? He seems to have ridden off unexpectedly before the conclusion of this event, whereat Edward Hall tells us 'many men mused'.[23] The details of the King's behaviour suggest a mind in turmoil. Norris was one of those who accompanied Henry when he left the tiltyard, and the latter seems to have taken advantage of the short ride from Greenwich to Westminster to persuade Norris to confess the truth. It was only when he persisted in his denial that his arrest was ordered, and then not until the following morning. At the same time Anne was herself arrested, and George, who seems to have been intent on finding out what was going on, was taken into custody later the same day.[24] So the timing of Henry's conviction presents some difficulties. Was he persuaded a week earlier, when he decided to postpone the Calais trip? Or on the evening of the 29th when he heard about Anne's indiscreet remarks? Or did something happen during the tournament which finally converted him? The suggestion is that Cromwell informed him of Smeaton's confession in the course of that day, and that it was the receipt of that news which caused his sudden departure, and his confrontation with Norris.[25] That is plausible, because what is clear is that Cromwell had won and over the next few days consolidated his advantage by building a case against the Queen which would admit no rebuttal. Francis Weston and William Brereton, both members of the Privy Chamber, were also arrested and charged with the same offence, although how they came to be identified as suspects is not clear. What is clear is that they both, along with Henry Norris, denied any wrongdoing. As Sir Edward Baynton, who had been involved in the interrogations, wrote to William Fitzwilliam a few days later, the problem was 'that no man will confess anything against her, but all-only Mark of any actual thing. Whereof (in my foolish conceit) it should much touch the King's honour if it should no further appear ...'.[26]

In other words to secure a conviction on the evidence available would involve overt pressure on the court of a kind which the King was not supposed to apply. Nevertheless, by using circumstantial stories, of which there was a great abundance, Cromwell soon had enough for his purpose, and juries were empanelled on 9 May. Indictments were found with convincing details of dates and places where the alleged offences took place, and their trial was ordered for the 12th. It was obviously intended, by securing the conviction of the accomplices first, to leave the trials of the principals as foregone conclusions. And so it transpired. The juries were packed with Cromwell's clients and agents, who did their duties as required and all the four defendants were condemned to a traitor's death.[27]

Meanwhile Anne was her own worst enemy. Taken to the Tower with a handful of attendants, she began to indulge in inconsequential chatter which seems, as reported, to have had an hysterical edge to it. While consistently denying the charges against her, she recalled a number of flirtatious conversations of the kind which were bound to arouse suspicion. Flirting seems to have been second nature to her, and Norris and Smeaton were not the only ones on the receiving end of her attentions. She seems at the same time to have indulged in a certain ribald humour at the King's expense, casting doubt upon his virility in a manner which was bound to arouse the ire of a man who was notoriously sensitive on that subject.[28] Brought before the Lord Marshall's court on 15 May, she and her brother were separately tried, and in spite of a composed and intelligent defence, both were found guilty. The Lord Marshall was the Duke of Norfolk, who in spite of being Anne's uncle was sufficiently alienated from her to be a reliable agent for such a service. Their father, the Earl of Wiltshire apparently wished to serve on the court but was excluded, although whether on the grounds of his blood relationship or to spare his feelings is not apparent. The only substance to the charges against Rochford was provided by his known affection for his sister, and by the regular access to her which their blood relationship guaranteed. Nevertheless, he was indicted and found guilty of certain specific offences, incest being particularly obnoxious both in the eyes of the law and of the King.[29] Witchcraft was not mentioned, but one of the charges specifically levelled against Anne was that she had conspired to poison both Mary and Henry Fitzroy, an indictment which seems to have owed its provenance to the King's personal conviction, and for which the supporting evidence is nebulous. When the news of her condemnation reached him, Henry's first thought was, typically, for himself, and how he had been abused by this notorious woman. The conservative party in the court rejoiced, but Cromwell, knowing the volatility of the King's emotions, could not afford to relax until she was safely dead.

He assiduously encouraged Henry's quite irrational belief that his wife had had a hundred lovers, and even Chapuys, who had no time at all for Anne or her family, found the proceedings against her 'very strange'.[30] He was not alone in his reaction, and for the first time in her life the ex-Queen found some public sympathy. Archbishop Cranmer, who had been close to her, even made a half-hearted attempt to intercede for her, an attempt which it took all Cromwell's vigilant control over access to the King to frustrate. Above all, the remnants of the Boleyn faction must be kept away. That was one of the reasons why Lord Rochford was pursued with such fury. After Anne he was the most formidable member of that party, and nothing but his death would prevent the possibility of his making a come-back. 'Stone dead', as was to be observed of the Earl of Wentworth over a century later 'hath no fellow'. Sir Francis Bryan was only allowed to see Henry when he had been summoned to court and briefed by the Secretary. Sir Thomas Wyatt was imprisoned, but not charged, and even such humble functionaries as George Taylor, Anne's Receiver General, were hugely relieved once the investigations were over.[31] No one who had had regular access to the Queen could assume that he was safe until she was dead. Only the Earl of Wiltshire appears to have escaped suspicion, and that was by making the extent of his religious estrangement from Anne's agenda sufficiently obvious. Whether he believed the wild charges levelled against his daughter we do not know, but given his silence on the subject, probably not. Anne seems to have spent the last few days of her life in a mixture of tearful despair and religious devotions. There had been some talk of despatching her to a nunnery, and at times she clung to that as a hope of life. At others she discussed the details of her own execution with Sir William Kingston, the Lieutenant of the Tower, with apparent relish.[32] The omens were not good. On the 17th, Archbishop Cranmer was constrained to find some pretext for dissolving her marriage to Henry – that marriage which he had pronounced good and true only three years earlier. Because the cause papers have disappeared, we do not know the reason which was found, but it could not have been her subsequent adultery. That could have been a ground for ending the marriage, but not for declaring it null in the first place.[33] Anne was being erased from the record as though she had never been, and their daughter consequently became illegitimate. George was executed on the 17th, making a suitable scaffold speech in which, without confessing to the truth of any of the charges against him, he submitted to the law, and admitted that he deserved death for having been a 'great reader of the scripture', but a poor follower thereof.[34]

Then at noon on the 19th, it became Anne's turn, the Calais executioner, who used a sword rather than an axe, having been specially imported for the occasion. Whatever her sins may have been, she made a splendid exit. She is reported as saying:

> Good Christian people, I have not come here to preach a sermon; I have come here to die. For according to the law and by the law I am judged to die, and therefore I will speak nothing against it. I have come hither to accuse no man, nor to speak of that whereof I am accused and condemned to die, but I pray God save the King and send him long to reign over you, for a gentler and more merciful prince there never was ... And thus I take my leave of the world and of you all, and heartily desire you all to pray for me ...[35]

It could hardly have been a more composed or orthodox departure, and even Chapuys was impressed. The formalities were quickly completed, and her body was committed for burial beside that of her brother in the chapel of St Peter ad Vincula.

So the King had his desire, and was free to marry again, which he proceeded to do with what many considered to be indecent haste, taking Jane Seymour as his wife on 30 May, just eleven days after Anne's death. Pope Paul III was encouraged, now that Anne and Catherine were both dead, to believe that England's relations with the Holy See might be renegotiated. The Emperor was also optimistic of the same outcome, and before the news of Jane Seymour's advent reached him was talking of a possible Portuguese bride for Henry.[36] However, the man who gained most from the demise of the Boleyn party was undoubtedly their chief rival, Thomas Cromwell, who now had no obvious challenger for the King's confidence. The Dukes of Norfolk and Suffolk, in spite of the prestige of their rank, were no competition in terms of political astuteness, or in their ability to read the King's moods. Nor was Jane Seymour, who was totally lacking Anne's political intelligence, and seems to have had no agenda beyond that of general pacification. She was a meek and submissive soul; just what Henry needed after his bruising confrontation with Catherine and the constant edginess of his relationship with Anne.[37] Her brother Edward became Earl of Hertford in the wake of her elevation, but the Seymours did not constitute a party in the same sense as the Boleyns, and did not have the same type of agenda. In spite of his acquiescence in all that had happened, the Earl of Wiltshire now found himself excluded from the inner circle of the council, and lost the office of Privy Seal to Cromwell on 29 June. He did not give up, but rather seems to have set out to recover his position. He served the King loyally during the Pilgrimage of Grace in the autumn of 1536, paid his subsidy assessment in full, and was assiduous in attending the ceremonies of the Garter. In January 1538 he was back at court, and according to one report 'well entertained'. When his wife Elizabeth died later in the same year there was even talk of his marrying Margaret Douglas, the King's kinswoman by virtue of being the daughter of his sister Margaret by her second marriage.[38] However, his health was probably failing by then, and he died at Hever on 29 March 1539, having recovered neither power nor influence.

But was Anne guilty of any or all of the offences which were alleged to destroy her and the power of her family? Professor Ives thinks not, arguing that the evidence against her was flimsy and circumstantial, and would not stand up for a moment in a modern court of law.[39] Professor Bernard thinks differently, without denying the validity of the modern comparison. He takes much more seriously the Countess of Worcester's testimony, and the stories related to it, arguing that Anne's notorious flirtatiousness did occasionally stray over the boundary into actual sexual misdemeanours.[40] The women of her Privy Chamber did indeed know what was going on, and it was from their testimony that the case against her and her accomplices was formulated. The reason why all this did not come out at the time lay in the legal protection which the Queen's reputation enjoyed under the Treasons Act of 1534. 'No one,' as de Carles observed, 'on pain of martyrdom, dared say anything to the detriment of the Queen.' Without denying the possibility that these were all opportunistic fantasies, dreamed up when Cromwell was obviously dredging for dirt, Professor Bernard nevertheless argues for their cumulative plausibility, although whether all those subsequently condemned were guilty is another matter.[41] With regard to the charges of incest brought against her brother, there is more agreement. Bernard points out that even according to Chapuys, Rochford was accused only 'by presumption', and that no actual witnesses were brought to accuse him. It is probably wisest to believe that this was a politically motivated charge, brought for the purpose of removing him from the scene, and that it was plausibly dressed up in the 'certain other little follies' in which an affectionate brother and sister had indulged.[42] The generally hostile attitude of the trial jury would have been sufficient to secure a conviction, in spite of his 'prudent and wise' defence, which many at the time thought had earned him an acquittal. On Anne's sexual conduct as a whole, the jury may still be regarded as out, although in the absence of any more conclusive evidence it is probably wisest to return a 'not guilty' verdict, while admitting that her demeanour at various times during her reign gave perfectly genuine causes for suspicion.

Although they had not been instrumental in bringing it about, the friends of Princess Mary rejoiced greatly at the fall of the Boleyns, and particularly at the execution of Anne. Taken along with the annulment of her marriage that had, in their eyes, restored a level playing field – a view which they shared with the Pope and the Emperor, as we have seen. However, the thing that they had not grasped was the seriousness with which Henry took his role as Supreme Head of the Church. This, he was quite convinced, was how God intended his Church to be run. Also he had committed himself by authorising the Bishops' Book, and by giving the royal assent to the Act dissolving the smaller monasteries, both intrusions upon ecclesiastical jurisdiction as that was traditionally understood.[43] He also knew perfectly well that the Act of Supremacy and the dissolution of his first marriage were two sides of the same coin. Consequently there could be no question of receiving his daughter back into favour unless she recognised that supremacy, and her own illegitimate status. Mary did not recognise this fact either. As far as she was concerned, the breakdown of relations with her father had been entirely the responsibility of 'that woman', and given what we know of their mutual recriminations, that is not surprising. So Nicholas Carew, the Poles and the Courtenays were encouraging her in what was soon demonstrated to be an illusion. Chapuys was not so sure. In an interview with Henry before Anne's execution, but when her fate was already decided, he had been told:

> ... as to the legitimation of our daughter Mary ... if she would submit to our Grace, without wrestling against the determination of our laws, we would acknowledge her and use her as our daughter, but we would not be directed or pressed herein ...[44]

And even if she did submit, there was no guarantee of her legitimation. Realising the conditional nature of the King's reaction, he wisely advised Lady Shelton, who was still in charge of the joint household in spite of her Boleyn kindred, not to receive any of Mary's former servants who were regularly turning up at Hunsdon expecting to be reinstated.[45] The King now had two illegitimate daughters and the household which cared for them had no particular designation.

Felicitations arrived from everyone, except the one person who mattered. Henry sent no word to Hunsdon, and as the suspense became unbearable, it occurred to Mary that she was expected to make the first move. On the 26th she wrote to Cromwell, asking for his intercession with her father, now that the great obstacle to their reconciliation was no more. The Secretary appears to have replied promptly – his letter does not survive – giving her to understand that obedience was looked for as the first condition for reinstatement.[46] 'Obedience' however, is flexible term, and on the 30th she wrote again, offering to be 'as obedient to the King's Grace as you can reasonably require of me'. Apparently satisfied that she had met his conditions, the next day she wrote to her father, in terms of disarming innocence, acknowledging her offences and begging for his blessing. Unfortunately she also made it clear that her submissiveness reserved her conscience. She would obey him in all things:

> Next to God ... humbly beseeching your highness to consider that I am but a woman and your child, who hath committed her soul only to God, and her body to be ordered in this world as it shall stand with your pleasure ...[47]

Since both the points upon which he required her submission, the ecclesiastical supremacy and her mother's marriage, were covered by this reservation, from his point of view she had conceded nothing and he did not deign to reply. Instead he approved the drawing up of a set of articles to be presented to her which would leave no room for equivocation or evasion. Chapuys and Cromwell were both on tenterhooks, although for very different reasons. It was no part of the Secretary's plans for a reconciliation with the Emperor to see his cousin imprisoned, or worse still executed for high treason.[48] Meanwhile, buoyed up by a false optimism which may have derived from her friends at court, that the King would change (or had changed) his mind, on 7 June she wrote again to Cromwell. This time she expressed her joy that her father 'had withdrawn his displeasure', and asked for some token from the King, so that she might visit the court and pay her respects. On the 10th she wrote to Henry, asking for his blessing, and this time copied it to Cromwell with a covering note asking not to be pressed further than her conscience would bear. This last was precisely what neither Henry nor Cromwell wanted to hear, and few days later, probably on the 15th, a commission headed by the Duke of Norfolk visited her at Hunsdon requiring an answer to two straight questions: would she repudiate the authority of the

Bishop of Rome, and would she accept the nullity of her mother's marriage?[49] In a stormy and emotional confrontation, she rejected both demands, and the crisis which both Cromwell and Chapuys had dreaded had now arrived. Technically Mary was guilty of treason, and the judges recommended that she be proceeded against. The council went into emergency session, with her friends the Marquis of Exeter and Sir William Fitzwilliam excluded. Sir Anthony Browne and Sir Francis Bryan were arrested for idle chatter concerning the Lady Mary's status, and the whole court seems to have been in a state of high tension.[50]

By this time Chapuys was arguing in favour of submission, on the ground that in the face of such cruel pressure no oath could be binding in conscience. Nevertheless it seems to have been Cromwell who broke the deadlock, by sending her a letter of unequivocal submission which she was merely required to sign. According to the ambassador, she signed it without even reading it, but it appears from her reaction that she knew very well what she was about, and her effusive letter to Cromwell a few days later indicates an immense gratitude for his intervention.[51] Perhaps some such casuistry as Chapuys had suggested was involved, and Mary was much later to indicate that she felt an overwhelming guilt at her surrender, but at the time the prevailing reaction was one of relief. The whole court relaxed, and on 6 July the King and Queen visited Hunsdon, staying for two days. In Rome it was believed that she would now be recognised as heir, and that Henry would return to the Catholic Church. Such self-deception was unwarranted, because Mary had after all submitted to her father, not the other way round. Her chamber was in due course restored, and when the Pilgrims of Grace took her name in vain in the autumn of 1536, she gave them not the slightest encouragement.[52] From then until the end of her father's reign, Mary gave no sign that her change of heart was not genuine. She even wrote to the Emperor, asking him not to try and use her as lever against her father, and Chapuys was reduced to making rather far fetched excuses. He even at one point suggested that she should secretly apply to the Pope for a dispensation for her action, an idea which she at once repudiated. If Anne's execution marks the point at which Cromwell triumphed over the Boleyns, then Mary's submission marks the point at which he triumphed over those conservative forces which had supported him in his first coup. He was reviled by the Pilgrims as the King's bear leader, but what the events of the spring and summer of 1536 really prove is his skill in manipulating Henry's moods. It was always the King who made the crucial decisions, but Thomas Cromwell who presented the options, restricted choices, and showed the way in which desired objectives could be achieved.

With the death of the Countess Elizabeth in 1538 and of the Earl of Wiltshire in 1539, the direct line of the Boleyns came to an end. Thomas was constrained to surrender his earldom of Ormond in February 1538, but Piers outlived him by only a few months, and the titles of Ormond and Ossory then descended without dispute to his son James Butler.[53] The earldom of Wiltshire became extinct on his death, not passing to his brother James, as might have been expected. It was resurrected for William Paulet, Lord St John, in 1551 and James died childless in 1561. In the last few years of Henry's reign the Boleyns were represented in the next generation by the Careys, Henry and his sister Catherine, and, of course, by Elizabeth. As a small child, she was left in limbo by her mother's rejection, but seems to have been well cared for in a household the head of which was notionally her sister Mary, and in 1543 at the age of ten was reintegrated into the royal family by the efforts of her last step-mother, Catherine Parr.[54] It was probably at this stage that she began to share lessons with her six-year-old brother Edward, and quickly began to display that intellectual precocity and sharpness which were to characterise her for the rest of her life. In July 1544 she wrote the first of her surviving letters to Catherine, in Italian, although there is no evidence that the Queen would have been able to read it. This was schoolroom exercise, in which she lamented her separation from her parents, occasioned by Henry's campaigning in France and by Catherine carrying out the duties of Regent in his absence.[55] It probably indicates no more than that Catherine was at Whitehall while Elizabeth and Edward were at St James. In spite of the Queen's good offices, Henry showed no inclination to legitimate either of his two daughters; indeed he could not do so without repudiating many of his policies over the years. What he did do, remarkably enough, was to include them both in his final Succession Act of 1544. If his son Edward, his undoubted heir, were to die childless, then the crown was to pass to Edward's half sister Mary, provided that she married with the consent of the council. If Mary also died childless, then the succession came to his other daughter Elizabeth, with the same condition attached. The terms of this Act were to be confirmed or altered by the terms of his last will and testament. In the event they were confirmed unchanged.[56] This was altogether unprecedented. Never before had an illegitimate child of the royal house been included in the succession to the Crown. Nor had any female successfully claimed the throne, although one, Matilda, had had a realistic claim in the twelfth century. It was as comprehensive an example of the new sovereignty of parliament as the Act of Supremacy, and was probably accepted only because no one thought that the hypothetical would ever happen. In fact it determined the succession to the English crown down to 1558.

Meanwhile, Elizabeth was growing up. Various marriages were suggested for her, but none came to anything because of her ambiguous status. Kate Champernowne (better known by her married name of Kate Ashley), having guided her young charge through the first steps of her learning, secured the services of Roger Ascham as her tutor, with the results which we have already noticed.[57] In December 1544, she presented Catherine with her own translation of Margaret of Angouleme's *Miroir de l'ame pecheresse* as a New Year's gift. She was eleven by this time, and one wonders whether she had any inkling of her mother's connection with the author. Probably not, because it was a suitable gift to pass between members of the evangelical party in the court, to which Ascham and Catherine Parr both belonged.[58] Elizabeth was thirteen when her father died, and though she is supposed to have wept copiously at the news, no one knows her real feelings. Her father had been a formidable and rather distant figure. Her stepmother, however, was different and she was living, along with her sister Mary, on the Queen's side of the court at the time. Catherine, however, was thirty-five and had endured three virtually sexless marriages. Consequently she was desperate for a real man, and quickly succumbed to the advances of Thomas Seymour, the brother of the Earl of Hertford. Mary, seeing which way the wind was blowing, made haste to move out of the ex-Queen's household, but Elizabeth more innocent, or perhaps more inquisitive, did not follow suit. Seymour and Catherine were secretly married in the spring of 1547, and Elizabeth, presumably, was given a ringside view of the pleasures and hazards of married life.[59] Then in the summer of 1548, while his wife was unavailable to him through pregnancy, Thomas Seymour began to make passes at Elizabeth. She was fourteen by this time, and very attractive. What passed between them probably amounted to no more than horseplay, but it was clearly enough to awaken the girl sexually. Catherine caught them in a compromising embrace, and she was sent away in disgrace to cool her ardour at the Dennys, Lady Denny being Kate Ashley's sister.[60] In September, Catherine died in childbirth, and before the end of the year, Seymour was pursuing Elizabeth again, this time speaking of marriage. Such a proposal, without the consent of the council, was treason, and was one of the charges levelled against Thomas when he was arrested in January 1549. The other charges related to plotting against his brother the Lord Protector, and were probably more substantial, but this was the one with the highest profile. Seymour was attainted and executed in March 1549, and we really do not know what Elizabeth's reaction may have been.[61] In a sense he had been a pest, but he had also contributed to the girl's education in a manner which no tutor was free to do. She now knew that she was attractive to men, especially to older men, and that discovery was exhilarating. She also knew the hazards as well as the pleasures of sexual adventures. She had undergone a primary training in the art of flirtation, and it had been extremely enjoyable, while it had lasted. Above all, she had awakened her maternal talents for sexual encounters, showing just the same ability which Anne had displayed at a similar age in the court at Mechelen. The hazards of politics were to bring her to the throne unmarried at the age of twenty-five in 1558, and during the intervening years she had learned also the survival techniques necessary for a person in her position, including the repressing of her own sexuality.[62] But she also came to the throne with a well developed sense of what it meant to be a woman in the masculine dominated world of sixteenth-century politics. Unlike her sister Mary, who had been bewildered by the problems of gender, Elizabeth knew that it offered opportunities for manipulation and control which no man could enjoy. It remained to be seen how this third Boleyn girl would exploit her position.

# 9

# HENRY CAREY, LORD HUNSDON –
# THE BERWICK YEARS

Henry Carey, Anne Boleyn's nephew, was treated as royal kindred almost from the start. We know nothing of his early education, which would have been in the hands of his stepfather, Sir William Stafford, but he was literate, inclined to the reformed religion, and appears to have been trained as a soldier. Born on 4 March 1526, he would have been two when his father died in the summer of 1528, and eight when his mother re-married in 1534. As we have seen, she cut herself off from the court by that action, but was partly rehabilitated after Anne's fall, and his wardship was granted to her once it had reverted to the Crown. Henry would have been about ten by that time, and Mary seems to have been content to leave his training to her husband. However, it was she who held the wardship, and when she died in 1543, Henry was still underage. His care therefore reverted to the Crown, and, probably by agreement with Sir William, he was taken into the royal household, where his presence is recorded for the first time in 1545, when he was nineteen. It was therefore the King, or someone acting for the King, who authorised his marriage on 21 May 1545 to Anne, the daughter of Sir Thomas Morgan of Arkestone, Herefordshire, a part of the world with which he had no known connection.[1] In spite of being arranged, this marriage was to be a long and happy one, producing six children who survived infancy, of whom the first, George, was born in 1546 or 1547. Anne outlived her husband, dying at an advanced age in 1607. In the summer of 1545, Henry also obtained his first military experience, serving as an officer of horse under John Dudley, Viscount Lisle, the Lord Admiral, in the force which Lisle raised for the defence of Portsmouth. His appointment involved no action, because the French never landed and there is no suggestion that Henry served in the fleet.[2] However, he must have impressed Lisle who chose him, at the age of twenty, to accompany his mission to negotiate peace with the French, which was agreed at Camp in March 1546. He received £40 in expenses for that trip, which can barely have covered the outlay.[3] He was therefore about five weeks short of his twenty-first birthday, and already well established in the royal service, when King Henry died on 28 January 1547.

The town of Buckingham had been a parcel of the possessions of William Carey, and came to Henry when he achieved his majority. He celebrated his acquisition by sitting for the borough in the parliament which met in November 1547, and on 5 May 1548 he was granted livery of his lands, which had come to him both from his father and his mother, having 'attained the full age of twenty one years'.[4] The reason for the delay lay in Chancery procedure and not in any difficulty which he may have had in getting his right recognised, because the livery was effectively back dated to March 1547. These properties included the manor and lordship of Rochford in Essex, and it appears to have been there that Henry and Anne resided when not at court. During Edward's reign he was regarded as a useful player, but definitely of the second rank and his relationship with the Duke of Somerset, for instance, is not known. Since he was selected to accompany the Marquis of Northampton to France again in 1551, he must have made the transition to the Earl of Warwick successfully. His rights in the town of Buckingham were confirmed in November 1552, but that was related to a plan to sell the whole lot to one Robert Brown of Horton. He conveyed the package to Brown in January 1553, which would seem to indicate that his finances were in a mess.[5] This conveyance would also account for the fact that he did not sit for Buckingham in either of the parliaments of that year. Having come to some arrangement with Brown, however, he resumed his seat in both the parliaments of 1554 and in that of 1555. In 1554 he departed early from the November session without licence, for which he was presented in King's Bench, although no action was taken against him or against the large number of others who had similarly defected. In 1555 he voted with Sir Anthony Kingston against the Exiles Bill, and thereby earned himself some additional black marks from the government. That may help to account for the fact that he found himself in the Fleet for debt early in 1557, although he managed to raise enough backers to be freed on recognisance on 19 May.[6] Throughout Mary's reign he managed to hang on to a minor (and probably honorary) position at court, as a Carver in the Chamber, which, given the fact that he was a known Protestant sympathiser serves to demonstrate the truth of Edward Underhill's assertion that there was no place to 'shift the Easter time' better than Queen Mary's court. He was also, and more significantly, a Gentleman of the Household to Princess Elizabeth. This he must have owed to his kinship with the Princess, which would not have commended him to the Queen, but unfortunately it did not carry sufficient income to support the lifestyle to which he obviously aspired.

Elizabeth's accession on 17 November 1558 transformed his circumstances. From being kindred to a possible heir to the throne, he was now a cousin of the reigning monarch. Before the end of November he had been knighted, and his position in the royal chamber confirmed. The Queen then set about to alleviate his poverty. On 13 January 1559, the day before she entered London for her coronation, she created him Baron Hunsdon, in which capacity he attended on her over the next few days, and on 12 March granted him the stewardships of various lucrative royal manors.[7] Then on 20 March she did something that was exceedingly rare for her, and endowed him lavishly with lands, allegedly worth £4,000 a year, 'for the maintenance of his rank and station', which if true would have placed him among the half dozen wealthiest peers in the kingdom.[8] On 28 June he was granted the wardship of Clement Tanfeld, and on 3 July another clutch of stewardships, including that of Leominster in Herefordshire, which carried a fee of £10 a year in addition to the rights. Finally, on 31 October 1560 he was given an office at court, which carried with it rights of access to the royal person. It was not the Mastership of the Horse, that was already spoken for, but the rather humbler position of Chief Keeper of the Hawks. Elizabeth enjoyed her hawking, and that no doubt mattered more to Hunsdon than the £40 salary which the post carried – although every little helped.[9] In 1561 he was given the more prestigious (and lucrative) office of Captain of the Band of Gentlemen Pensioners in recognition of his closeness to the sovereign. Not surprisingly, we find no more evidence of straightened circumstances. The new baron had received the former royal residence of Hunsdon along with the other lands conveyed to him on 20 March, and took up residence there along with his growing brood of children. George, aged thirteen in 1560, was entered in that year as a Fellow Commoner at Trinity College, Cambridge, which not only indicates a good grounding in the classics, but an enlightened attitude to education of the part of the Careys. It would be a few years yet before some time at the university was a part of every gentleman's *cursus honorem*.[10]

Meanwhile, Henry, whose dissident connections, or lack of substance, seem to have kept him off the Commissions of the Peace during Mary's reign, served for Bedfordshire and Essex in 1562 and 1564, and for Hertfordshire and Kent as well in the latter year. He was also a commissioner for Gaol Delivery in Warwickshire and several contiguous counties at the same time, and for the collection of the subsidy in May 1564.[11] Had he discharged all these duties conscientiously, he would have had little time to spend at court, but the evidence is that he placed attendance on the Queen ahead of mere administrative responsibilities. He witnessed the creation of Robert Dudley as Baron Denbigh and Earl of Leicester on 28 September 1564, and seems to have enjoyed good relations with the powerful favourite, although what his attitude had been in the critical days of his courtship of Elizabeth in 1560, the records do not reveal. If he was opposed to the prospect of their marriage, then he had the good sense to keep his opinion to himself. Since he was not a councillor, this would not have been too difficult, and his first priority had to be to please his mistress. In 1564 he was sent on an honorific embassy to France to present the Garter to the French king, a mission which he again owed to his known closeness to Elizabeth.[12] By 1565 he is alleged to have belonged to the 'affinity' of the Earl of Sussex, which was opposed to Leicester, but the evidence for that is hearsay. In whatever capacity, his services were obviously appreciated, because at the end of October 1565 he received a further grant of land in Berkshire. On this occasion he seems to have been a mere agent because the very next day he alienated his acquisitions to the Lord Treasurer, the

Marquis of Winchester, who presumably felt less sure of his own favour. Since he had been one of those opposed to Dudley's suit, that is not hard to account for, but that he should have found it desirable to use Hunsdon in this way is highly significant of their respective positions in the court.[13] Whether Elizabeth had a high opinion of his capabilities or not, we do not know. What we do know is that he was her kinsman, and that she appreciated his loyalty. If she resented her favour being circumvented, as it was by the Lord Treasurer, then she gave no sign. Indeed she probably appreciated his subtlety.

Between 1560 and 1568 Henry Carey was a man about the court, weaving his way carefully between the opposing factions, but without any major office. He was not a member of the Privy Council, and appears to have served on only the one diplomatic mission, although he did interest himself in the affairs of Mary of Scotland.[14] It was Nicholas Throgmorton and Thomas Smith who negotiated the treaty of Troyes in 1564. When remonstrating with Mary in October 1564 about the interest which the Queen of Scots was showing in Elizabeth's marriage, the Queen wrote of 'the talk in the French court at the signing of the peace'. 'I will not say,' she went on, 'whether it were my Lord of Hunsdon or any of his company', who had reported this talk to her. If it were he, then he must have collected the gossip at second hand.[15] He seems to have been a man whom the Queen found congenial. He attended the creation of Thomas Sackville as Lord Buckhurst on 8 June 1567, and shortly after was granted, along with his son George, various stewardships in Bedfordshire and Buckinghamshire, including the prestigious one of Ampthill, which was in the process of reconstruction at that time. The reconstruction was never completed and the house gradually fell into ruin, but that was not Lord Hunsdon's fault.[16] His sister Catherine was also one of the Queen's closest female friends, and that brought Sir Francis Knollys into the charmed circle of the royal kindred.

However, this comfortable situation was about to change. In May 1568 Mary Stuart, having escaped from Lochleven Castle, and failed in a bid to recover her throne, fled across the border into England, which immediately created a problem with the regency government of Scotland, acting in the name of the infant King James, which Elizabeth did not recognise. Nevertheless, the Earl of Moray was in command of the situation, and he demanded Mary's return. Elizabeth was not prepared to concede that, and relations grew tense.[17] Consequently the Queen decided that she needed a man whom she could trust absolutely in the key border region. There was nothing much wrong with the Earl of Bedford, who held the governorship of Berwick, except that he was never there, and Elizabeth needed someone on the spot. On 25 August 1568 she appointed Henry Carey to this crucial office of trust, and the following day named him as Keeper of the East March, with the implicit understanding that he would live on his post. He visited the North-East in company with Sir Francis Knollys early in September, and consulted with the merchants of Newcastle about the Danzig trade, but appears not to have stayed very long.[18]

Lord Hunsdon was back in February 1569, when the Regent Moray asked for his support in a border clearing operation, but again it is not clear how long he stayed. It was to be several months before he made his way north again, and by then the circumstances had changed. 1569 was the year in which the politics of the court may well have outweighed the needs of the borders. It started with the Queen's decision in December 1568 to borrow the money destined for the Duke of Alba's troops in the Low Countries. The

Genoese ships carrying this treasure had ended up in Southampton to escape a gale in the Channel, and Elizabeth impounded the cargo, announcing that she would take it up herself. This was technically permissible, because the money still belonged to the bankers, but Alba was understandably annoyed and embargoed English trade. This development in turn provoked Cecil's opponents in the council, who blamed him for this outcome, to conspire against him, with the intention of undermining the Queen's confidence.[19] At the same time the court was equally, although rather differently, divided over the Duke of Norfolk's plan to marry the Scottish queen. A number of traditional peers were in favour of this move, because the Duke was a conformist in his religion, and such a marriage might have neutralised the Catholic threat which Mary presented. Among his supporters were the Earl of Sussex, the President of the Council in the North, and the Earls of Northumberland and Westmorland, who were not at court. Elizabeth allowed both these plots to fester for a while, and then in the late summer, declared herself unequivocally. Cecil enjoyed her full confidence, and under no circumstances would she countenance a marriage between her premier peer and the Queen of Scots.[20] How dare anyone suggest such a thing! She gave the Duke a piece of her mind, and he withdrew in a huff to his estates. During September there were rumours that he was plotting rebellion, but he seems to have been disorientated by the vehemence of the Queen's reaction. At the beginning of October he set off to return to the court, but before he could reach it he was arrested and taken to the Tower. This left his supporters in an ambiguous situation, and most of them, like Cecil's detractors, ran for cover. In the north, however, the reaction was rather more hostile. The Earls of Northumberland and Westmorland, as well as being supporters of Norfolk, were

also Catholics and sympathetic to the Queen of Scots. Rumours
began to spread of an intended rebellion in County Durham, and
the Earl of Sussex, not free from suspicion himself, was ordered
to summon them to court to give an account of themselves.[21]
Interpreting this instruction freely, at the end of October he
summoned the earls to York, and professed himself satisfied with
their explanations. At the same time he wrote to Cecil, expressing
his incredulity that the Duke of Norfolk should be suspected of
treason: 'I have always loved him above all others, her Majesty
excepted ...', he declared. Nevertheless, the Secretary should be
under no illusions as to where his primary allegiance lay, and the
cloud of suspicion lifted.[22] He had, however, been deceived by the
northern earls, who, in a general mess of misunderstandings, and
egged on by more aggressive inferiors, raised the standard of revolt
and marched on Durham. On 13 November, Sussex proclaimed
them both, and all their adherents, traitors.[23]

For the time being the royalist position in the north looked
bleak, and Sussex reported that he was unable to raise a reliable
army to encounter the rebels. The Yorkshire gentry were sitting
on their hands, and the commons were religiously disaffected. He
suggested that an army be raised in the south, and this was done.
Lord Clinton was placed in command of the levies of Lincolnshire
and the Earl of Warwick those of his own county. At the same time,
on 16 November, Lord Hunsdon was ordered back to the north,
with a general commission to support Sussex in any way that he
could.[24] It was assumed that the garrison of Berwick, being paid
professionals, would remain loyal, and so it proved. Hunsdon met
Sir Ralf Sadler at Hull on the way north, and they both joined
Sussex at York on the 24th. Sadler was very experienced in the
affairs of Scotland, and a staunch friend of Sir William Cecil, while

Hunsdon represented the Queen's confidence. Within a few days they were both writing to Cecil praising the loyalty and diligence of the Lord President, who, they reckoned, had turned the situation in Yorkshire around so that the rebels were now likely to find 'scant comfort' in the county.[25] Sadler remained with Sussex at York, but Hunsdon proceeded to Berwick, with instructions to levy troops and to liaise with Sir John Forster, the Warden of the Middle March. On 2 December Cecil wrote that Lord Scrope, the Warden of the West March, was under similar orders, meanwhile Clinton and Warwick were advancing from the south. By that time the crisis was virtually over, because reluctant though the men of Yorkshire might have been to turn out for the Queen, they proved even more reluctant to join the rebels. That force, originally estimated at 4,000 foot and 1,000 horse, gradually diminished as they advanced south, and was not replenished. Their best chance of success would probably have been a cavalry raid on Tutbury, where Mary was being held, but on 25 November she was removed to the greater security of Coventry. On the 24th the rebels reached Bramham Moor, near Leeds, still about fifty miles from Tutbury, and their best chance was clearly gone. They would not have known of the move, but on the 25th they began to retreat.[26] There had been no battle, but the momentum had gone out of their movement. By 30 November they were back at Brancepeth, County Durham whence they had set out full of hope less than a month before, and in spite of a late boost from the taking of Barnard Castle, they began to disperse what was left of their force. By the end of December they had taken refuge in Scotland, which no doubt prompted a mission to the Regent, undertaken by George Carey on 22 December.

Meanwhile, Sussex had advanced to Newcastle, and was sending joint reports with Hunsdon to the council in London. Neither was very happy with the scale of the operation being mounted from the south, considering the large numbers involved to be unnecessary.[27] In spite of their dissatisfaction with the religious settlement, the gentlemen of Yorkshire were far too astute to want to be associated with a failed rebellion, and were now anxious to prove their loyalty to the Queen. Besides, Clinton and Warwick were behaving in a heavy handed fashion which was likely to cause more trouble than it solved. Sussex himself was by no means lenient, and on 4 January 1570 he reported that no fewer than 305 men had been executed in County Durham by the exercise of martial law, including 30 townsmen of Durham itself.[28] The north would not quickly forget the consequences of arousing the Queen's anger. However, the story was not quite concluded, because there was a rather curious aftermath in a remote corner of the borders. Leonard Dacre had lost what he considered to be his birthright in the family estates to the Duke of Norfolk in a lawsuit back in June. Norfolk was the guardian of the young Lord Dacre, who was the son of his late duchess by a previous husband, while Leonard was his uncle.[29] When Lord Dacre died in May 1569, the succession and the lands were in dispute between them. Neither was in favour with the Queen, the Duke for the reasons already noticed and Leonard because he was an ardent supporter of Mary Stuart. Nevertheless, the verdict had gone to the Duke and the pair were, apparently, reconciled. Leonard was thus still in the south when the northern rebellion erupted, and although he was strongly sympathetic to the earls, he was not in a position to be of much assistance to them. He returned to the borders during December, and belatedly attempted to rescue their enterprise, using the substantial Dacre affinity as his base and endeavouring to solicit assistance from the borderers on the Scottish side. From his base at Naworth he even seemed briefly to menace Carlisle. At first the seriousness of this did not appear. Sussex and Hunsdon advanced to Hexham in the last days of December, but finding nothing worthy of their attention returned to Berwick, from where Hunsdon reported on the 30th, greatly commending his colleague's service. Being at Hexham, he declared, 'did little service', which suggests that Dacre's mobilisation had not yet progressed very far.[30] However, the threat quickly developed during January, and by the end of the month Lord Hunsdon had been ordered to apprehend him. Leading out his mixed force of borderers and garrison troops from Berwick, he confronted Dacre's retainers and Scots, said to number 3,000, near Naworth on 20 February. The battle was sharp, but decisive, and the rebels fled, leaving some 300 dead on the field. Dacre joined the earls in Scotland, and Naworth fell to the royal army without a siege.[31] The Queen, who had complained at one stage that she was not being kept properly informed, was vastly relieved by the news of this victory, and sent Hunsdon a personal letter of congratulation, in which she addressed him as her 'dear kinsman'.[32]

For the next few months Carey remained in the north, negotiating with the Scottish council, which was (more or less) in control of the country after the assassination of the Earl of Moray on 27 January. The country was divided between the King's men, who were Protestant and supported the young King James, and Queen's men who were (mostly) Catholics, and who wanted her reinstated. The Earl of Westmorland had slipped through this net and ended up in the Low Countries, but the Earl of Northumberland was held in prison by the King's party. Hunsdon busied himself about the business of his extradition. On 20 October 1571 he was briefed for another mission to the new regent, the Earl of Mar,[33] but had for the time being no success, reporting on 16 November that there was no prospect of his being surrendered. Meanwhile, Mar was in urgent need of military support. In Hunsdon's opinion, 4,000 men would be needed for the task, but Elizabeth did not respond. The Earl of Northumberland was eventually sold to the English for £2,000 in May 1572, but it was not until July, after the Earl of Lennox had replaced Mar as regent, that he was handed over. He was executed at York on 22 August. Meanwhile, Elizabeth was much exercised over how best to support the King's men without stirring up the French to intervene on the other side, and briefly sent the Earl of Sussex against the Hamiltons, who were the chief of Mary's supporters, drawing him back only when he threatened to be too successful. Hunsdon busied himself about his charge in Berwick, reporting on 27 April that he had ridden the borders in pursuit of Leonard Dacre, who was being protected by the reivers of Teviotdale, but without, apparently, any success. He also, rather mysteriously, intervened on behalf of the Countess of Northumberland, who, if the accounts are accurate, had been a great 'setter on' of the rebellion and was certainly a staunch Catholic. She wrote thanking him for his 'comfortable letters', and he was constrained to do some explaining to his mistress, who seems, understandably, to have taken his interest amiss.[34] It may have been by his connivance that she escaped into Scotland later in 1570, and was not included in her husband's extradition. She was, however, in great hardship, and was cared for by sympathisers both in Scotland and after she had made her way to the Netherlands. On reaching the Low Countries she prudently retired into a convent, and died at Namur in October 1596.[35]

The rank and file of the rebels, those who had not been executed under martial law, were tried by a special commission of Oyer and Terminer during the summer of 1570, and 199 of them were hanged. Lord Hunsdon sat on this commission ex officio, but his role is not distinguishable from that of the other justices.[36] The more substantial of the offenders were dealt with by Act of Attainder in the spring parliament of 1571, and a wholesale confiscation of lands and other property followed. Henry Percy, Thomas's brother, was allowed to succeed to a much reduced earldom of Northumberland in the following year, but the earldom of Westmorland and the barony of Dacre became extinct.[37] The lands of these and the other attainted gentlemen passed first into the hands of the Crown, and then were redistributed to the loyal gentry of the north. On 30 May 1571, Lord Hunsdon received his share of the loot, a substantial proportion of the lands of Leonard Dacre, in Cumberland and Derbyshire, which were still extensive in spite of his failure to secure the main inheritance.[38] Those lands were also possessed by the Crown, not as a result of Dacre's attainder but by that of the Duke of Norfolk, which passed in the same session. Hunsdon had been well supported by his family during his action in the north. His son George was knighted at Berwick in May 1570, and the Edward Carey 'Groom of the Privy Chamber', who was deputed to take possession of the lands and goods of Sir John Neville on 11 January was almost certainly his third son. Presumably, both served alongside their father in his campaign, but whether they distinguished themselves in any way is not on record. In spite of the fact that Henry was re-appointed to the keepership of the East March in 1571, and reappears in Berwick from time to time over the next few years, the whole family seems to have moved its main base of operations back to the south once the fall-out from the rebellion had ceased. Lord Hunsdon was a witness to the creation of Sir William Cecil as Lord Burghley on 25 January 1572, and George sat as MP for

Hertfordshire in the parliament of 1571.[39] On 20 March 1573, Henry was appointed to the High Commission for the Northern Province, and that must have taken him at least as far as York from time to time. Unfortunately it is not known how often he sat. He was by this time considered to be something of an expert on Scottish and border affairs, a position which he seems not to have relished, and was determinedly, even violently, opposed to the pretensions of the Scottish queen, at a time when Elizabeth was trying to negotiate her way out of the trouble which that lady was causing her. Sir Francis Knollys appears to have aroused his ire at one stage by suggesting that his son George, then aged twenty-six, would be a suitable groom for Mary, but Hunsdon did not see the joke – if any was intended![40] He had a different destination in mind for George, and on 29 December 1574 the latter married Elizabeth, the daughter of Sir John Spencer of Althorp, Northamptonshire, an ancestor of the present Earl Spencer. In spite of what seems to have been a somewhat prickly nature, he carefully steered a middle course in religious disputes and favours continued to be granted to him. On 31 July 1574 he got a couple of plums, neither particularly generous in financial terms, but both in recognition of his status as a courtier. First he was made Keeper of Hyde Park, with all the rights of herbage and pannage which were attached to that office, and the same day Keeper of Somerset House in the Strand, which had been the Queen's London residence during her sister's reign and must have carried many painful memories for her.[41] He took up residence there, and used it as his London home until the time of his death. In November 1575 he was back in the north-east, where he was reported as hanging thieves with great enthusiasm, although how long he was present, and whether this characterisation was justified, is not known.[42]

On 16 November 1577 his political career moved up a notch with his appointment to the Privy Council. Whereas Mary had tended to rely on a rather diverse group of advisers, and had allowed the council to become unmanageably large, Elizabeth reverted to the practice of her father's later years, and treated her council as an elite group of State servants, most of them senior office holders. Hunsdon was not a minister in that sense, and his appointment was rather a reflection of the confidence which Elizabeth reposed in him.[43] Nevertheless, he became an assiduous attender at meetings, appearing 125 times in 1578–80, as compared to 177 attendances by Lord Burghley, who was the acknowledged work horse. Only in 1581–2 did his appearances drop to 41, and that was because he was away in Scotland from March to September. In 1588 he put in 91 appearances (as compared to 100 by Burghley), and appeared for the last time on 1 July 1596, just three weeks before his death.[44] At the time of his appointment he was fifty-one years old, and was regarded as something of an elder statesman.

Jurisdiction within the verge of the court traditionally belonged to the Lord Steward, at this time Edward Fiennes, Earl of Lincoln. However, for some reason which is not clear, Elizabeth was not satisfied with this arrangement, and on 20 February 1579 constituted a special commission of Oyer and Terminer to hear criminal cases which arose within the verge and gave that commission to Henry Carey.[45] It may have been that the council was alarmed at the rising threat of political assassination, in which case it would have made sense to grant a special jurisdiction to the Captain of the Queen's chief bodyguard. It seems that the Steward's civil authority over mere misdemeanours was not affected, nor is there any evidence that he resented this intrusion upon his traditional rights. Meanwhile, Sir George Carey's career was advancing alongside that of his father. In 1572 he sat in parliament again, this time for Colchester, and served on the Commission of the Peace for Essex, which perhaps indicates that he had taken over responsibility for Rochford. On the other hand, in 1584 he sat for Hampshire, and thereafter for Middlesex, both counties in which he held property and for which he acted as a Justice, so it is not safe to assume a connection between his parliamentary seat and his place of residence.[46] He was primarily a courtier, and in 1578 was appointed a Marshall of the Household, which was a virtual sinecure, carrying official duties only at the time when the accounts were due to be audited. In 1583 George received also two apparently incompatible promotions, that as Constable of Bamburgh Castle in Northumberland, and that as Governor of the Isle of Wight. The Bamburgh office he discharged by deputy, and there is no evidence that he ever visited it, but the governorship was a different matter altogether. He conducted an extensive correspondence over several years with Burghley and Walsingham about the security of the island, conducted musters and arranged for troops to be stationed there.[47] He was on the spot during the critical summer of 1588, and retained the post until he succeeded to his father's offices in 1596.

In 1583 occurred the Throgmorton plot. Worked out in Paris, and involving agents of the Guises, Mary Queen of Scots and the English Catholics, this aimed at the assassination of the Queen and at a joint Spanish and French invasion to install Mary on the English throne. Bernardino de Mendoza, the Spanish ambassador, was put in touch with Francis Throgmorton, a young English aristocrat, whose job would be to mobilise the Catholics in support of the invasion, and to provide essential information about English troop deployment. Charles Paget, the exiled brother of Lord Paget, visited England secretly more than once in pursuit of this objective. Unfortunately for them, Walsingham's spies were already on to Throgmorton, and the council had good warning of what was afoot. Toward the end of 1583 he was arrested as a 'privy conveyor and receiver of letters to and from the Scottish Queen' and a series of interrogations was established.[48] During one of his visits, Charles Paget had talked with his brother, and, it was suspected, with Philip Howard Earl of Arundel. Arundel was placed under arrest and on 24 December Lord Hunsdon and Sir Walter Mildmay were given the invidious task of questioning him. What questions they may have asked we do not know, but Arundel denied any involvement with Paget and his schemes, and there the matter was allowed to rest.[49] Throgmorton himself, against whom the evidence was clear if circumstantial, was tried and executed, and Mendoza was expelled in January 1584. Hunsdon and Mildmay were obviously selected for this duty because both were notoriously hostile to Catholics in general and to the Queen of Scots in particular. In February the former sent to Walsingham a set of notes which he had compiled on the recusant problem, and on the seminarians who were at the heart of it, indicating the names of prominent suspects of whom he was aware. It is unlikely that these told the Secretary anything which he did not know, but it was accepted in the spirit in which it was intended.[50]

Meanwhile, the affairs of Scotland were unsettled. King James was still underage, and the Earl of Arran was Regent, but Mary had not given up hope of being reinstated as a joint ruler, and a complicated three way negotiation between Arran, Mary and the English Council was underway. At this point James complicated the issue still further by taking as his favourite Esme Stuart, a kinsman of the late Earl of Lennox who had been brought up in France and was a Catholic. Mary naturally took this to be good omen, and began to work to undermine Arran. Hunsdon, as the council's resident expert on Scottish affairs, was deeply involved in support of the Regent, and he tended to see eye to eye with Lord Burghley on this issue.[51] Leicester on the other hand was suspicious because he believed that Hunsdon nursed a secret ambition to marry either his daughter or his niece (Sir Francis Knollys' daughter) to the young King of Scots. Walsingham was also suspicious because one of Burghley's nephews, Sir Philip Hoby, was married to another Carey daughter and he thought that kinship was taking precedence over policy. In July 1584 he wrote:

> Touching the by-course between Lord Hunsdon and the Earl of Arran, there is nothing to help it but time and trial. You know Lord Hunsdon's passion, whose propinquity in blood doth somewhat prevail to enable his credit to more harm than good. And yet he should not herein greatly prevail were he not countenanced by the Lord Treasurer, who dealeth strangely in the action of Scotland.[52]

Strangely or not, Burghley was dealing cautiously both with Scotland and its queen, far too cautiously for Walsingham's taste, who wanted a more robust defence of the reformed faith. He suspected the Lord Treasurer of using Hunsdon as a catspaw against Leicester, whom neither of them trusted, 'although, God wot, he be but a weak one'.[53] He was sent to the King of Scots again in June 1584, at Arran's suggestion, which gives some point to Walsingham's concern.[54] Burghley was trying to conciliate both James and his mother at this point, knowing that the Queen was in two minds, and obviously felt the need to have her closest kinsman in the council on his side. That he was a weak support is merely

Walsingham's opinion, and is not borne out by other evidence. In any case Esme Stuart was ousted in 1583, and the Earl of Arran in 1585, leaving James (more or less) in control. Meanwhile, Mary's involvement in the Babington plot forced Burghley and Hunsdon into a tactical withdrawal, which neither of them was reluctant to make. Although the Lord Treasurer's professions of friendship apparently deceived Mary at the time, they had been made in the interests of a cause which was now discredited, and the evidence suggests that both of them were heartily glad to see the back of her.[55] Elizabeth herself treated all the parties in this tangled situation to the rough side of her tongue, and Walsingham confessed to Burghley in June 1584 that he had received 'hard speeches' over his attitude to Scotland, but that was in the context of informing him that her Majesty was in a foul mood, particularly with Lord Hunsdon, in case he should be thinking of using the latter as a means of access.[56] However, his loss of favour, if such it was, does not seem to have affected him adversely. He was re-appointed to the captaincy of the Gentlemen Pensioners in 1583, and served as Lord Lieutenant of Hertfordshire from 1583 to 1585, both positions of trust. Then in July 1585 the Lord Chamberlain, Charles, Lord Howard of Effingham was appointed Lord Admiral in place of the deceased Earl of Lincoln, and Henry Carey was named in his place.[57] The summit of his career as a courtier had now been reached. He was fifty-nine, and his kinship with the Queen had paid its full dividend.

Hunsdon, however, was still not an officer of state, and over the next two years he seems to have busied himself with routine council business, authorising a warrant for the building expenses at Portsmouth, and keeping an eye on Scotland, which he was no doubt expected to do. In February 1588, Lord Admiral Howard wrote to Walsingham that he had received 'advertisement' from Hunsdon relating to the affairs of the north, and was relieved to hear that the King of Scots was running 'a true course'. This presumably meant that he was resisting the blandishments of some of his Catholic peers to become involved in Philip of Spain's plans against England, and must have been sent to the Admiral in his military capacity.[58] It may well be that Hunsdon was reluctant to communicate directly with the Secretary because of the tensions which existed between them. He remained a conscientious attender at council meetings, in spite of his commitments elsewhere, but had presumably written to Howard in case he did not see him at a meeting. Howard, like Walsingham, was one of the workhorses of the council, and he wrote because he considered that his tidings needed to be 'of record' rather than through any lack of personal contact. Since 1585 Hunsdon had shifted his lord lieutenancy from Hertfordshire to Norfolk, which was a maritime county and therefore more likely to come under attack, and in the summer of 1588 mustered the county in preparation for Philip's expected invasion. He was still, however, spending a good deal of his time in the north-east, where he also had responsibility for the East and Middle Marches, although intelligence out of Scotland suggested that the threat from that quarter was minimal.[59] By July of 1588 he was back in the south and took personal command of the household and other troops designated for the protection of the Queen's person, in the event of Parma affecting a landing. In that capacity he would have been with the army at Tilbury on 9 August when Elizabeth made her famous speech, although there is no record of his reaction. By that time the crisis was effectively over, and the Armada, defeated at Gravelines, was streaming north in an effort to escape. On 22 August Sir George Carey, monitoring the situation from his position on the Isle of Wight, was able to write to his father that a 'great fleet' was reported to be between the Orkneys and Fair Isle, which would have been approximately the location of Medina Sidonia's ships by that date.[60] A few weeks later a number of them were wrecked on the Irish coast. At some point early in 1589 the Queen rewarded her Lord Chamberlain for his service in this crisis, with a licence to export 20,000 broadcloths over the next six years without paying duty. This did not mean that Lord Hunsdon had turned merchant in his declining years, but that he would have been able to sell his licence for a substantial sum to those who were in the business. This was typical of Elizabeth's cash-cautious style at this time, more famously typified by the grants of monopolies in the manufacture of such commodities as soap and playing cards, which enabled the recipients to sell their rights, and obtain their rewards at the cost of the consumer, to whom the price would have been enhanced.[61]

By this time, Lord Hunsdon was settled at the court, although he still retained his interests in the north. In 1592 it was noted again that no one knew 'the Scottish causes' better than the Lord Chamberlain, who should be consulted over any matter relating to King James or his conduct over the English succession.[62] He also held Norham Castle of the Queen, and the fishing rights in the river Tweed, which had come to the Crown from the bishopric of Durham by a statute of the first year of her reign. These would have gone along with his governorship of Berwick, a post which he continued to hold, and would have been leased out to those with the relevant interests, while Norham would have been in the hands of a reliable deputy.[63] He continued to be busy almost to the end, but his health was giving way, and in March 1596 the Earl of Essex reported to Sir Robert Sidney, the Governor of

Flushing that he was likely to die. In the event he survived until 23 July when he expired at Somerset House at the age of seventy. The Queen's personal reaction is not known, but he was one of the last of her early favourites, and his death severed a link with her mother which she must surely have valued.[64] Her feelings are probably best gauged by the fact that she promptly bestowed the chamberlainship upon his son George, who became the second Lord Hunsdon. George's brothers Henry, Robert and Edward were also in the royal service, so the image of her cousin lived on in his descendants. The elder Henry is alleged to have been discontented that he was never promoted to an earldom in spite of his closeness to the Queen, but Elizabeth's creations at that level were so few that it is not surprising. Moreover, although his services were worthy, and extended over many years, they lacked the distinction of her lord admirals, created Earls of Lincoln and Nottingham respectively in 1572 and 1597. In spite of her early flutter with the Earl of Leicester, the Queen was not anxious that it should appear that she was promoting peers primarily for kinship to herself. Her affection for her cousin is probably best expressed in the fact that she paid for his funeral, which cost her £800, and gave Lady Hunsdon and her daughters £400 by way of a gift in November 1596. Shortly after, on 5 December she also took the most unusual step of conferring the keepership of Somerset House upon Ann, with all the rights and fees dependent upon that office, and the following July gave her an annuity of £200, which would have made her virtually independent of her son.[65] George, as we have seen, sued unsuccessfully for the earldom of Ormond in 1597, and may have done his own chances no good by being notoriously opposed to the pretensions of the Earl of Essex. He would probably have been raised to a superior title by King James, who was much more generous than his predecessor, but he died at the age of fifty-six on 8 September 1603, before the King had got around to thinking about him. His mother outlived him, dying at Somerset House in 1607. His son, Henry, the third Lord Hunsdon, was created Viscount Rochford in 1621, in what must have been a deliberate echo of his family history, and Earl of Dover on 8 March 1628. When his son John, the second Earl, died in May 1677 the senior branch of the Carey line became extinct.[66] It was left to the descendants of George's younger brothers to carry the Carey descent down to the present day.

There was only one stain on the married life of Henry Carey, and that is the existence of an illegitimate son, one Valentine Carey, who became Bishop of Exeter in 1621 and died in 1626.[67] He must have been born about 1560, and the name of his mother is not known, but he appears to have been acknowledged and educated at his father's expense. Ann, who was herself the mother of at least six children, left no recorded opinion of her husband's waywardness, and perhaps she did not mind very much. She and Henry must often have been apart as he pursued his various official duties, and it is even possible that she never found out. Like his uncle, Lord Rochford, Lord Hunsdon left a legacy to the Church of England.

# ELIZABETH I, THE BOLEYN DAUGHTER – THE DUDLEY YEARS

It needs to be remembered that Elizabeth I had two grandfathers – King Henry VII and Sir Thomas Boleyn, and that Anne Boleyn was her mother. She had been less than three years old when Anne was executed, and would hardly have noticed her absence. Her mother had been an occasional visitor to the daughter's household rather than a regular presence, and the child's affections were probably more focussed upon her nurse. Nevertheless, she had her mother's genes, and they included not only her deviousness and acute political intelligence, but also her sexuality. We are told that Elizabeth 'gloried' in her father, and had learned his way of doing business. 'She intends to have her way absolutely as her father did,' observed the Count of Feria a few days before her accession; and indeed she inherited her imperious demeanour as well as her colouring from Henry VIII.[1] She never spoke of her mother, but promoted her Carey relations, not only Henry but also his wife Anne, his sister Catherine and Catherine's husband Sir Francis Knollys. Elizabeth owed her evangelical upbringing to Catherine Parr rather than to Anne, and her outright Protestantism to her brother Edward and his tutors, but she must have been aware of her mother's reputation as a promoter of reform, and determined to tread in her footsteps. Sexually, her encounter with Thomas Seymour had taught her caution, and she was careful not to allow any man's name to be associated with hers as long as Mary was alive. Philip had been keen to marry her to a loyal Catholic and Habsburg supporter, and had endeavoured to match her with the Duke of Savoy. However, she had rejected all overtures on the pretext that she was not ready for such a commitment, realising perfectly well that his real objective was to limit her freedom of action if (or when) she should come to the throne.[2] She had affected a puritanical plainness of dress, and professed a complete lack of interest in sexual activity, lest it lead to her entrapment in an unfavourable marriage. When she came to the throne, therefore, at the age of twenty-five, she suddenly found herself the most attractive bride in Europe, and free to chose whatever partner she liked.

In his despatch of 14 November, Feria speculated on who would be in favour and who out when the new regime took effect. Among those not presently councillors, he mentioned the Earl of Bedford, Sir Peter Carew and Sir William Cecil as likely to be promoted. He also referred to Lord Robert (Dudley), although without any particular emphasis.[3] He reported that Elizabeth regarded talk of her marriage to the Earl of Arundel as a joke, and beyond that it was Lord Paget's opinion that there was no one outside the kingdom or within it upon whom she had an eye. Sir William Pickering was mentioned (although not by Feria) as a possibility, but this seems to have been on no stronger grounds than that he was fine upstanding man, and worthy of any damsel's favour. Although she talked to the ambassador with remarkable freedom, this was one subject that was not discussed between them, and he declined to speculate. It was, however, a live issue for her council as soon as she had one, and her first parliament in January 1559 petitioned her to marry. Her reply was typically devious, outlining the circumstances which had hitherto deterred her, she went on:

Although my youth and words may seem to some hardly to agree together, yet it is most true that at this day I stand free from any other meaning that either I have had in time past or have at this present. With which trade of life I am so thoroughly acquainted that I trust God, who hath hitherto preserved me and led me by the hand, will not now of his goodness suffer me to go alone.[4]

She would marry, but in God's good time, and taking careful thought for the well being of her realm. She knew perfectly well that it was not out of any solicitude for her happiness that this course was urged upon her.

And albeit it might please Almighty God to continue me still in this mind to live out of the state of marriage, yet it is not to be feared but that he will so work in my heart and in your wisdoms as good provision by his help may be made in convenient time, whereby the realm shall not remain destitute of an heir ...[5]

Elizabeth did not, however, place this at the head of her list of priorities. God had given her a realm to rule, not as a consort but as a sovereign, and it remained to be seen whether she could square the duties which that imposed upon her with the submissiveness required of a sixteenth-century wife. Her sister Mary had faced that same difficulty, and had never satisfactorily resolved it, while her own mother, although not a sovereign, had faced a similar conflict between her political instincts and her conjugal duty. Under the stern eye of Henry VIII, that had led to disaster, but Elizabeth was answerable to no one but God, and perhaps He would sympathise. John Aylmer saw her as being two distinct persons, the one public and the other private. Responding to a conventional argument he said:

You say God hath appointed her to be subject to her husband ...
therefore she may not be the head. I grant that, so far as pertaining
to the bands of marriage, and to the offices of a wife, she must
be a subject; but as a Magistrate she may be her husbands head.
Why may not the woman be the husband's inferior in matters of
wedlock, and his head in the guiding of the commonwealth.[6]

Elizabeth, however, rightly perceived that this dichotomy would not
work. A sovereign who was also a wife needed to be emancipated
from the normal constraints of matrimony, and it would be very
difficult to find a husband on those terms.

However, such thoughts did not deter her from entering the
European marriage market, where her price could well be unique.
It is not clear what conditions her former brother-in-law, Philip of
Spain, had in mind when he proposed to her in December 1558,
except that it would have been a highly political marriage.[7] The
story that he had become enamoured of his attractive sister-in-
law before his wife's death unfortunately belongs to the world
of historical fiction. Philip was concerned to continue the Anglo-
Spanish alliance which was currently fighting against France, and
any consideration of personal or sexual gratification was distinctly
secondary. Realising this perfectly well, Elizabeth politely declined
his offer. The prospect of a Habsburg alliance was nevertheless an
attractive one, particularly to the council, and a positive response
was made to the suggestion of the Archduke Charles, a younger son
of the Emperor Ferdinand, as a candidate. The Queen's reaction
was equivocal. She professed her preference for the single life, but
recognised the legitimacy of concern about the succession, and did
not reject him out of hand. Consequently in 1559 a protracted and
convoluted negotiation began, which concentrated particularly

on the nature of the Archduke's position as King of England, and on the religious rights which might accompany any marriage.[8] Charles (and his advisers) naturally insisted upon the mass as the minimum concession, and while some members of her council might have been willing to concede this, Elizabeth herself was adamantly opposed. Whether this was out of genuine conviction, or a desire to protract the negotiations in the interests of national security is not apparent, but by 1565 the exchanges were becoming unreal, and collapsed eventually in 1567, to widespread sighs of relief from the more committed Protestants in Elizabeth's court.[9]

While this negotiation chugged discouragingly ahead, the Queen, operating on a different level of reality, had fallen in love. This time it was not rather theoretical arguments about gender and authority which created the imperative, but sex. Elizabeth knew she was a woman like any other, but since the Seymour episode had kept herself on a tight leash. However, the attractiveness of Robert Dudley proved too much for her defences. She began a flirtation of which her mother might have been proud. He was the third son of John Dudley, Earl of Warwick and Duke of Northumberland, and they had known each other in a sense since both were adolescents at King Edward's court.[10] They had shared the perils of Mary's reign, and had even been lodged in the Tower at the same time in 1554, although it is unlikely that that experience improved their acquaintance. After their release, their friendship had been maintained, and it is even rumoured that she borrowed money off him at one juncture, although her financial circumstances should have been a good deal easier than his. At that time he was living the life of a country gentleman in Norfolk, married since 1549 to Amy, the daughter of Sir John Robsart. Elizabeth's accession to the throne led to an immediate recall to the court, and she almost immediately conferred upon him the office of Master of the Horse, a position worth £1,500 a year, and carrying regular rights of access to the royal person.[11] His prospects were transformed overnight, and within about six months it was being rumoured that he was putting his rights of access to improper use. Kate Ashley, Elizabeth's Principal Gentlewoman and general chaperone, became understandably anxious at these rumours, declaring that in showing herself so affectionate towards him, her honour and dignity were becoming sullied.[12] Dudley's favour was also creating unhealthy rivalries within the court, because the older nobility resented him bitterly as the son of a parvenue, and one moreover who had been executed for high treason. The Duke of Norfolk blamed the difficulties of the Habsburg marriage negotiations on these reports of the Queen's behaviour, while a number of young hopefuls hitched their wagons to his in the hope of rising with him. She was not only flirting with a young man of no lineage, she was also flirting with a married man, whom she could not be intending to marry. Early in 1560 the rumours subsided, because everyone, including the Queen was preoccupied with the affairs of Scotland, but no sooner had William Cecil returned to London with the completed treaty of Edinburgh than they began again. Cecil himself was in despair, and spoke of resigning the secretaryship, more because of Elizabeth's behaviour than because the success of his Scottish labours had been largely ignored in the orgy of lustful speculation.[13] It was widely believed that Dudley had designs on his wife's life, so that he might be free to marry the Queen; and then in September it happened. Amy was found dead at the foot of the stairs in Cumnor Hall, which she and Robert were renting while he was occupied at court. The circumstances were suspicious, and all fingers pointed at Robert Dudley.

Any forensic examination of Amy Dudley's death is likely to be inconclusive.[14] The servants had been given a day off, which looks suspicious but could be entirely innocent. It has been argued that a fall down stairs would have been unlikely to be fatal, and was not the real cause of her death. On the other hand, it was reported at the time that she was unwell, with a 'malady in one of her breasts', which sounds like breast cancer, which, undiagnosed and untreated, would have given her brittle bones. Lord Robert was carefully kept away from Cumnor while the coroner's jury considered the evidence, and indeed was as keen as anyone that the jury should operate free from any suspected interference. The Queen was equally cautious, and kept him away from the court while the deliberations were on-going. The coroner's court returned a verdict of death by misadventure, and that should have been the end of the matter; but of course it wasn't.[15] One anonymous chronicler noted that 'the people say she was killed by reason that he [Dudley] forsook her company without cause'. The people no doubt said lots of other things, because Dudley was not popular, and careful though she was, the Queen's reputation was tarnished. Sir Nicholas Throgmorton at the French court, was assailed with ribald humour:

> ... one laugheth at us, an other threateneth, an other revileth her Majesty, and some let not to say what religion is this that a subject shall kill his wife, and the prince not only bear withal but marry with him ...[16]

Throgmorton's distress was typical of that suffered by loyal defenders of the Queen's position, and it became obvious that to marry Dudley would be political suicide. The rumours did not go away, and years later the author of *Leicester's Commonwealth* accused Sir Richard Verney, the owner of Cumnor, of making away with Amy on the orders of her husband. This was admittedly a virulently polemical tract, but it reflected what was widely believed in London at the time.[17] Dudley did all the right things. He spent nearly £2,000 on his wife's funeral, and wore mourning for about six months, but when he returned to court in October he received a number of marks of personal favour, and believed, unrealistically, that his hopes of marriage were still alive. Quite typically, Elizabeth sent out ambiguous signals, and frictions within the court built up again. The nobility were rumoured to be ready to rebel if the marriage took place, and there was an affray between Dudley's servants and those of the Earl of Pembroke.[18] Nevertheless, anyone who openly slandered the favourite was in danger of the royal wrath, and William Cecil (who was as opposed to the marriage idea as anyone) was forced to behave with the utmost discretion. At the same time, in November 1560, the Queen drew back from the idea of conferring a title on Robert, and since this would have been a necessary precursor to marriage, it may be that by then she had decided that the idea was impossible, although that is by no means clear. She would not have forgotten that her father had conferred the title of Marquis of Pembroke upon her mother nearly thirty years before, with just such an intention. What is clear is that Elizabeth was in considerable distress of mind. As a woman she desired Dudley wholeheartedly, and could barely keep her hands off him in public, but as a queen she recognised the likely outcome of any decision to marry him. It would probably cost her crown, and that meant more to her than any man. It is even possible that she was party to a devious ploy by Lord Robert in February 1561 to secure the backing of King Philip for the match, in return for some form of toleration for English Catholics.[19] The only evidence for these exchanges comes from De Quadra, the Spanish ambassador, who may have misrepresented their intention, but it seems that Dudley was in earnest, and it can only be surmised that Elizabeth was playing her usual double game. It is hard to credit that she was aware of Lord Robert's alleged offer to reconvert the realm to Catholicism in return for the King of Spain's support. Her Church, like her Crown, meant more to her than sexual gratification.[20]

Elizabeth nearly died of the smallpox in October 1562, and for about a week anxiety was intense. There was much speculation about the succession in the event of her death, one party supporting Lady Catherine Grey, and another the Earl of Huntingdon. The Queen was powerless to prevent these discussions, but she said two things which relate to her relationship with Dudley, and which in the circumstances are highly revealing. In the first place she swore that, in spite of appearances, they had never had sexual intercourse, and in the second place she wanted him made protector of the realm if she should die.[21] This provision indicates that she was prepared to leave the succession to be decided by her council, and that her trust in Lord Robert was undiminished, but that she had not committed herself to him physically, and would never do so. Although he remained her favourite, he was henceforth confined politically to membership of the Privy Council, where he quickly assumed a dominant role, usually in opposition to Sir William Cecil. It was largely through his influence that the Queen intervened in the affairs of France in 1562–3, and burned her fingers badly when the Huguenots settled with the government and turned against her.[22] Her trust in his judgement was never entirely restored. Ironically enough, his elevation to the earldom of Leicester, which occurred on 29 September 1564 had more to do with her rather far-fetched idea that he would be a suitable husband for the Queen of Scots than for herself. How seriously this idea was intended is not very clear, and Mary was not amused at being offered Elizabeth's 'cast off lover', but whether this was ever more than a game played between them is not apparent. Dudley apparently professed himself willing to do his duty, but never regarded it as a realistic proposition.[23] As Earl of Leicester he was properly endowed with landed estates, including the magnificent castle of Kennilworth where in 1575 he entertained his royal mistress with lavish splendour, endued with dramatic representations of true love, perhaps in a forlorn and belated hope that she would change her mind about marrying him. By the time of these entertainments Robert was in an adulterous relationship with Lettice, Countess of Essex. This was, of course, kept secret, but after her husband died in September 1576, their intimacy increased and she became pregnant. In the spring of 1578 he secretly married her at Kennilworth.[24] Inevitably Elizabeth found out, and became immensely and quite irrationally angry. Robert was man like any other, and could not be satisfied indefinitely with the kind of platonic relationship which was the most that she was prepared to offer. The fact that he had enjoyed a rather similar association with Lady Douglas Sheffield remained unknown to her. He seems to have made his peace privately with his irate mistress, because although his wife was banished from the court, it appears that his reign as royal favourite continued unchecked. Lettice was not satisfied with secrecy. A secret marriage could be too easily repudiated if circumstances should change, so they went through a public ceremony before witnesses in September, and Elizabeth seems to have reconciled herself to the situation.[25] It was, after all, only a return to that which had appertained before September 1560, except that the Queen was now over forty, and even the keenest advocates of matrimony now recognised that it was probably too late to secure the succession. She had been conducting a diplomatic flirtation with the Duke of Anjou since 1572, and that continued in a fitful fashion, with endless wrangling over religious rights, and what powers the Duke would enjoy in England. At this stage there was no sexual frisson in those discussions whatsoever.[26]

Meanwhile, Elizabeth ruled as no man could have done. A king, if he were of suitable age, was expected to show military prowess, ideally on the field of battle, but a least in the war games of the tilt and the tournament. Such a role was not possible for a queen, and Mary had deliberately distanced herself from all such entertainments, but Elizabeth embraced them enthusiastically. She became the 'Queen of Fairie', presiding glamorously, where every courtier was supposed to wear her favour in the lists, and to offer her their tribute of daring-do. Using the tropes of the courtly love tradition, she became the unattainable but desirable lady, with whom all her servants were supposed to be in love.[27] Even aging ministers of State were required to play this game, accepting the reward of a smile or a small favour in lieu of the more substantial rewards that they might reasonably have expected. She also made remorseless use of the female stereotype. A woman was supposed to be fickle, and to change her mind? Very well, she would procrastinate endlessly, in order to demonstrate that she alone could make certain critical decisions. Let them wait! She would not be taken for granted, and probably rejoiced when her council was divided, because that gave her more freedom of action.[28] This was particularly demonstrated in her relations with Spain, where she continued to give Philip's ambassadors bland assurances of goodwill while allowing (and

even encouraging) the remorseless depredations of her freebooting
subjects, particularly John Hawkins and Francis Drake. She was a
mere woman; how could she know about such things? Two other
aspects of her foreign policy especially demonstrate this feminine
style of diplomacy – her relationship with the Dutch rebels and
her search for a husband. This latter was a unique operation
which took her agents and representatives to Sweden, Vienna and
Paris over more than twenty years.[29] There they were expected to
respond positively to all the suggestions made, but also to insist
on personal visits by the prospective grooms, and to avoid any
outright commitment, particularly on the question of religious
concessions. Over the years she was pursued in this fashion by Eric
of Sweden, the Archduke Charles (as we have seen), Henri, Duke
of Anjou and Francois, Duke of Alencon. With Eric the lack of
real interest soon became mutual, and he went in pursuit of Mary
of Scotland. With Charles and Henri the negotiations broke down
over religion, and with Francois time eventually foreclosed the
exercise in a very interesting way in 1581. From 1578 onward the
Queen was endeavouring to persuade her council to accept Anjou
(as he had then become), largely, it would seem, as a means of
forestalling his proposed intervention in the Netherlands, but the
negotiations hung fire.[30] Then in August 1581 the Duke resolved
to come in person to secure his prize, and Elizabeth succumbed
to those charms which were so lacking in the eyes of her subjects.
In what looks like an onrush of menopausal sexuality, she kissed
him and swore that she would marry him. Her councillors and the
ladies of her chamber were alike appalled, and spent the whole
of the following night talking her out of her resolution. They
succeeded and the next day she told the Duke that she had changed
her mind. He departed, cursing the fickleness of women, and that

was the end of her matrimonial adventures.[31] Contemporaries and historians alike have debated this curious episode. Was the Queen serious, even briefly, or was it another ploy aimed at getting rid of him? In a way it was symbolic of her whole attitude to marriage, in which the needs of the woman and of the politician were in constant tension. She probably would have married, if the conditions had been right, but they never were, and in the end she backed out of each negotiation on the ground of incompatibility, usually religious. This makes all her proposals look like episodes of foreign policy, unrelated to real emotion, but that was probably not the case. She metaphorically dangled her person before the courts of Europe in the hope of finding a satisfying relationship, but at the end the price in terms of surrendered authority, was always too high. Like her sister, Mary, although in a different way, Elizabeth was a victim of that culture which made it impossible to be both a ruler and wife. At the beginning of her reign, John Aylmer had proposed that a solution could be found, but it turned out not to be the case, and the Queen paid with a lifetime of frustration for the power which she cherished. God, who had given her a realm to rule, did not chose to find her a husband who would share that burden in a satisfactory way, and perhaps it could not be done.[32]

Her relationship with the Dutch was female mainly in its deviousness, because for more then twenty years she continued to express goodwill towards Spain, which ruled the country, while permitting her subjects to support the rebels there in any way that they chose. It was an exercise in brinkmanship, postulated on the theory that Philip did not wish to add her to his list of enemies, and it worked. In 1565 the obvious English sympathy with the Protestant 'Compromise' movement led the Regent, Margaret of Parma, to impose a trade embargo, until that proved to be more damaging to Antwerp than it was to London, and in 1568 Elizabeth anticipated the Duke of Alba's money, intended to pay his troops, leading to another embargo.[33] Between 1568 and 1572, while negotiating with Alba to get this lifted, she was giving refuge to those fugitives from his regime known as the Sea Beggars – pirates in effect – who preyed on Flemish shipping. In 1572, in what was ostensibly a conciliatory gesture, she expelled the Sea Beggars, only for them to cross to Brill, seize the town and give the revolt against Alba a new lease of life. Nobody knows whether that outcome was intended or not.[34] Thereafter there were always rebels in arms against the Spanish authorities, and Elizabeth turned a blind eye to those military volunteers who went over in considerable numbers to help them. Such service not only got hot-headed young men out of the country, but enabled professional soldiers to secure the up-to-date experience which they needed to train the local levies upon which the English government relied for the defence of the realm, whether against foreign invasion or domestic rebellion. Most of the county muster-masters of the 1570s had seen service in the Low Countries, and short of going to war herself that provided the best means of supplying such a need.[35] It was not until 1585 that this ambiguous policy was finally exposed by the situation following the assassination of William the Silent. Then the Queen was faced with the stark alternatives of open intervention or standing aside while the revolt was suppressed. That was no choice, faced with the prospect of unchallenged Spanish power on the other side of the North Sea, and the result was open war, but Elizabeth was still negotiating with the Duke of Parma as the armada sailed up the Channel.

The Queen disliked war for a number of reasons, several of them gender related. In the first place it was very expensive, and she hated asking her subjects for money almost as much as they disliked paying it. However, she was also very aware that, unlike a king, there was no glory to be gained for her upon the field of battle. Women, even queens, did not lead armies, and this meant that she was deeply suspicious of those men who could. Like her father, she disliked the pretensions of the nobles of lineage, and especially their military culture, which had survived half a century of discouragement from her father and grandfather.[36] The best way to avoid calling upon their services was to avoid war, and that she did successfully for nearly thirty years. Such limited campaigns as were fought in the early years saw the Duke of Norfolk commanding in Scotland in 1560, and the Earl of Warwick in France in 1562–3, but the latter was a peer of her own creation and the Duke was no great soldier. Neither was likely to come home in triumph and upstage their mistress. When she was forced into war in 1585, she gave the principal land command to her favourite the Earl of Leicester, and then recalled him in disgrace when he accepted (on her behalf) the governor generalship, which was contrary to his instructions.[37] For serious fighting, both in the Low Countries, Brittany and Ireland she preferred to rely on professionals like Sir John Norris and Lord Mountjoy, who had technical competence and no social pretensions. One of the reasons why she favoured the 'sea dogs' was that they were good sea fighters, the other reason was that they were men of humble origin, and entirely dependent upon her for their wealth and status. Elizabeth was very conscious of the fact that her mother's principal opponents had been the old nobility, who had regarded her as a parvenue, a description which they also applied, *sotto voce*, to the Tudors.[38] When Elizabeth donned armour and went to harangue her troops at Tilbury in 1588, she was consciously abandoning her habitual gender role, but that was in an emergency, and in spite of her rhetoric she was not called upon to fight. Although Elizabeth was very reluctant to admit that there were any aspects of government not 'pertinent to women', war was definitely off limits. Ironically, she was to spend almost a third of her reign fighting Spain, and successfully outfaced that most military of monarchies.

If Elizabeth had been a consort, then her husband would have condemned her for adultery with Robert Dudley, in much the same way as her mother had been condemned for her liaison with Henry Norris. The evidence would have been similar, persuasive but circumstantial and probably misleading. As it was, their relationship continued, sexual in its nature, but increasingly political in its expression. In 1585 she sent him to the Low Countries, in command of her forces there, but recalled him when he became embroiled in the politics of that divided country.[39] He resented this and they quarrelled bitterly, but he never forfeited his special relationship, and when he died in September 1588, it transpired that the Queen had kept all his letters, even those which most revealed his hurt at her lack of trust in him. In spite of his marriage and her continued celibacy, it was a lovers' relationship in every respect short of full consummation.[40] When she had invested him with the Garter, way back in 1559, she had deliberately tickled the back of his neck, and that kind of playfulness endured in their dealings with each other, until the very end of his life. We do not, of course, know what kind of a woman her mother would have been if she had lived into her fifties, but the similarities between mother and daughter are so marked, that we can probably reconstruct the hypothetical Anne of the 1550s in the person of Elizabeth.

The Earl of Leicester left no legitimate son, and he was eventually, in 1618, followed in his title by his nephew Robert

Sidney. He did, however, leave a stepson, Robert Devereux, the second Earl of Essex, Lettice's son by her first marriage, who had succeeded to his father's title at the age of ten in 1576.[41] As a ward of the Crown, his education was in the hands of the Master of the Wards, Lord Burghley, who sent him to Trinity College, Cambridge at the precocious age of twelve in 1578. His mother appears to have had little or no say in this process, which was probably just as well because she was barred from the court after her marriage to Leicester, and the Queen never forgave her. Unlike many young noblemen, Devereux seems to have taken his education seriously, and actually proceeded to the Master of Arts degree in 1582.[42] He may well have seen very little of his stepfather by that time, and it was probably Burghley who introduced him to the court in 1584, when he was eighteen years old. He was an immediate success, particularly with the Queen, being very handsome and having excellent manners. He was to become in due course the son which she had never had, and he quickly became his stepfather's protégé. In 1585 he accompanied Leicester to the Netherlands, and raised a band to serve under him, for which either Leicester or Burghley must have paid since he had not yet achieved his majority. In the field he quickly began to display that combination of personal courage and bad military judgement which was to mark his later career. In spite of his irresponsible conduct, he showed bravery in some small scale actions, and that gave his stepfather sufficient excuse to knight him. He also earned the friendship of Leicester's kinsman, Sir Philip Sidney, and inherited the latter's sword when he was killed in action at Zutphen in 1586.[43] When Leicester was recalled in November of that year, the Earl of Essex accompanied him, but was not politically important enough to share the former's disfavour. Indeed he quickly slotted back into the routines of the court, and by the spring of 1587 was clearly the Queen's new favourite. Still short of his twenty-first birthday, it was noted that he was spending a great deal of time in her company:

> When she is abroad, nobody [is] near her but my Lord of Essex; and at night my Lord is at cards, at one game or another with her [so] that he cometh not to his own lodging till the bird sing in the morning …[44]

Perhaps it is also true that she enjoyed his conversation, being a young man (relatively) fresh from the university, and no doubt well stocked with that classical lore which she so much appreciated. The Earl of Leicester had become lord steward of the household in succession to the Earl of Lincoln in 1584, and his former office of master of the horse had been left vacant. Now in September 1587 it was conferred upon the Earl of Essex, who thus acquired a post not only famous for the intimacy with the sovereign which it carried, but also worth £1,500 a year. Since he would have taken livery of his father's lands at about the same time, on achieving his majority, he became within a few weeks a man of substance, which was just as well because his tastes were running to expensive clothes and entertainments, and his expenditure was soon running ahead of even his sizeable income.[45] When the Earl of Leicester died in the following year, it seemed to observers that he was immediately born again in the person of his brilliant twenty-two-year-old stepson. Yet those who were close to the Queen knew that their relationships were very different. Robert Dudley had been an old and dear friend, in spite of their tiffs and disagreements – a former lover with a very special place in her heart. Robert Devereux was young and handsome and dashing, just the kind of lad to bowl over an ageing spinster, but the sexual element in their relationship, if it existed at all, was quite different in its nature. Elizabeth would never have taken Devereux as a lover, even if he had been willing; rather he was part of the fantasy world of sexual delusion which she created around herself in the later years of her life.[46] This was a world in which courtiers were still supposed to love the Queen, and bombarded her with flattery, telling her she was the most beautiful woman in the world, a pathological lie which both she and they understood. It was world of make believe, and into this world the Earl of Essex with his youthful good looks and skilful word play fitted perfectly. He was to an extent also self deceived, believing himself to be great soldier and a statesman who was only waiting his chance to take over the realm as he had already taken over its mistress. Elizabeth loved these fantasies, and pandered to them, but they did not for a moment deceive her. Beneath the powder and the paint and the wigs which appearances demanded, her shrewd political brain was still in full working order. Which was why the Earl of Essex found himself less important than he thought that he should have been in the political world of the 1580s.[47]

In truth, Essex was a deeply flawed character, lacking the substance that Robert Dudley had had, even as a young man. He was incurably vain – proud of his ancient lineage, his good looks and his imagined talents. He was intelligent, but chronically lacking in judgement, and was a slave to passionate emotions which he could neither conceal nor control. He made all the mistakes which an impulsive young man could make, but never learned from them, choosing to regard the hostile reactions of his fellow courtiers as evidence of jealousy and of conspiracy against him, never of his own impulsiveness. In July 1587, in the course of the summer progress, he quarrelled with Elizabeth herself, taking umbrage at some disparaging remarks about his mother which the Queen (who could not stand her) had made in a fit of bad temper. He then compounded his error by trying to blame Sir Walter Raleigh, a rival favourite, for turning the Queen against him, and stormed out of the house where the court was assembled, declaring that his affections were 'so much thrown down' that he was off to Flanders – no doubt to seek redemption on the battlefield.[48] He seems to have regarded his success at court as some kind of birthright, and reacted with blank incomprehension to Elizabeth's ill humour. Such a reaction would have been suicidal for most courtiers, but not for Essex. The Queen chose to regard it as an amusing tantrum, and peremptorily summoned him back to court. He seems to have had no idea what a narrow escape he had had, and in April 1589 he again left the court without licence, this time in a desperate effort to repair his parlous financial situation by joining what he took to be the plundering expedition led by Drake and Norris to Portugal. On 1 April he wrote to Sir Francis Knollys that his debts were 'at least two or three and twenty thousand pounds', and that her Majesty had been so good to him that he could not ask her for more, so there was 'no way left but to repair myself by mine own adventure'.[49] He apparently commandeered one of the Queen's ships and set off as a kind of freelance addition to the expedition. A few days later Drake and Norris were appraised of this unwanted addition to their party, and instructed that when located he was to be returned to London. After a brief panic he was found, and ignominiously sent back.[50] Again his transgression was forgiven, and in 1590, when he returned to pleading his financial plight, the Queen granted him his stepfather's monopoly on the importation of sweet wines, which brought him an income of £2,500 a year, and transformed his circumstances – for the time being.

In 1591 he was humoured, if that is the right word, by being given command of an expeditionary force sent to help Henry IV in Normandy.[51] He made a mess of his assignment, and this again led to a falling out with the Queen, but once again when he returned in October he managed to wheedle and flatter his way back into favour, aided on this occasion by the fact that Sir Walter Raleigh had disgraced himself by getting one of the Queen's young ladies (Bess Throgmorton) with child in the summer of 1592. Against all the seeming odds, he was appointed to the Privy Council on 25 February 1593, and gathered round him a clientele of young hopefuls who saw him as the rising star in the political firmament.[52] By this time he was locked into a feud with Lord Burghley's equally up and coming son, Sir Robert Cecil, and petulantly regarded every set back to one of his clients as the result of Sir Robert's scheming. Having aroused the hostility of the powerful Cecils, he was skating on thin ice, but for the time being continued to lead a charmed life in the eyes of the Queen. In 1596 he was given what he craved most, a chance to redeem his military reputation, and on 1 June sailed as joint commander (with Lord Charles Howard) of the expedition against Cadiz. This was one of the great successes of the war against Spain, and Essex should have returned covered with glory. Instead he chose to sulk, because his rash strategic advice had been rejected by the council of war, and he felt that Howard had been given more than his due credit for the victory.[53] To add insult to injury, Sir Robert Cecil had been appointed to the vacant secretaryship while he was away. As usual, the Queen blandly ignored his tantrum, and gave him the command of another fleet, this time to intercept the Spanish American treasure fleet, in July 1597. The so-called 'Islands voyage' was a complete fiasco. That was not the Earl's fault, because it was the weather which ruined it, but it did not sweeten his temper, or improve his standing in the council, which now began to matter to him. Lord Burghley died on 4 August 1598, and his lucrative mastership of the Court of Wards, which Essex coveted, was not immediately reassigned. This was probably due to Elizabeth's distress at the death of her old friend and servant, rather than anything to do with Devereux, but he typically took it as a personal affront and made his displeasure clear. Then in 1599 he inadvertently talked himself into appointment as Lord Lieutenant in Ireland.[54] His brief was to tackle the growing menace of the Tyrone rebellion, and he could have regarded it as a golden opportunity to display himself as England's finest soldier. Instead he interpreted it as a plot by Sir Robert Cecil to get him away from the court, and he went to Ireland in a dangerous frame of mind. Having wasted his resources, and signed a disadvantageous truce with Tyrone, he decided to return to England without licence to explain his actions in person. Preceded by rumours of treason, on 24 September he quitted Dublin and headed straight for the court.[55] Intending make his peace as usual with the only person who mattered, he burst unexpectedly upon the Queen, and was immediately placed under arrest. If Sir Robert Cecil was responsible for his disfavour, then Essex had walked straight into a trap, because this time Elizabeth was not to be placated. After nearly a year under house arrest, in August 1600 the Earl was released, but he was not permitted to return to the court, and his sweet wine monopoly was reassigned, threatening him with complete ruin. After more than a decade, he could no longer be regarded as a wayward youth, and the Queen was bitterly disappointed in him.[56] For all his charm, he was taking himself far too seriously, and this time he had been dramatically disobedient. She may also have remembered that he claimed an ancient lineage, and may have been taking her favour for granted. The one thing Elizabeth Tudor could not endure was to be taken for granted. It had been part of her royal strategy from the beginning of her reign never to allow her ministers to do that, and she was not going to endure it now from the hands of a wayward noble. As she observed when terminating his monopoly 'an unruly horse must be abated of his provender, that he may be the easier and better managed'.[57] By the end of 1600 Essex's debts had mounted again to £16,000 or thereabouts, and he was desperate.

By this time he had lost all respect for his sovereign, regarding her as a prisoner of the Cecil clique, which would have to be removed if his favour were to be restored. He seems to have had no doubt but, that having been achieved, he would find her as responsive as before. In that he seriously misjudged Elizabeth, who was by this time totally alienated, and probably reproving herself for her long folly in putting up with him. She was by this time an old lady, and many of her subjects were finding her tiresome, but the old mystique still worked in public, her sexuality an inexhaustible source of fascination and speculation. We do not know what Anne Boleyn would have been like at the same age, but the chances are that she would have been rather similar. Then in February 1601 Essex staged his abortive coup in London, deluding himself that he was a hero to the citizens, and that they would back him against the Cecils.[58] However, it was not the Cecils with whom he had to deal, but the Queen. He was arrested, tried and executed, a victim of his own hubris and self glorification. Elizabeth is alleged to have been deeply disturbed by the fate of her one time 'son', but the evidence for that is dubious. After working on her susceptibilities for many years, he had eventually behaved inexcusably, and paid the lawful price. Elizabeth was not vindictive, and many of her outbursts of rage were so much play acting. She was accustomed to toying with her servants, and once they learned the rules of this game, that had worked well enough, although even William Cecil found it irritating at times. Similarly Anne Boleyn had played with her servants, teasing them with sexual innuendos, only unfortunately for her, she had a suspicious husband in the background. The third Boleyn girl was true to her family traditions, except that she never placed herself in a position where she was expected to be obedient to a lord and master. By being a sovereign, and therefore able to please herself, Elizabeth avoided the fate of most sixteenth-century women.

# CONCLUSION: A POLITICAL FAMILY?

The Boleyns were one of a number of families which served the Tudors through several generations. The Howards were such another, and the Talbots and the Stanleys. However, the Boleyns were unique in that they owed their influence to the sexual prowess of their women rather than to the military or political talents of their men. Sir Thomas was courtier and diplomat of note before his daughters attracted the attention of Henry VIII, but Henry Carey owed his career almost entirely to being Elizabeth's kindred on the distaff side. He was competent, but not of the same level of ability as William Cecil, and lacked the charismatic personality of the Earls of Leicester or Essex. He was a courtier rather than a statesman or a soldier, and the same description might be applied to his grandfather. Without the court connections supplied by his wife, Elizabeth Howard, Sir Thomas Boleyn might well have lived out his life as a country gentleman, and married his daughters into similar families. The marriages of his own father and grandfather had given him court connections, but these might well have lapsed without the marriage which his father negotiated for him with the daughter of the Earl of Surrey. As it was, he became a member of the Howard affinity, and that gave him access to the Prince of Wales, who promoted him after his accession. He became thereafter the King's own man, and owed his first diplomatic assignment to the fact that the King liked him, and that his wife was a favoured member of the Queen's Privy Chamber. Sir Thomas was a successful diplomat, but he is not known to have had any political agenda. He got on comfortably with Cardinal Wolsey, without being in any sense dependent upon him, and it was only the chance that his daughter Mary caught the King's eye that singled him out from other royal servants of the second rank, like Sir Henry Wyatt and Robert Wingfield.

Mary's talents appear to have been strictly domestic. She was pretty and biddable, and raised no objection to being used for the King's pleasure. She was all that a mistress ought to be, so self effacing that we have difficulty in tracking her relationship with Henry, and entirely innocent of any political agenda. If she raised any difficulty about being placed in a morganatic marriage with William Carey, we have no record of the fact, and at the end we are left speculating about when she commenced conjugal relations with her husband. Both her husband and her father derived benefits from her complacency, receiving grants of land and office, but there is no suggestion that she was rewarded herself. After William's death she can be glimpsed about the court, but the circumstances of her second marriage to William Stafford remain mysterious, or why should it have provoked the wrath of her family. Mary's story is that of a court lady of a certain type at the disposal of a monarch of an arbitrary disposition. It is not remotely political, and she played no part in the infighting of the court. Her father is alleged to have fallen out with Cardinal Wolsey over the controllership of the Household, but there is no sense in which he was important enough for that to have mattered. Wolsey was not going to lose any sleep about having quarrelled with Sir Thomas Boleyn. The kind of personal link which the latter enjoyed with the King was hardly of the kind that could be acknowledged in public. Mary's importance in this story is mainly as the mother of Henry and Catherine, particularly Henry through whom the Boleyn genes were to be transmitted to subsequent generations.

Anne was completely different, and it is with her advent that the politics of sexuality become important. However, it needs to be remembered that it was power at second hand. Even Anne, who had her own independent ideas, and patronage of her own, exercised her authority in and through her husband. Henry was always in charge, even in the days when some diplomats thought that he was overshadowed by Cardinal Wolsey. Wolsey himself never made the same mistake, which is why he viewed the advent of Anne with increasing alarm. Here was a rival with access to the King that no mere minister could rival, and he knew Henry well enough to realise his susceptibility to pillow talk. Anne had been trained in France to regard sex and politics as two sides of the same coin, and saw courtly love for what it was – a part of the competitive role play of male courtiers. However, the lady did not have to be a passive recipient of these attentions. By playing a positive part herself she could raise the stakes for the male competitors, which could result in brinkmanship of a most exhilarating kind.[1] Anne's matrimonial adventures before the King took her up were conventional enough. Being used like a chess piece in her father's and grandmother's play for the Ormond inheritance was what any girl of her status could expect, and although she does not seem to have approved of these manoeuvres, she would have been powerless to resist had the negotiation succeeded. Her affair with Henry Percy was no more than a gesture of independence, and although she was seriously put out by its quashing, she was equally powerless to do anything about it. Indeed her silence on that subject afterwards, and the emphasis upon her virginity indicates that it was a purely platonic relationship, no matter what Percy may have been motivated to claim. It was the King who gave Anne and her family a political role. Before 1526 she was simply a lady of the court with whom Henry had chosen to play the game of courtly love. She was unusually sophisticated, thanks to her training in France, but not distinguished in any other way. Her father owed his treasurership of the Household and his promotion to a viscountcy to his own status as a courtier, and neither was an appointment of much political significance. It was Henry's desire to end his marriage and make Anne his second queen which elevated her whole kindred into the status of a political party.

For nearly seven years this desire dominated the politics of the court, and spilled over into foreign policy, as the King struggled against both Pope and Emperor to bring it about. There is abundant evidence that it was Anne who kept him to his task, using her father, her brother and their friends as seemed most appropriate at the time. This gave the whole party a political agenda, centred on the securing of the annulment, which led first to a pro-French stance in the ongoing battle between Francis and Charles, and secondly to the overthrow of Cardinal Wolsey. They became powerful, but only because of their capacity to influence the King. Others, like the Duke of Suffolk joined them for some activities, without being sympathetic to their main agenda. Officially, the Duke of Norfolk was their leader by virtue of his rank, but his ambition did not extend much beyond securing Anne's position as queen. He was quite happy to see Viscount Rochford promoted to the earldom of Wiltshire in 1529, and George Boleyn used on diplomatic missions, but drew back when the younger Boleyns began to support an evangelical agenda which followed up the logic of their political position. Norfolk remained pro-French, but was rapidly eclipsed after 1532 by the rising star Thomas Cromwell, who allied himself with the Boleyns mainly as a matter of convenience.[2] It was Anne who held Henry's attention, but Anne was not a member of the council, and the King was conscientious in consulting his council over every important decision. Consequently it was necessary to manage the council, and although Anne could have some input into that through her father, it fell mainly to Cromwell. By 1535 the so-called 'Boleyn party' in the council was held together mainly by support for the King's second marriage, and the Royal Supremacy which essentially maintained it. They remained dominant largely because Catherine remained alive, and the King became increasingly committed to the supremacy. The Duke of Norfolk and the Earl of Wiltshire remained in this affinity, but it was effectively driven by Anne and by Thomas Cromwell.

The events of April and May 1536 are mainly significant in demonstrating how little real power the Boleyns actually had. As long as they were acting as agents for the King, they were effective, but when Henry changed his mind, they were absolutely helpless. The King changed his mind for a variety of reasons, as we have seen, but the critical factor was that he chose to trust Cromwell rather than Norfolk or Wiltshire – or Anne. There was no struggle in the council at that point; the only struggle was in the mind of the King, and once that mind was made up, Anne was destroyed. The whole imposing edifice of the 'Boleyn ascendancy' disappeared within a matter of days. Norfolk survived, but was politically unimportant. What followed was a sharp struggle between Cromwell and those conservatives who had allied with him to get rid of Anne – a struggle which Cromwell won by securing the submission of the Princess Mary in July 1536. It was not necessary to destroy the Earl of Wiltshire, because he was not politically effective. He lost his office as Lord Privy Seal and retired from the fray. It was necessary to destroy George, partly because the charges of incest against him were an essential aspect of the charges against his sister, and partly because he had the political will and intelligence to remain dangerous. Sir Henry Norris had to be executed for the same combination of reasons, and because he was a member of Privy Chamber who had been (and might be again) close to the King. For the next four years it was Cromwell and his allies, like Sir Thomas Audley, who dominated the King's council and influenced his mind. He attempted, unsuccessfully, to reach agreement with the Emperor, and then even less successfully, to negotiate with the Schmalkaldic League.[3] Politically the Boleyns were in eclipse, represented in the corridors of power only by the infant princess Elizabeth, who remained mainly as a symbol of a dead passion, and as a burden upon the chamber finances. In 1540 Cromwell was destroyed in his turn by those conservative forces which he had outwitted in 1536, who succeeded in convincing the King that he was a sacramentarian, and 'bounced' Henry into executing him in much the same way that he had been 'bounced' into disposing of Anne. Norfolk's triumph, however, was short lived, as the indiscretions of his other niece, Catherine Howard, led to the indictment of his whole family (the Duke excepted) for misprision of treason in December 1541 and destroyed the Howard ascendancy as well. During the last three or four years of her life, Mary Carey received a few favours from the Crown, but neither she nor her husband were politically significant. The most important thing that happened to the Boleyns during the last few years of Henry's life was the inclusion of Elizabeth in the order of succession laid down in 1544. This did not mean that the King was regretting what he had done to her mother, but simply that he was facing the reality that he had one legitimate son (who was a child) and two illegitimate daughters, a fact of which his last queen, Catherine Parr, had made him acutely aware. Neither he nor anybody else anticipated that both his son and his elder daughter would die childless, or that the great queen who was to reign for forty-five years would be Anne Boleyn's daughter.

The removal of Henry's overwhelming presence in January 1547 changed the politics of the court fundamentally, because first Protector Somerset and then the Earl of Warwick were in possession of real power, and not of influence.[4] The Boleyns however, scarcely feature in the battles of Edward's reign. Mary was the acknowledged leader of the conservative opposition, and Elizabeth scarcely features except when her brush with Thomas Seymour contributed to the latter's execution on charges of treason. Henry Carey lurked on the fringes, with a minor post at court and a seat in the House of Commons, while the Earl of Wiltshire's younger brother, James, (who is very easily forgotten), continued to live at Blickling. He did his duty on various kinds of commission, but in other respects led the life of a country gentleman. If he had any residual contacts with the court, they are not apparent.[5] Mary's accession changed the profile, because Elizabeth was now the heir, unacknowledged by the Queen, but recognised by the political nation. She became the symbol of opposition, rather than its leader, because the latter would have been far too exposed a position. She spent time in prison for suspected involvement with Sir Thomas Wyatt, and Mary made it clear that she did not wish Elizabeth to succeed her because of 'certain respects in which she resembled her mother'.[6] It was probably association with religious reform that the Queen had in mind, rather than her sexuality, but the painful memories of Mary's adolescence might have been equally responsible. At the time when this remark was made, in the winter of 1553–4, the Queen had every intention of marrying and providing the realm with an heir of her body, so Elizabeth's claim was a hypothetical one. Mary's marriage, however, failed, and her husband Philip of Spain disclaimed any interest in claiming the realm in the event of her death. He knew the disposition of the English, and knew that it would mean fighting a civil war to force himself onto the throne. So he accepted Elizabeth's right, and brought her to the forefront of politics by seeking to marry her to the Duke of Savoy. By the time that the Queen's health went into terminal decline in the autumn of 1558, it was clear that Elizabeth would be the next queen, and that Anne Boleyn's unmarried daughter would be faced with all the challenges of ruling England. Fortunately for her, Mary's second parliament had cleared up the constitutional propriety of having a woman on the throne, and had declared that her powers would be the same as any 'of her predecessors, kings of this realm'.[7] It remained to be seen how she would cope.

In a sense the whole story of Elizabeth's reign could be entitled 'the Boleyns in power', but that would be unrealistic because she derived her claim and a fair bit of her personality from her father. What is realistic, however, is to look at how she addressed the issues arising from her gender and sexuality, because that was her inheritance from her mother. Direct comparisons are not possible, because Anne was never a sovereign, and her power always lay in her ability to manipulate her husband. Elizabeth had no husband, but she did have a council and lovers of various degrees of intimacy whom she also had to control. As we have seen, she spent almost half her reign coping with pressures from within the realm that she should marry, and nobody knows whether, or when, she decided that that would not work. One international negotiation succeeded another, and all ended in failure because there was no way in which the obligations of a ruler could be squared with the duties of a wife. What these did do, however, was to provide a theme by which foreign policy could be conducted. This was a theme which no king could have used because of the differences between a male and a female consort, the latter being a mere adjunct and the former a king matrimonial. Elizabeth's objective was to maintain the security and integrity of her realm, without having to fight major wars in order to do so. So she played the feminine card for all that it was worth, and for more than twenty years it worked. A king could not have expected to retain his authority, either at home or abroad, without fighting, but she could, and did. She also had to deal with her council and courtiers, all of whom were men. She had, admittedly, a female Privy Chamber to retreat to when the pressures of the masculine world became intolerable, and that had a politics of its own, but it was not a centre of power in the same sense that Henry VIII's Privy Chamber had been.[8] Courtiers, ultimately, would do as they were told, but councillors were a different proposition. Elizabeth took seriously her obligation to rule with counsel, but was denied the kind of male bonding which had traditionally determined relations between kings and their advisers. It was one thing for councillors to pretend to be in love with their mistress, but quite another to admit any degree of intimacy. The relationship which fitted her predicament best was that which she enjoyed with William Cecil, which was that of a niece with a surrogate uncle. This enabled her to quarrel with him, and reject or ignore his advice, without ever forfeiting that special relationship which underpinned her regime for almost forty years. Elizabeth modelled all the associations which mattered to her on aspects of the family. The Earl of Leicester was her 'husband' (without any of the rights which real marriage would have conveyed), Lord Burghley was her 'uncle', the Earl of Essex her 'son' and so on. Henry Carey, who was her real cousin, was much favoured and employed, but does not really feature in this make believe family. Elizabeth also played the female card in other ways. She threw tantrums in which neither the recipients nor the observer knows where the play-acting ended and the real rage began. She even became violent on occasions – with her female attendants. She procrastinated endlessly when she was expected to be decisive, but whether out of a genuine inability to make up her mind, or out of a mischievous desire to keep her servants on their toes, no one is very certain. Sometimes events made up her mind for her, and sometimes she eventually came to a resolution – as with the fate of Mary of Scotland – but never did her indecisiveness matter in the long run. Similarly she changed her mind. Having resolved to send Sir Francis Drake to sea in 1585, she countermanded his instructions, but only when he was safely out of sight of land! These devices had her councillors hopping up and down with frustration, and even Cecil found her practices hard to take at times, but it all seems to have been in the service of never being taken for granted. At the beginning of her reign her councillors believed that, being a mere woman, she would follow their directions in everything, and that she was determined not to do. God had given England to her to rule, and she would be answerable to him, and not to a bunch of her own servants. In short, Elizabeth became a man manager of the sort that only a certain kind of woman can be, and that skill she undoubtedly inherited from her mother. Had she been a subject, and had she married, she would very probably have taken a risk too far, as Anne did, although probably not at such a cruel cost.

The only occasion in which her control slipped and almost fell was in her early relationship with Robert Dudley, and that too carries echoes of her mother's misadventures. The kind of evidence of clandestine gestures, private rendezvous and ill-considered words which was produced against Anne at her trial could equally have been produced against the Queen in the summer of 1560. The court gossips were so certain that Dudley was her lover that they circulated rumours that the Queen was pregnant by him, and in France Catherine de Medici scoffed 'the Queen of England is to marry her horsemaster'.[9] Elizabeth was the queen, and no husband was going to call her to account, but public opinion did, and that opinion did not like what it saw. Her council were very worried, because apart from that minority which supported the idea, everyone assumed that such behaviour could only lead to a disparaging marriage. Just as Henry's courtiers had put two and two together, and concluded from Anne's words to Sir Henry Norris that she had a secret plan to poison the King, so Elizabeth's courtiers concluded that she was determined to marry Dudley. When his wife died in suspicious circumstances, it was generally believed that this was part of a most dishonourable plot, to which the Queen was privy. Had Elizabeth succumbed to the logic of the situation, and followed her own sexual inclinations, she would have married him; at which point William Cecil would have resigned, and the nobility would probably have risen in rebellion. None of this happened because the Queen got a grip on herself in time, and by a titanic effort of will succeeded in converting a lover into a friend. What would have happened if Anne had seen the warning signs in time, and never conducted that fatal flirtation with Sir Henry Norris? Would Cromwell have found some other means of getting rid of her, or would he have swallowed the reverse and renegotiated his relations with the Boleyns? Such uncertainties, depending as they do upon the personal reactions of monarchs, are inevitable when dealing with a personal monarchy. Contemporary culture made the sexual peccadillos of women more important than those of men, because a woman's honour was bound up with her chastity in a way which was not true of men. Elizabeth recognised this later in her reign when she became 'the Virgin Queen', and used the integrity of her own body as a symbol for the inviolable sovereignty of her realm. No king could have used such imagery, least of all the much married Henry VIII, but a queen could only retain full control by eschewing marriage, and thereby turning the succession into a lottery. For Anne no such choice was available, and she was forced to put her sexuality to the service of her political agenda. Unfortunately in doing so she gave hostages to fortune which eventually destroyed her.

By comparison with Elizabeth, Henry Carey is unimportant, except that it was through him that the Boleyn line was continued. He does not seem to have inherited his mother's sexual appetite, or if he did it was mostly absorbed by his marriage. Only the existence of Valentine Carey suggests any hint of Mary's waywardness. He was a staunch Protestant, and that he undoubtedly owed to his upbringing, but there is no suggestion that he was sympathetic to the puritan lobby which developed in the court after 1570. Insofar as he played a part in the factional rivalries of the period, it was as a supporter of William Cecil, but he was not a prime mover in any cause, and his opinion on some of the issues which divided the council is not known. What is known is that he was a strong opponent of Mary of Scotland, and sympathetic to the King's men in that country, which attitude he derived partly from his Protestantism, and partly from long and varied experience of dealing with successive regency governments. He had no military pretensions, and apart from his encounter with Leonard Dacre, very little experience. He was a follower rather than a leader, and gives the impression of being regarded as a safe pair of hands. Elizabeth seems to have been fond of him, but whether for his personal qualities, or out of a sense of duty to a kinsman is not very clear. She endowed him lavishly, both with lands and with minor offices, and eventually made him her Lord Chamberlain, but he was not a favourite in the same sense as Lord Burghley, let alone the Earl of Leicester. In fact his political career was low key, and that applied even more to his son and successor George. George was given the important office of Governor of the Isle of Wight in his father's lifetime, and the lord chamberlainship after his death. Both of these offices he seems to have discharged to the satisfaction of the Queen, but there is no suggestion that these services were regarded in anyway as distinguished. His younger brother Robert was created Earl of Monmouth in 1626, and his son Henry, the third Lord Hunsdon, Viscount Rochford in 1621 and Earl of Dover in 1628.[10] However, apart from a nod to his family history in the title of Rochford, these appear to have been promotions which arrived with the rations rather than being rewards for exceptional service.

So should the Boleyns be regarded as a political family, in the same sense as the Howards or the Cecils? Probably not, because it was the women who were the leaders and movers, and the men the followers, in a manner altogether exceptional. Anne was a remarkable politician, in a way which neither her sister nor her father were. This was a quality which she shared to some extent with her brother, but not with her sister's children. Her daughter was even more remarkable, and it is through Elizabeth that the family's claim to fame really lies. A unique combination of her father's intelligence and imperious personality with her mother's sharp wit and feisty sexuality, she demonstrated how a woman's body could contain the heart and stomach of a king. For Elizabeth alone the historian should be grateful to Sir Thomas Boleyn and his offspring.

# NOTES

## 1 Origins – the Blickling Years

1. *History of Parliament, Biographies* (1936), p. 90.

2. *Calendar of the Patent Rolls, 1452–61*, p. 216.

3. A. B. Beavan, *The Aldermen of the City of London* (1904), I, pp. 90, 272; II, pp. 10, 164.

4. *History of Parliament*, loc cit.

5. *Cal. Pat., 1446–1452*, pp. 130, 225.

6. Ibid, p. 472. Gascony fell to the French in 1453.

7. *History of Parliament, loc.cit.*

8. Ibid.

9. Charles Ross, *Edward IV* (1974), pp. 166-7.

10. R. Sharpe, *Letter Books of the City of London* (1894–9). Letter Book L, p. 19.

11. *ODNB*, sub Thomas Boleyn. Thomas Butler was the brother and heir of John Butler, 6th Earl of Ormond, who died in October 1476.

12. *Cal. Pat., 1476–85*, pp. 343, 466. William Boleyn's story is complicated by the fact that there was another William Boleyn, described as a gentleman, who was a collector of taxes in Lincolnshire in 1463, and for the Port of Boston in 1485. However, that William appears to have died in 1491. *Cal. Fine., 1461–1471*, p. 104, and *Cal. Fine., 1485–1509*, pp. 36-7, 136.

13. Ibid, pp. 397, 490.

14. *Calendar of the Close Rolls, 1485–1500*, no. 143.

15. *Cal. Pat., 1485–1494*, pp. 294, 349.

16. *ODNB*. The Earl of Surrey was restored to his father's dukedom of Norfolk in 1514. His son, who succeeded him in the dukedom in 1524, married Anne, a younger daughter of King Edward IV.

17. It was normal practice for noblemen and major gentry to run these schoolrooms when they had children of an appropriate age. It was also quite usual for children to be sent to other suitable homes for their upbringing, although there is no sign of that happening in this case.

18. *Calendar of the Fine Rolls, 1485–1509*, no. 668. *Cal. Pat., 1494–1509*, no. 273.

19. *ODNB*. The birth dates of all Thomas's children are conjectural. See G. W. Bernard, *Anne Boleyn: Fatal Attractions* (2010), pp. 4-19.

20. Ibid, p. 5.

21. *Cal. Pat., 1494–1509*, pp. 479, 484. On enfeofment to use, see K. B. MacFarlane, *The Nobility of Later Medieval England* (1973), pp. 76-8, 217-219.

22. *Cal. Fin., 1485–1509*, no. 829, 11 November 1505.

23. S. T. Bindoff, *The House of Commons, 1509–1558* (1982), sub. James Boleyn.

24. Ibid.

25. Ibid. The earldom of Wiltshire was revived for William Paulet, Lord St John, in 1550.

26. For Jane Rochford's behaviour in the summer of 1541, see D. Loades, *The Tudor Queens of England* (2009), pp. 144-8 and L. B. Smith, *A Tudor Tragedy* (1961), pp. 173-207. Jenny Rowley-Williams, *Jane Rochford*, (2011).

27. Bindoff, *House of Commons*.

28. *Letters and Papers … of the Reign of Henry VIII*, I, no. 698. He was supporting Sir Charles Brandon.

29. For Henry's essentially backward looking attitude at this time, and particularly his obsession with Henry V, see J. J. Scarisbrick, *Henry VIII* (1968), pp. 23-4. He commissioned a life of his hero, which was translated into English in 1513, and edited by C. L. Kingsford in 1911.

30. *Calendar of State Papers, Spanish*, II, p. 44. Scarisbrick, *Henry VIII*, p. 26.

31. Garrett Mattingly, *Catherine of Aragon*, (1963), p. 97.

32. Scarisbrick, *Henry VIII*, pp. 26-7.

33. Polydore Vergil, *Anglica Historia*, ed. D. Hay, (Camden Society, 1950), p. 163.

34. Edward Hall, *Chronicle* (ed. 1806), pp. 520 et seq.


## 2 *Thomas at Court – the Hever Years*

1. *Letters and Papers*, I, nos. 81 (11 May 1509), 707 (27 February 1511).

2. Ibid, no. 1186. War had been declared at the end of April. Scarisbrick, *Henry VIII*, p. 29.

3. *Letters and Papers*, I, no. 1229.

4. *L & P*, I, no. 1448. Eric Ives, *The Life and Death of Anne Boleyn*, (2004), p. 11.

5. *L & P*, I, no. 2055.

6. Ibid, no. 1279. On Thomas's ease of manner, both with the Archduchess and the King, see Ives, *Life and Death*, pp. 11, 18.

7. *L & P*, I, no. 1587.

8. Edward Echyngham to Wolsey, 5 May 1513. Alfred Spont, *Letters and Papers relating to the War with France, 1512–1513* (1897), pp. 145, 53.

9. For a discussion of the deployment of this household, see Charles Cruikshank, *Henry VIII and the Invasion of France* (1990), pp. 30-31. His Chamber Staff totalled 579.

10. Ibid, pp. 105-7.

11. *Calendar of State Papers, Venetian*, II, no. 316.

12. F. Nitti, *Leo X e la Sua Politica* (1892). Scarisbrick, *Henry VIII*, p. 51.

13. *L & P*, I, no. 2964.

14. For an assessment of Mary's character, see *ODNB* sub Mary Stafford.

15. *L & P*, II, no. 1501. A total of eighteen courtiers took part in this performance.

16. S. J. Gunn, *Charles Brandon, Duke of Suffolk* (1988) , pp. 35-8.

17. *L & P*, II, no. 125, 6 February 1515.

18. *Cal. Ven.*, II, nos. 594, 596, 635.

19. For a full discussion of Wolsey's manoeuverings at this juncture, see P. Gwynn, *The King's Cardinal* (1990), pp. 613-8.

20. *L & P*, II, nos. 1309, 1573, and p. 1470.

21. Ibid, no. 1277.

22. *State Papers of Henry VIII*, (1830–52), II, 35, 49, 58. D. B. Quinn, 'Henry VIII and Ireland, 1509–1534', *Irish Historical Studies*, 12, 1961, p. 331.

23. *L & P*, II, no. 1517.

24. Ibid, nos. 3756, 3783.

25. Garrett Mattingly, *Catherine of Aragon*. For Catherine's jointure, see *L & P*, II, no. 1363.

26. *Cal. Ven.*, II, 1074. Scarisbrick, *Henry VIII*, p. 71.

27. There were violent protests against the intrusion of a foreigner. Charles had been born in Ghent, and brought Netherlandish

advisers with him, who were much resented. The revolt is known as the *Comuneros*.

28. *L & P*, II, nos. 4469, 4475.

29. *L & P*, III, no. 70. The danger lay in the fact that Charles now controlled three of Francis's five possible frontiers – the Low Countries, Germany and Spain. The fourth was the English Channel, and the fifth, where conflict was most likely, was in northern Italy.

30. BL. Cotton Vitellius B xx, ff.165, 170. *L & P*, III, nos. 240, 241. Scarisbrick, *Henry VIII*, pp. 98-101.

31. *L & P*, III, no. 306.

32. Ibid, no. 702. J. G. Russell, *The Field of Cloth of Gold* (1969), p. 57.

33. *Cal. Ven.*, III, no. 108.

34. Wolsey appears to have been attempting to impute some disloyalty to Sir Thomas early in 1515, although nothing came of it. *L & P*, II, nos. 124, 125. On the promise of the comptrollership, see ibid, III, no. 223.

35. *L & P*, III, no. 1004, 1011. Surrey tended to take the Irish side in this dispute.

36. Ibid, no. 1762.

37. Ibid, no. 1994.

38. Hall, *Chronicle*, p. 462. D. Loades, *The Tudor Navy* (1992), pp. 105-6.

39. *L & P*, III, nos. 2333, 2481.

40. Ibid, no. 3008.

41. Ibid, no. 2982. Helen Miller, *Henry VIII and the English Nobility* (1986), p. 19.

42. *L & P*, III, no. 3213. Wolsey wrote that Charles was 'encouraged' by the efforts of Bourbon, but Henry was expecting

the latter to advance on Paris.

43. S. J. Gunn, 'The Duke of Suffolk's March on Paris in 1523', *English Historical Review*, 101, 1986, pp. 596-634.

44. *State Papers of Henry VIII*, VI, pp. 221, 233 *Cal. Span., Further Supplement*, p. 318.

45. *L & P*, III, no. 3386.

46. *L & P*, IV, no. 137.

47. *State Papers*, IV, pp. 120 et seq. Scarisbrick, *Henry VIII*, p. 133.

48. Ibid, p. 138.

49. Ibid, p. 140.

50. G. W. Bernard, *War, Taxation and Rebellion in Early Tudor England* (1986), p. 99.

51. Hall, *Chronicle*, pp. 699, 701-2.

52. *L & P*, IV, no. 1298.

53. TNA SP1/55, ff.14-15. *L & P*, IV, no. 5807. Miller, *Henry VIII and the English Nobility*, pp. 20-21.

54. D. Loades, *Mary Tudor; the Tragical History of the First Queen of England* (2006), pp. 22-3.

55. *L & P*, IV, no. 1939.

## 3 *Mary & the King's Fancy – in & out of Favour*

1. J. Gairdner, 'Mary and Anne Boleyn', and 'The Age of Anne Boleyn', in *English Historical Review*, 8, 1893, pp. 53-60 and *EHR*, 10, 1895, p. 104.

2. E. W. Ives, *The Life and Death of Anne Boleyn* (2004), pp. 15-17. G. W. Bernard, *Anne Boleyn; Fatal Attractions* (2010), pp. 5-6.

3. G. de Boom, *Marguerite d'Autriche-Savoie et la Pre-Renaissance* (Paris, 1935), p. 118. Ives, *Life and Death*, p. 16.

4. *Letters and Papers*, I, no. 3348 (3), 3357.

5. *L & P*, II, I, no. 224. S. J. Gunn. *Charles Brandon, Duke of Suffolk* (1988). pp. 35-38.

6. *L & P*, I, nos. 826, 827. Scarisbrick, *Henry VIII*, pp. 57-8.

7. Claude had been born on 13 October 1499. Lancelot de Carles in Ascoli, *L'Opinion*, lines 37-42.

8. *Cal. Ven., 1509–1519*, no. 1235. Giustinian and Surian to the Signory, 16 June 1519.

9. Ibid no. 1269.

10. *L & P*, II, p. 1539. The King made an offering of 6s 8d. at the wedding.

11. *L & P*, XII, I, no. 822.

12. *L & P*, III, no. 559. Hall, *Chronicle*, p. 631.

13. For a discussion of the succession issue, see D. Loades, *The Tudors* (forthcoming).

14. John Hale, the Vicar of Isleworth confessed in the early 1530s that one of the priests of the Brigittine nunnery of Syon '... did show to me young master Carey saying he was our sovereign lord the king's son by our sovereign lady the Queen's sister ...' TNA SP1/92, f. 37. *L & P*, VIII, no. 567. Bernard, *Anne Boleyn*, p. 22.

15. *L & P*, III, no. 3358. N.A. M. Rodger, *The Safeguard of the Sea* (1997), p. 477.

16. *L & P*, IV, no. 4409 (misdated), see *ODNB*.

17. *ODNB*.

18. Philip Mowat, *History and Antiquities of the County of Essex* (1768), Vol.I, p. 154.

19. *L & P*, V, no. 306.

20. *The Manner of the Triumph at Calais and Boulogne* (1532), in A. F. Pollard, *Tudor Tracts* (1903), p. 7.

21. S. T. Bindoff, *The House of Commons, 1509–1558* (1982).

22. *L & P*, VII, no. 1554.

23. Ibid, no. 1665.

24. Bindoff, *House of Commons*.

25. *L & P*, XII, no. 822. Ibid, XIV, no. 236.

26. Ibid, no. 572. 22 November 1539.

27. *L & P*, XVII, no. 1012. Grants in October 1542.

28. *L & P*, XVIII, no. 832. Idem, XIX, no. 273.

29. *L & P*, XVIII, nos. 421, 19 April 1543, 478, 1 May. William was one of several gentlemen similarly charged.

30. *L & P*, XVIII, no. 623 (66).

31. *L & P*, XXI, under 'undated grants in 1546'. This grant is clearly misdated, since it refers to Mary as 'widow, one of the daughters of the late Earl of Wiltshire and Ormond, and lately wife to William Carey deceased ...' It must have been made at some point between 1539 and her own death in 1543. Her marriage to William Stafford is ignored.

32. Bindoff, *House of Commons*.

33. *L & P*, XX, no. 418.

34. *Acts of the Privy Council*, IV (1552–4), 24 June 1554.

35. C. H. Garrett, *The Marian Exiles* (1938/66), pp. 295-6.

36. Ibid. Bindoff, *House of Commons*.

## 4 *Anne & the Grand Passion – the Paris Years*

1. Hugh Paget, 'The Youth of Anne Boleyn', *Bulletin of the Institute of Historical Research*, 54, 1981, pp. 162-70.

2. Ibid, p. 166. Ives, *Life and Death of Anne Boleyn*, p. 19.

3. For a discussion of the political significance of these images, see Anglo, *Spectacle, Pageantry and Early Tudor Policy*.

4. G. de Boom, *Marguerite d'Autriche-Savoie et la Pre-Renaissance*, p. 123.

5. Ives, *Life and Death*, p. 23.

6. G. W. Bernard, *Anne Boleyn*, pp. 7-8.

7. De Carles in G. Ascoli, *La Grande-Bretagne devant l'Opinion Francaise*.

8. John Taylor's account of the campaign. BL Cotton MS Cleo. C v, ffs.64 et seq. *L & P*, I, no. 2391.

9. Paget in *BIHR*, p. 167.

10. Ives, *Life and Death*, pp. 27-8.

11. S. J. Gunn, *Charles Brandon, Duke of Suffolk*, pp. 29-30.

12. De Carles in Ascoli, *La Grande-Bretagne*, lines 39-51.

13. Ives, *Life and Death*, p. 29. Blois was Claude's own, but was nevertheless the site of Francis I's first major building project. R. J. Knecht, *Renaissance Warrior and Patron: the Reign of Francis I* (1994), pp. 114-6, 134-7.

14. *L & P*, II, nos. 4440-1, 4462. Rymer, *Foedera*, XIII, p. 624.

15. *State Papers of Henry VIII*, VI, p. 56.

16. J. G. Russell, *The Field of Cloth of Gold*, (1969) p. 123.

17. It is possible that Sir Thomas's wife, Elizabeth, was also present among Catherine's ladies, because she had been a member of the Queen's Privy Chamber since 1509.

18. Ives, *Life and Death*, pp. 32-3.

19. This was Edward Herbert's opinion in the seventeenth century. Herbert, *History of England under Henry VIII*, ed., White Kennett (1870), p. 399. See *Cal. Span. Supplement*, 1513–42, p. 30. *L & P*, III, no. 1994. Ives, *Life and Death*, pp. 32-3.

20. *L & P*, II, no. 1277.

21. *L & P*, III, no. 1628. *State Papers*, II, p. 49. D. B. Quinn, 'Henry VIII and Ireland', *Irish Historical Studies*, 12, 1961, pp. 318-44.

22. *L & P*, III, no. 1762.

23. S. G. Ellis, *Tudor Ireland* (1985), pp. 104-5.

24. Hall, *Chronicle*, p. 631. *L & P*, III, no. 1559.

25. Nicholas Sander, *The Rise and Growth of the Anglican Schism*, ed. D. Lewis (1877), p. 25.

26. George Wyatt in *The Life of Cardinal Wolsey, by George Cavendish*, ed. S. W. Singer, (1827), p. 424. George Wyatt was writing in about 1597, deriving his information from Anne Gainsford, then very aged, who had known Anne Boleyn as a young woman.

27. For the latest round in these investigations, see Bernard, *Anne Boleyn*, pp. 15-18. The most satisfactory explanation is that given by Ives, *Life and Death*, pp. 63-83.

28. *The Life and Death of Cardinal Wolsey by George Cavendish*, ed. R. S. Sylvester and D. P. Harding, in *Two Early Tudor Lives* (1962), p. 32.

29. Ibid, pp. 33-4.

30. Ibid, pp. 34-5.

31. Ibid, p. 36.

32. Bernard, *Anne Boleyn*, pp. 72-8.

33. For a summary of this speculation, and a suggested timetable see Ives, *Life and Death*, pp. 81-92.

34. Guy Bedouelle, 'Les scruples du roi Henry VIII', in Bedouelle and Le Gal, *Le 'Divorce' du roi Henry VIII* (1987), pp. 26-8.

35. Fernando Felipez, the messenger, defeated an attempt to intercept him in France by travelling by sea. Scarisbrick, *Henry VIII*, p. 157.

36. Ives, *Life and Death*, p. 90.

37. *Cal. Ven.*, 1527–29, p. 432.

38. *The Love Letters of Henry VIII*, ed. H. Savage (1949), pp. 40-41.

39. Ives, *Life and Death*, pp. 85-6.

40. *Love Letters*, pp. 29-30.

41. A pendant diamond was the symbol of a constant heart. Chaucer, *Roman de la Rose*, line 4385.

42. *Love Letters*, pp. 34-6.

43. *State Papers*, I, nos. 205, 225, 230. Scarisbrick, *Henry VIII*, pp. 146-7.

44. His specific target appears to have been Renée, the 2nd daughter of Louis XII.

45. Hall, *Chronicle*, p. 707.

46. When the legitimation of the Beauforts was confirmed by Henry IV in February 1407, the phrase *excepta dignitate regali*, was inserted, on the insistence of Archbishop Arundel. E. F. Jacob, *The Fifteenth Century*, p. 105.

47. B. Murphy, *Bastard Prince: Henry VIII's Lost Son* (2001), pp. 110-12.

48. Scarisbrick, *Henry VIII*, pp. 163-5.

49. Ibid, p. 203

50. *L & P*, IV, no. 5604. Stefan Ehses, *Romische Dokumente zur Geschich der Ehesscheidung Heinrichs VIII von England, 1527–1534* (1893), p. 107.

51. *Cal. Span.*, 1527–29, pp. 789, 831.

52. Hall, *Chronicle*, p. 754.

53. *Love Letters*, pp. 36-7, 48.

54. Hall, *Chronicle*, p. 756.

## 5 Thomas, Earl of Wiltshire – the Westminster Years

1. *Letters and Papers*, IV, no. 3619. November 1527.

2. *State Papers*, I, p. 261. *L & P*, IV, no. 3361.

3. *L & P*, IV, no. 1963. Scarisbrick, *Henry VIII*, p. 142.

4. *Calendar of State Papers, Venetian*, IV, p. 105.

5. *State Papers*, I, pp. 191 et seq. *L & P*, IV, no. 3186.

6. Nicholas Pocock, *Records of the Reformation*, I, pp. 22 et seq. Scarisbrick, *Henry VIII*, pp. 159-60.

7. Ibid, p. 162.

8. *L & P*, IV, no. 3644.

9. The envoy chosen was Silvester Darius, a papal collector, chosen for his neutrality. For an account of his mission, see *L & P*, IV, nos. 4269, 4637, 4802, 4909-11.

10. Ives, *Life and Death*, pp. 100-01.

11. Stefan Ehses, *Romische Dokumente*, pp. 48 et seq.

12. Scarisbrick, *Henry VIII*, pp.13-5. H. A. Kelly, *The Matrimonial Trials of Henry VIII* (1976), pp. 59-60.

13. Ibid, p. 67.

14. Ehses, *Romische Dokumente*, pp. 89 et seq.

15. The court record is calendared in *L & P*, IV, nos. 5695, 5697-8. Kelley, *Matrimonial Trials*, p. 87.

16. George Cavendish, *The Life and Death of Cardinal Wolsey*, ed. R. S. Sylvester, (EETS, 1958), p. 89.

17. G. Walker, *John Skelton and the Politics of the 1520s* (1988).

18. *L & P*, IV, no. 5742. Ives, *Life and Death*, p. 121.

19. *L & P*, IV, no. 5996.

20. Miller, *Henry VIII and the English Nobility*, p. 25. D. Loades, *Henry VIII, Court Church and Conflict* (2007).

21. *ODNB*.

22. Nichols, *Narratives of the Days of the Reformation*, p. 242.

23. MacCulloch, *Thomas Cranmer*, p. 47.

24. Graham Nicholson, 'The act of Appeals and the English Reformation', *Law and Government under the Tudors*, pp. 19-30.

25. David Wilkins, *Concilia Magnae Britanniae et Hiberniae*, (1737), III, pp. 727 et seq.

26. P. L. Hughes and J. F.Larkin, *Tudor Royal Proclamations*, I, p. 193.

27. *Cal. Ven.*, *1526–33*, no. 567. His return was reported on 4 August, ibid, no. 598.

28. Ibid, no. 682. An Italian narration of England.

29. Ibid, no. 694.

30. *L & P*, IV, no. 672, undated but ascribed to 1531.

31. N. Pocock, *Records of the Reformation*, II, pp. 385-421. Kelly, *Matrimonial Trials*, p. 123.

32. Wilkins, *Concilia*, III, pp. 725 et seq. Scarisbrick, *Henry VIII*, pp. 274-5.

33. Mattingly, *Catherine of Aragon*, p. 231.

34. Scarisbrick, *Henry VIII*, p. 300.

35. Hall, *Chronicle,* p. 790. *Cal. Span,* *1531–33*, p. 508. *L & P*, V, no. 1370.

36. Ives, *Life and Death*, pp. 157-61. *L & P*, V, no. 1256.

37. R. J. Knecht, *Francis I* (1982), pp. 226-30. Francis, like Clement, did not want the general council to which Henry had appealed.

38. Bernard, *Anne Boleyn*, p. 62.

39. *Cal. Span.*, *1531–33*, p. 602. S. E. Lehmberg, *The Reformation Parliament*, pp. 161, 168.

40. *Cal. Span.*, *1531–33*, p. 609. *L & P*, VI, no. 180. For a discussion of the various rumours circulating about this marriage, see Bernard, *Anne Boleyn*, pp. 66-7, and Ives, *Life and Death*, pp. 170-71.

41. Wilkins, *Concilia*, III, pp. 756 et seq.

42. Ives, *Life and Death*, p. 158.

43. Ibid, p. 171.

44. *L & P*, VIII, no. 121.

45. *L & P*, VI, no. 407.

46. *The noble tryumphaunt coronacyon of quene Anne wyfe unto the most noble kynge Henrye the viii* [RSTC 656], reprinted in Pollard, *Tudor Tracts*, pp. 9-29.

47. *Cal. Span.*, *1531–33*, p. 704.

48. *L & P*, VI, nos. 953, 998.

49. Hughes and Larkin, *Tudor Royal Proclamations*, I, pp. 209-10.

50. *Cal. Span.*, *1531–33*, pp. 721, 724. Ives, *Life and Death*, p. 183.

51. Hall, *Chronicle*, p. 805.

52. De Carles, in Ascoli, *L'Opinion*, lines 183-5.

53. Ives, *Life and Death*, pp. 185-6.

54. 26 Henry VIII, c.13. *Statutes of the Realm*, IV, pp. 18-22.

55. *L & P*, VI, no. 1485.

56. *Cal. Span.*, *1534–35*, p. 57. *L & P*, VII, no. 214.

57. *L & P*, VIII, no. 1031.

58. *L & P*, IX, no. 90.

59. T. S. Freeman, 'Research, Rumour and Propaganda: Anne Boleyn in Foxe's "Book of Martyrs"', *Historical Journal*, 38, 1995, pp. 802-10.

60. G. R. Elton, *Reform and Renewal*, (1973) p. 23.

61. Ives, *Life and Death*, p. 285.

## 6 The Boleyns as a Political Faction – the Whitehall Years

1. TNA SP1/54, fs. 234-43. *L & P*, IV, no. 5749. Lord Darcy was later to be executed for his involvement in the Pilgrimage of Grace.

2. *Cal. Span.*, *1527–29*, pp. 885-6.

3. Ives, *Life and Death*, pp. 115-6.

4. BL Cotton MS Otho C.x, f.220. Gilbert Burnet, *History of the Reformation*, ed. N. Pocock (1865), I, p. 104.

5. *State Papers*, VII, p. 102 et seq. *L & P*, IV, no. 4897.

6. The petition was eventually sent on 12 June 1530. *Cal. Span.*, *1530–33*, nos. 354, 366.

7. Ives, *Life and Death*, p. 114.

8. *State Papers*, VII, p. 170. *L & P*, IV, no. 5519.

9. TNA SP1/54, fs. 234-43. J. A. Guy, *The Public Career of Sir Thomas More* (1980), pp. 206-7.

10. Cavendish, *Life and Death of Cardinal Wolsey*, ed. R. S. Sylvester (1962), p. 97.

11. *L & P*, IV, no. 5816.

12. *Correspndence du Cardinal Jean du Bellay*, ed. R. Scheurer (1969), I, 16, pp. 52-3.

13. Scarisbrick, *Henry VIII*, p. 233.

14. Du Bellay, *Correspondence*, I, 24, pp. 70, 72.

15. *State Papers*, I, p. 344. L & P, IV, no. 5936.

16. According to Thomas Alward. H. Ellis *Original Letters Illustrative of English History*, (1824–46), I, pp. 307-10.

17. Scarisbrick, *Henry VIII*, pp. 235-6.

18. *L & P*, IV, no. 4477. D. Knowles, 'The Matter of Wilton', *Bulletin of the Institute of Historical Research*, 31, 1958, pp. 92-6.

19. *L & P*, IV, no. 4477.

20. Cavendish, *Life and Death of Cardinal Wolsey*, p. 104 et seq.

21. Ibid, p. 123.

22. Ibid, p. 120.

23. *L & P*, IV, no. 6720. *State Papers*, VII, p. 212.

24. Stephen Gardiner had originally been in Wolsey's service, but he switched his loyalty to the King in 1527–28, and became

his secretary in July 1529. Thereafter he was active in securing Wolsey's fall. Glyn Redworth, *In Defence of the Church Catholic: the Life of Stephen Gardiner*, (1990), pp. 23-26.

25. This group also included Lord Montague, the son of the Countess of Salisbury, Sir Thomas Arundel and Sir Henry Parker. Mattingly, *Catherine of Aragon*, p. 288.

26. *L & P*, V, no. 879. Scarisbrick, *Henry VIII,* p. 329.

27. Ives, *Life and Death*, pp. 55-7.

28. Notably *The Glass of the Truth*, and *The Articles Devised*. Apparently Anne attempted to persuade Henry to make use of Tyndale's *Obedience of a Christian Man*, but did not succeed. Bernard, *Anne Boleyn*, p. 111.

29. A. D. Cheney, 'The Holy Maid of Kent', *Transactions of the Royal Historical Society*, 2nd series, 18, 1904, pp. 107-30.

30. D. Knowles, *The Religious Orders in England*, III, pp. 182 et seq.

31. Cheney, op. cit.

32. Scarisbrick, *Henry VIII*, p. 322.

33. Ibid.

34. *L & P*, VI, no. 1572.

35. Pocock, *Records of the Reformation*, II, pp. 523 et seq. Scarisbrick, *Henry VIII*, p. 323.

36. *L & P*, VII, no. 1483, VIII, no. 176.

37. Ives, *Life and Death*, pp. 277-80.

38. BL Royal MS 20. B. xvii, f.1. Ives, *Life and Death*, p. 269.

39. William Latymer, 'Treatyse', f.24.[Bod. MS Don. C. 42]. Ives, *Life and Death*, p. 279.

40. Ibid, p. 280.

41. T. S. Freeman, 'Research, Rumour and Propaganda; Anne Boleyn in Foxe's 'Book of Martyrs', *Historical Journal*, 38, 1995,

pp. 797-819. Foxe, however, was careful not to describe her as a martyr.

42. Ives, *Life and Death*, pp. 272-3. Bernard, *Anne Boleyn*, pp. 98-108.

43. Other bishops, such as Nicholas Shaxton and Thomas Goodrich also seem to have owed their promotion to her influence. Alexander Ales, 'Letter to Queen Elizabeth', TNA SP70/7, ff.1-11. *Calendar of State Papers, Foreign, 1558–9*, no. 1303.

44. The former figure comes from George Wyatt, 'The Life of Queen Anne Boleign', in the *Life of Cardinal Wolsey*, ed. S. W.Singer, (1827), p. 443 and the latter from Foxe, *Acts and Monuments* (1583), p. 1082.

45. Ives, *Life and Death*, pp. 170-71.

46. Ibid, p. 163.

47. Mattingly, *Catherine of Aragon*, pp. 258-73, 280-308. Catherine's revised household was costing the King about £3,000 a year.

48. T. F. Mayer, *Reginald Pole, Prince and Prophet* (2000), pp. 13-61.

49. David Loades, *Henry VIII: Court, Church and Conflict* (2009), p. 102.

50. David Loades, *Mary Tudor: a Life* (1989), p. 75.

51. Ibid, pp. 82-3.

52. Ibid, pp. 77-8. Randall Dodd did yeoman service for Mary in this respect.

53. *Cal. Span.*, *1534–5*, p. 67.


## 7 George & Jane – the Grimston Years

1. Ives, *Life and Death*, p. 10. His self-confessed weakness in Latin makes it less likely that he attended a university.

2. *L & P*, III, no. 2214.

3. *L & P*, IV, no. 4779.

4. Peter Gwyn, *The King's Cardinal* (1990), pp. 613-15.

5. *L & P*, IV, no. 6539, 31 July 1530.

6. *L & P*. IV, nos. 5945, 5996, 6073. The Duke of Albany had, allegedly, gone to Scotland without Francis's consent.

7. *Cal. Ven.*, *1526–33*, 10 March 1530, p. 567.

8. *L & P*, IV, no. 6115.

9. *ODNB*.

10. Ibid.

11. *L & P*, VI, no. 1164. Ives, *Life and Death*, p. 293.

12. According to Richard Hilles, who was forced into exile after Anne's death. *The Zurich Letters*, ed. H. Robinson (Parker Society, 1842), I. p. 200.

13. Ives, *Life and Death*, p. 262.

14. J. P. Carley, *The Books of Henry VIII and his Wives* (2004), pp. 129-33.

15. Carley, 'Her moost lovyng and fryndely brother sendeth gretyng', in M. P. Brown and S. MacKendrick, *Illuminating the Book*, (1998), p. 272.

16. Ibid, p. 277.

17. *L & P*, VIII, no. 1062. Duke of Norfolk and Lord Rochford to Cromwell.

18. G. Burnet, *History of the Reformation*, I, p. 316. The dependence on Anthony Anthony is speculative.

19. *L & P*, 10, no. 1010.

20. *ODNB*.

21. L. B. Smith, *A Tudor Tragedy* (1961), pp. 121-3.

22. Loades, *The Tudor Queens of England* (2009), pp. 143-8.

23. Culpeppers's testimony. *L & P*, XVI, no. 1339.

24. Loades, *Tudor Queens*, p. 152.

25. *L & P*, VI, no. 180. MacCulloch, *Thomas Cranmer*, p. 86.

26. *Lords Journals*, I, p. 77. *L & P*, VI, no. 944. R. J . Knecht, *Francis I* (1982), pp. 229-31.

27. Statutes 25 Henry VIII, caps.20, 22. *Statutes of the Realm*, III, pp. 462-4, 471-4.

28. *L & P*, VI, no. 954.

29. *L & P*, VII, no. 922 (16).

30. *L & P*, VIII, no. 662.

31. *L & P*, VIII, nos. 609, 1105.

32. *L & P*, VIII, no. 686.

33. Knecht, *Francis I*, p. 235. *L & P*, VIII., no. 909.

34. *Cal. Span., 1536–38*, pp. 19, 28.

35. Ives, *Life and Death*, p. 328.

36. *L & P*, X, no. 878. Contrast with Henry Norris, worth £1,327, and William Brereton at £1,236.

37. Retha Warnicke, *The Rise and Fall of Anne Boleyn*, (1989), pp. 214-19. Ives, 'Stress, Faction and Ideology in early-Tudor England', *Historical Journal*, 34, 1991, p. 199.

## 8 The Fall of the Boleyns – the Tower Days

1. Notably by Eric Ives, George Bernard, Retha Warnicke and Maria Dowling. Ives, *The Life and Death of Anne Boleyn* (2004), Bernard, *Anne Boleyn: Fatal Attractions* (2010) (and in numerous articles), Warnicke, *The Rise and Fall of Anne Boleyn* (1990), and Dowling, 'Anne Boleyn and Reform', *Journal of Ecclesiastical History*, 35, 1984.

2. Sir John had a large family, including several daughters, and it is thought to have been his inability to produce dowries for them all which accounts for Jane's unmarried state at the age of twenty-seven.

3. *Cal. Span., 1536–38*, p. 39.

4. Ibid, pp. 39-40.

5. Knecht, *Francis I*, p. 275.

6. Charles Wriothesley, *A Chronicle of England, 1485–1559*, ed.W.D. Hamilton (Camden Society, 2nd series,11, 1875), I, p. 32.

7. Ives, *Life and Death*, p. 296. Anne was about thirty-five at the time, and could have been approaching the menopause.

8. Ibid. The miscarriage was unexpected, and no skilled midwife would have been in attendance.

9. Warnicke, *The Rise and Fall of Anne Boleyn*.

10. *Cal. Span., 1531–33*, p. 28. Ives, *Life and Death*, pp. 298-9.

11. *L & P*, X, no. 670.

12. Among other things, he saluted her in the Chapel Royal. *Cal. Span., 1536–38*, pp. 54, 75, 89, 91-8.

13. It was this opposition which prompted Henry to haggle in his dealings with the Imperial ambassador, in spite of an apparent consensus in his council in favour of a deal. *L & P*, X, no. 699.

14. R. W. Hoyle, 'The origins of the dissolution of the monasteries', *Historical Journal*, 38, 1995, pp. 284-99.

15. Ives, *Life and Death*, p. 316.

16. Bernard, *Anne Boleyn*, p. 163.

17. *State Papers*, VII, pp. 683-8.

18. Wriothesley, *Chronicle*, I, pp. 189-91.

19. S. E. Lehmberg, *The Later Parliaments of Henry VIII*, (1977), pp. 25-28.

20. Bernard, *Anne Boleyn*, pp. 151-61.

21. Ives, *Life and Death*, p. 320.

22. Cavendish, *The Life of Cardinal Wolsey*, ed. Singer, pp. 451, 456.

23. Hall, *Chronicle*, p. 819.

24. Cavendish, *Wolsey*, ed. Singer, p. 451.

25. *Cal. Span., 1536–38*, pp. 107-8.

26. Cavendish, *Wolsey*, ed. Singer, pp. 458-9.

27. Ives, *Life and Death*, pp. 338-40.

28. Rochford was apparently given a writing containing her statement, for his comment. He then read it out publicly in court. Wriothesley, *Chronicle*, p. 39.

29. Bernard, *Anne Boleyn*, pp. 168-9.

30. *L & P*, X, no. 908.

31. N. H. Nicholas, *The Privy Purse Expenses of Henry VIII*, (1827), pp. 97, 112, 168.

32. Ives, *Life and Death*, pp. 334-6.

33. The only possible impediments which could have been used in this context must have existed before the marriage had taken place. It could have been the King's relationship with Mary, or Anne's precontract with Henry Percy (if any such had existed).

34. S. Bentley, *Excerpta Historica*, (1831), p. 263.

35. *The Papers of George Wyatt*, ed. D. Loades (Camden Scoety, 4th series, 5, 1968) p. 189.

36. *L & P*, X, pp. 888, 1161, 1227.

37. Loades, *The Six Wives of Henry VIII* (2009), p. 92.

38. *L & P*, XIII, I, no. 1419.

39. Ives, *Life and Death*, pp. 338-56.

40. Bernard, *Anne Boleyn*, pp. 161-82.

41. Ibid.

42. *L & P*, X, no. 908.

43. Statute 27 Henry VIII, cap. 28. *Statutes of the Realm*, III, pp. 575-8. For a discussion of the Bishops' Book and its revisions, see MacCulloch, *Thomas Cranmer*, pp. 185-97, 207-13.

44. Loades, *Mary Tudor*, pp. 98-9.

45. Ibid.

46. BL Cotton MS Otho C.X, f.283. *L & P*, X, no. 968.

47. BL Cotton MS Otho C.X, f.278. *L & P*, X, no. 1022.

48. Loades, *Mary Tudor*, p. 102.

49. BL Cotton MS Otho C.X, f.289. *L & P*, X, no. 1136.

50. Loades, *Mary Tudor*, p. 101.

51. Chapuys to the Emperor, 1 July 1536. *L & P*, XI, no. 7.

52. R. W. Hoyle, *The Pilgrimage of Grace and the Politics of the 1530s* (2001), pp. 347, 351.

53. *Handbook of British Chronology*, p. 496.

54. Susan James, *Kateryn Parr: the Making of a Queen* (1999).

55. *Elizabeth I: Collected Works*, ed. L. S. Marcus, Janelle Mueller and M. B. Rose (2000), pp. 5-6.

56. Statute 35 Henry VIII, cap.1. *Statutes of the Realm*, III, p. 955.

57. Loades, *Elizabeth I* (2003), p. 49.

58. Bodleian Library MS Cherry 36, ffs.2-4. *Elizabeth I: Collected Works*, pp. 6-7.

59. Loades, *Elizabeth I*, pp. 63-4.

60. Princess Elizabeth to Edward Seymour, Duke of Somerset, Lord Protector, September 1548. *Elizabeth I: Collected Works*, p. 22.

61. G. Bernard, 'The Downfall of Sir Thomas Seymour', in Bernard, *The Tudor Nobility* (1992).

62. She had been imprisoned during Mary's reign for suspected involvement in Sir Thomas Wyatt's rebellion, and had been pressed by Philip to marry the Duke of Savoy. Her reaction had been to adopt a very sober style of dress, and to keep a low profile.

## 9 *Henry Carey, Lord Hunsdon – the Berwick Years*

1. *ODNB.*

2. Ibid. For the action and deployment of the fleet, which involved the sinking of the *Mary Rose*, see D. Loades and C. S. Knighton, *Letters from the Mary Rose* (2002), pp. 106-120.

3. *L & P.*, XXI, no. 1235. Among the documents signed by stamp in 1546 is a grant to John Carey, Esquire of the Privy Chamber, who must have been a kinsman, of the 'rule' of Kynderweston Hundred, Wiltshire, with issues from the death of William Carey, until the full age of Henry Carey, William's son and heir.

4. *Cal. Pat., Edward VI*, II, p. 93.

5. *Cal. Pat., Edward VI*, III, pp. 250, 320.

6. *ODNB.*

7. *Cal. Pat., Elizabeth, 1558–60*, pp. 60, 90.

8. Ibid, pp. 115-7. W. MacCaffrey, *The Shaping of the Elizabethan Regime* (1969), p. 40. L. Stone, *The Crisis of the Aristocracy* (1965), p. 760.

9. *Cal. Pat., Elizabeth, 1558–60*, p. 415.

10. The Garter was also conferred on him in April 1561. *ODNB.* The takeover of schools and universities by the sons of gentlemen began in the early sixteenth century, and gradually took over from the older notion of a training in arms and manners. Joan Simon, *Education and Society in Tudor England* (1966), pp. 291-8, 333-368.

11. *Cal. Pat. Elizabeth, 1563–66*, pp. 22, 24, 42, 123.

12. The Garter was conferred on 24 June. *Cal. For., 1564–5*, no. 522. Conyers Read, *Mr. Secretary Cecil and Queen Elizabeth* (1965), p. 327. Sir Thomas Smith reported to Cecil on 27 June that 'there was never an ambassador better liked than Lord Hunsdon', *Cal. For.*, no.523.

13. *Cal. Pat, Elizabeth, 1563–6*, pp. 280, 285. D. Loades, *The Life and Career of William Paulet* (2008), p. 144.

14. *Calendar of State Papers Relating to Scotland*, II, various.

15.*Calendar of State Papers Relating to Scotland*, II, p. 86. A report of Thomas Randolf to Cecil, 24 October 1564.

16. *Cal. Pat., Elizabeth, 1566–9*, p. 119. H. M. Colvin, *The History of the King's Works*, Vol. IV, 1485–1660, pt. ii (1982), pp. 40-47.

17. Antonia Fraser, *Mary Queen of Scots* (1969). Alison Weir, *Mary Queen of Scots and the Murder of Lord Darnley* (2008), pp. 450-465.

18. *Cal. Pat., Elizabeth, 1566–69*, pp. 201, 327.

19. Conyers Read, 'Queen Elizabeth's seizure of Alba's pay ships', *Journal of Modern History*, 5, 1933, pp. 443-464. D. Loades, *The Cecils; Privilege and Power behind the Throne* (2007), pp. 88-9.

20. Loades, *Elizabeth I*, pp. 165-6.

21. MacCaffrey, *The Shaping of the Elizabethan Regime*, p. 229.

22. Conyers Read, *Mr. Secretary Cecil and Queen Elizabeth* (1965), pp. 331-3.

23. *Cal. SP. Dom., 1547–1580*, p. 348. This was followed up by a royal proclamation, issued at Windsor on 24 November, Hughes and Larkin, *Tudor Royal Proclamations*, II, p. 323.

24. *Cal. SP. Dom*, p. 346.

25. *The 1569 Rebellion*, edited by Sir Cuthbert Sharp (1840, reprint 1965), pp. 64-5. Conyers Read, *Mr. Secretary Cecil*, pp. 458-68.

26. Loades, *Elizabeth I*, p. 167. *The 1569 Rebellion*, pp. 83-4. On 30 November Sir Ralph Sadler wrote to Cecil 'the rebels are returned into the Bishopric'.

27. The Earl of Sussex to Sir William Cecil, 1 January 1570, ibid, pp. 130-32. *Cal. SP. Dom*, p. 356.

28. *The 1569 Rebellion*, pp. 133-4.

29. Read, *Mr. Secretary Cecil*, pp. 445-6.

30. *The 1569 Rebellion*, pp. 124-5.

31. *Cal. SP., Scotland, 1569–71*, p. 54. *Cal Dom. Addenda, 1566–79*, pp. 193, 241.

32. *Elizabeth I: Collected Works*, pp. 125-6.

33. *Cal. SP., Scotland*, I, pp. 329, 331.

34. *Cal. SP., Dom., 1547–1580*, p. 360.

35. *Rebellion of 1569*, Appendix, pp. 343-9.

36. Ibid, pp. 250-52. That he was a member of this commission may be ascertained from the number of pardons issued to offenders in whose conviction he had had a part. For example, *Cal. Pat., 1569–72*, p. 290. The commission itself does not appear to be recorded.

37. G. E. Cockayne, ed. Vicary Gibbs, *The Complete Peerage* (1910–59).

38. *Cal. Pat., 1569–72*, p. 212.

39. Ibid, p. 289. *Cal. SP. Dom., 1547–1580*, p. 370.

40. *Cal. Pat., 1572–5*, p. 169. Conyers Read, *Mr. Secretary Cecil*, pp. 409-10. *Cal. Scot., 1563–69*, pp. 530, 534, 540.

41. *Cal. Pat., 1572–5*, p. 328.

42. Captain Cockburn to Lord Burghley, 4 November 1575. *Cal. Scot.*, I, p. 393.

43. A. Weikel, 'The Marian Council Revisited' in J. Loach and R. Tittler, *The Mid Tudor Polity, 1540–1560* (1980). W. MacCaffrey, *Queen Elizabeth and the Making of Policy, 1572–1588*, (1981) pp. 436-7.

44. *Acts of the Privy Council, 1577–96*, passim.

45. *Cal. Pat., 1578–80*, p. 121.

46. P. W. Hasler, *The History of Parliament: The House of Commons, 1558–1603* (1981), sub George Carey.

47. ODNB. *Cal. SP. Dom.*, *1581–1590*.

48. Raphael Holinshed, *Chronicle* (ed. 1807–8), IV, p. 536. Loades, *Elizabeth I*, pp. 222-3.

49. *Cal. SP. Dom.*, *1581–1590*, p. 139.

50. Ibid, p. 161.

51. Conyers Read, *Lord Burghey and Queen Elizabeth* (1965), pp. 233-5.

52. Ibid, p. 289.

53. Ibid.

54. *Cal. SP. Scot.*, II, p. 473.

55. J. H. Pollen, *Mary Queen of Scots and the Babington Plot*, Scottish Historical Society, 1922. J. Wormald, *Mary Queen of Scots: a study in failure* (1988).

56. *Cal. SP. Dom.*, *1581–90*, p. 164. Walsingham to Burghley, 12 June 1584.

57. Ibid, p. 278.

58. Ibid, p. 463. Howard to Walsingham, 14 February 1588.

59. Read, *Lord Burghley and Queen Elizabeth*, p. 422.

60. *Cal. SP. Dom.*, *1581–90*, pp. 517, 534.

61. F. C. Dietz, *English Public Finance, 1558–1641* (1964), pp. 96-9. For Elizabeth's 'Golden speech' of 1601, see *Elizabeth I: Collected Works*, pp. 355-59.

62. *Cal. SP. Dom.*, *1591–94*, p. 268. Report of 11 September 1592.

63. Ibid, *1594–97*, p. 162.

64. Elizabeth did not, as far as I am aware, leave any record of her emotional reaction to Lord Hunsdon's death, but her attitude towards his family after his death suggests a warm attachment, as did her loyalty to him during his life. In that respect he resembled Lord Burghley, for whom her feelings are better known.

65. *Cal. SP. Dom.*, *1594–7*, pp. 309, 314. On 11 June 1597 the

Queen granted to Hundson's old friend Charles Howard, the Lord Admiral his office of Chief Justice in Eyre South of the Trent, with a fee of £100 a year. It is not clear when Hunsdon had acquired this office.

66. The junior branch, stemming from Robert, died out with Henry, his son, the second Earl of Monmouth, in June 1661.

67. *ODNB*.

## *10 Elizabeth I, the Boleyn Daughter – the Dudley Years*

1. 'The Count of Feria's despatch of 14th November 1558', edited by Simon Adams and Mia Rodriguez-Salgado. *Camden Miscellany*, 28, 1984, p. 331. He also observed that she was a very vain and clever woman and unlikely to be 'well disposed in matters of religion', which could be a description of her mother at the same age.

2. Loades, *Elizabeth I*, pp. 109-110.

3. Feria's despatch, p. 332.

4. *Elizabeth I: Collected Works*, p. 58.

5. Ibid.

6. Susan Doran, *Monarchy and Matrimony; the courtships of Elizabeth I* (1996), p. 8.

7. Philip is alleged to have said that in making this proposal, he was sacrificing himself in the cause of his country. Henry Kamen, *Philip II* (1997).

8. Doran, *Monarchy and Matrimony*, pp. 73-98, contains a very full description of these negotiations.

9. Ibid, pp. 97-8. The Howards were the only element in the English Court who supported the marriage unreservedly.

10. D. Loades, *John Dudley, Duke of Northumberland* (1996), p. 123. They allegedly shared Edward's lessons at the beginning of

the reign. They were both fourteen at that time, while he was ten, but it is just about feasible.

11. Derek Wilson, *Sweet Robin; a biography of Robert Dudley, Earl of Leicester* (1981), pp. 43, 78.

12. Caspar Breuner to Ferdinand I. Victor von Klarwill, *Queen Elizabeth and Some Foreigners* (1928), pp. 113-4.

13. Conyers Read, *Mr. Secretary Cecil*, pp. 192-3.

14. The best analysis of this controversial subject is still Ian Aird's article of 1956, although Chris Skidmore has recently added his contribution to the debate. Aird, 'The death of Amy Robsart', *English Historical Review*, 71, 1956, pp. 69-79.

15. Doran, *Monarchy and Matrimony*, pp. 42-45.

16. Throgmorton to Chamberlain, October 1560. TNA SP70/19, f.132.

17. Wilson, *Sweet Robin*, pp. 252-68.

18. Doran, *Monarchy and Matrimony*, p. 45.

19. Read, *Mr. Secretary Cecil*, pp. 203-205. De Quadra is the only source for this story, which must be regarded with a certain scepticism.

20. W. P. Haugaard, 'Elizabeth Tudor's Book of Devotions; a neglected clue to the Queen's life and character', *Sixteenth Century Journal*, 12, 1981, pp. 79-105.

21. *Cal. Span., Elizabeth*, I, pp. 262-4.

22. MacCaffrey, *Shaping of the Elizabethan Regime*, pp. 93-7.

23. Wilson, *Sweet Robin*, pp. 139-43.

24. Ibid, p. 226. *Cal. Span., Elizabeth*, I, p. 431.

25. Dudley Papers at Longleat, III, f.61.

26. Francois, Duke of Alencon, as he was at that time, had been proposed to Elizabeth by Catherine de Medici, his mother, when the negotiations with his elder brother Henri collapsed in 1571.

He became Duke of Anjou when Henri succeeded to the throne as Henri III in 1574. Doran, *Monarchy and Matrimony*, pp. 130-153.

27. Alan Young, *Tudor and Jacobean Tournaments* (1987), p. 153. Roy Strong, *The Cult of Elizabeth* (1977).

28. This is a view not shared by Susan Doran, who considers that Elizabeth preferred consensual advice. However, the way in which she played the Earl of Sussex against Dudley, and Cecil against both of them does not suggest that.

29. Doran, *Monarchy and Matrimony*, p. 21.

30. Conyers Read, *Lord Burghley and Queen Elizabeth* (1965), pp. 256-277.

31. *Cal. Span. 1580–86*, p. 226.

32. All the negotiations suggest that Elizabeth's requirements would have reduced the Crown Matrimonial to a mere cipher, because in addition to the limitations imposed upon Philip in 1554, there was a need for outward conformity to her Church settlement.

33. Conyers Read, 'Queen Elizabeth's seizure of Alba's pay ships'.

34. Hughes and Larkin, *Tudor Royal Proclamations*, II, pp. 357-8. Geoffrey Parker, *The Dutch Revolt* (1977).

35. L. O. Boynton, *The Elizabethan Militia* (1967).

36. D. Loades, *The Fighting Tudors* (2009), pp. 196-204.

37. *Elizabeth I: Collected Works*, pp. 269-74. Queen Elizabeth to Sir Thomas Heneage, her emissary to the Earl of Leicester, 10 February 1586, enclosing her letter to Dudley, bearing the same date.

38. Loades, *Elizabeth I*, p. 177. At his trial in 1572 the Duke of Norfolk tried to impugn the witnesses against him on the grounds that they were men of no substance – by which he meant lineage.

39. Wilson, *Sweet Robin*, pp. 278-9.

40. Simon Adams, *Leicester and the Court* (2002), pp. 138-41, 143-4, 146-9.

41. G. E. Cockayne, *Complete Peerage*.

42. *ODNB*.

43. L. B. Smith, *Treason in Tudor England; Politics and Paranoia* (1986), p. 200.

44. W. Camden, *The History of the Most Renowned Princess Elizabeth, Late Queen of England*, (1688), pp. 623-4.

45. W. B. Devereux, *Lives and Letters of the Devereux Earls of Essex, 1540–1646* (1853), I, p. 185.

46. Philippa Berry, *Of Chastity and Power: Elizabethan Literature and the Unmarried Queen* (1989), pp. 61-83.

47. Conyers Read, *Lord Burghley and Queen Elizabeth*, pp. 464-86.

48. Devereux, *Earls of Essex*, I, p. 184.

49. R. B. Wernham, *The Expedition of Sir John Norris and Sir Francis Drake to Spain and Portugal, 1589* (1988), p. 133.

50. Ibid, p. 134.

51. W. MacCaffrey, *War and Politics, 1588–1603* (1992), pp. 161-2.

52. Ibid, p. 472.

53. S. and E. Usherwood, *The Counter Armada, 1596: The Journal of the Mary Rose* (1983), pp. 118-9.

54. L. B. Smith, *Treason in Tudor England*, pp. 226-7. MacCaffrey, *War and Politics*, p. 522.

55. Smith, *Treason in Tudor England*, pp. 232-3.

56. Ibid, pp. 255-6.

57. Camden, *Elizabeth*, pp. 602-3.

58. Loades, *The Cecils*, pp. 217-8.

## Conclusion: A Political Family?

1. For a discussion of the origins of this game, see A. Kelly, 'Eleanor of Aquitaine and her courts of love', *Speculum*, 12, 1937.

2. G. R. Elton, *The Tudor Revolution in Government* (1953), p. 84.

3. These negotiations failed because the King was unwilling to subscribe to the Confession of Augsburg. One of the consequences of that failure was the Cleves marriage. Loades, *Henry VIII*, (2011) p. 285.

4. The form of acting in the King's name was strictly observed, but Edward was a child and had no control over their actions. M. L. Bush, *The Government Policy of Protector Somerset* (1975).

5. He received a few modest grants, such as that of Jane Rochford's 'stuff' at Blickling in September 1542, but there is no indication of significant patronage. *L & P*, XVII, no. 119.

6. *Cal. Span.*, XI, p. 393.

7. Statute 1 Mary, sess.3, cap.3. Jennifer Loach, *Parliament and the Crown in the reign of Mary Tudor* (1986), pp. 96-7.

8. David Starkey, 'Intimacy and Innovation; the rise of the Privy Chamber, 1485–1547' and Pam Wright, 'A Change of Direction; the ramifications of a female household, 1558–1603' in D. Starkey, ed., *The English Court from the Wars of the Roses to the Civil War* (1987).

9. Loades, *Elizabeth I*, p. 142.

10. G. E. Cockayne, *The Complete Peerage*.

# LIST OF ILLUSTRATIONS

1. Blickling Hall, Norfolk. A seventeenth century rebuilding of the 'fair brick house' constructed by Sir Geoffrey Boleyn. © Elizabeth Norton & the Amberley Archive. 2. Blickling church contains many Boleyn memorials, starting with Sir Geoffrey in a stained glass window. © Elizabeth Norton & the Amberley Archive. 3. The tomb of Thomas Howard, 3rd Duke of Norfolk, Anne Boleyn's uncle. He was originally interred at Thetford Abbey, then moved to Framlingham, where this memorial was erected. © Elizabeth Norton & the Amberley Archive. 4. Henry Howard, Earl of Surrey, who took part along with his father, the 3rd Duke of Norfolk, in the trials of Anne and George Boleyn. He was executed for treason in January 1547. © Elizabeth Norton & the Amberley Archive. 5. Thomas Boleyn, Earl of Wiltshire, who died at Hever Castle in Kent in 1539. From a monumental brass in St.Peter's church at Hever. © Elizabeth Norton & the Amberley Archive. 6. Isabella Boleyn, Sir Geoffrey's daughter, and Anne's great aunt. She married Sir John Cheyney, and her memorial brass remains in Blickling church. © Elizabeth Norton & the Amberley Archive. 7. Lady Anne Shelton, daughter of Sir William Boleyn of Blickling, and sister to Sir Thomas. She died in December 1555, and was buried at Shelton, ten miles south of Norwich. © Elizabeth Norton & the Amberley Archive. 8. Hever Castle, Kent. After the Earl of Wiltshire's death, Henry VIII purchased the castle from his heirs, and bestowed it on Anne of Cleves. When it reverted to the Crown on her death in 1557, Mary sold it to Sir Edward Waldegrave. © Hever Castle. 9. The 'Henry VIII bedroom' at Hever Castle. © Hever Castle. 10. The gardens at Hever. © Hever Castle. 11. A portrait of Anne Boleyn at Ripon Cathedral, Artist unknown; probably a seventeenth century copy. © Ripon Cathedral. 12. A lady, thought to be Mary Boleyn. Artist unknown. At Hever Castle. © Hever Castle. 13. Henry VIII, c. 1540. From the Great Gate at Trinity College, Cambridge. © Elizabeth Norton & the Amberley Archive. 14. Henry VIII, from the cartoon by Hans Holbein in the National Portrait Gallery. © Elizabeth Norton & the Amberley Archive. 15. From a bas relief depicting the Field of Cloth of Gold, 1520, which was something of a 'family reunion' for the Boleyns. © Jonathan Reeve JR1177b2p167B 15001550. 16. The meeting of the two kings, Henry VIII and Francis I, from the same bas relief. © Jonathan Reeve JR1177b2p167T 15001550. 17. Another depiction of the Field of Cloth of Gold, showing the temporary English palace which was built for the occasion. © Jonathan Reeve JR1151b66p1 15001550. 18. Thomas Wolsey from a drawing attributed to Jacques Le Boucq. © Jonathan Reeve JR1169b2p7 15001550. 19. Sir Thomas More by Hans Holbein. © Elizabeth Norton & the Amberley Archive. 20. Thomas Cranmer, Archbishop of Canterbury, by Gerhard Flicke. © Elizabeth Norton & the Amberley Archive. 21. William Warham, Archbishop of Canterbury, c.1528. By Hans Holbein. © Elizabeth Norton & the Amberley Archive. 22. Henry VIII and Anne Boleyn's initials entwined at King's College Chapel, Cambridge. © Elizabeth Norton & the Amberley Archive. 23. Detail from Holbein's design for a coronation pageant. It was staged on the eve of Anne's coronation, 31 May 1533. © Elizabeth Norton & the Amberley Archive. 24. Anne Boleyn's coronation procession approaches Westminster Abbey, 1st June 1533. This was an event boycotted by Catherine's supporters. © Jonathan Reeve JR968b42p404 15001600. 25. A view of London, showing the Tower, where Anne was taken following her arrest. By Claes Visscher, 1616. © Stephen Porter & the Amberley Archive. 26. The execution of Anne Boleyn, 19th May 1536. A nineteenth century reconstruction. © Jonathan Reeve JR965b20p921 15001600. 27. Princess Elizabeth, later Queen Elizabeth I, aged about twelve in 1545. © Jonathan Reeve JR997b66p40b 15001600. 28. Catherine Parr, Henry VIII's last Queen and Elizabeth's stepmother, from her memorial at Sudeley. © Elizabeth Norton & the Amberley Archive. 29. Elizabeth I at prayer from the frontispiece to Christian Prayers (1569). © Jonathan Reeve JR1168b4fp747 15001600. 30. Great Seal of Elizabeth I. © Jonathan Reeve JR1009b66fp181 15001600. 31. Signature of Elizabeth I. © Jonathan Reeve JR1013b66fp196 15001600. 32. Robert Dudley, Earl of Leicester, in old age. He was Elizabeth's favourite from the beginning of her reign until his death in 1588. A copy of a portrait, probably by William Segar. Ripon Cathedral. © Ripon Cathedral. 33. Engraved portrait of Elizabeth I by William Rogers c. 1595. © Jonathan Reeve JR1016b5fp26 15001600. 34. Thomas Seymour. Catherine Parr's fourth husband. While Catherine was unavailable to him through pregnancy, Thomas began to make passes at Princess Elizabeth. © Elizabeth Norton & the Amberley Archive.

# BIBLIOGRAPHY

*Manuscripts*
*In the National Archives*:
C66.
LC2, 5.
PC2.
SP1/54, 55, 92.
SP12, various.
SP70/19.
*In the British Library:*
Cotton MS Otho C. X; Vitellius B.XX.
Royal 20 B. XVII.
*At Longleat:*
Dudley Papers, III.

*Printed Documents, Calendars and Guides*
*Acts of the Privy Council*, ed, J. Dasent et al., (1890–1907).
Adams, S., and Rodriguez Salgado, M-J., 'The Count of Feria's despatch to Philip II of 14th November 1558', (*Camden Miscellany*, 28, 1984).
Ascoli, G., *La Grande Bretagne devant l'Opinion Francaise* (1927).
Bentley, S., *Excerpta Historica* (1831).
*Calendar of the Patent Rolls*, 1446–1509.

*Calendar of the Patent Rolls, Edward VI.*

*Calendar of the Patent Rolls, Elizabeth.*

*Calendar of the Fine Rolls, 1461–1509.*

*Calendar of the Close Rolls, 1485–1500.*

*Calendar of State Papers, Domestic, 1547–1597.*

*Calendar of State Papers, Foreign, 1547–1592.*

*Calendar of State Papers Relating to Scotland.*

*Calendar of State Papers, Spanish, and supplements.*

*Calendar of State Papers, Venetian.*

Cavendish. *The Life of Cardinal Wolsey by George Cavendish*, ed. S. W. Singer (1827).

Cockayne. G. E., ed. V. Gibbs, *The Complete Peerage* (1910–1959).

*Elizabeth I: Collected Works*, ed. L. S. Marcus, Janelle Mueller and M. B. Rose (2000).

Ellis, H., *Original Letters Illustrative of English History* (1824–46).

Garrett, C. H., *The Marian Exiles* (1938/66).

Hall, Edward, *Chronicle* (ed. 1806).

*Handbook of British Chronology*, ed. E. B. Fryde et al. (1986).

Holinshed, Raphael, *Chronicles* (ed. 1807–8).

Hughes, P. and Larkin, J. F., *Tudor Royal Proclamations* (1964–9).

*Journal of the House of Lords* (1846).

*Letters and Papers, Foreign and Domestic … of the Reign of Henry VIII*, ed. J. S. Brewer et al. (1862–1910).

Loades, D., *The Papers of George Wyatt* (Camden Society, 4th series, 5, 1968).

Loades, D. and Knighton, C. S., *Letters from the Mary Rose* (2002).

Nicholas, J. G., ed., *Narratives of the Days of the Reformation* (Camden Society, 77, 1859).

Nicholas, N. H., *The Privy Purse Expenses of Henry VIII* (1827).

Pocock, Nicholas, *Records of the Reformation: The Divorce, 1527–1533* (1870).

Pollard, A. F., *Tudor Tracts* (1903).

Robinson, H., ed., *The Zurich Letters* (Parker Society, 1842).

*Romische Dokumente zur Geschichte der Eheschidung Heinriches VIII von England, 1527–1534*, ed. Stefan Ehses (1893).

Rymer, T., *Foedera, Conventiones* etc. (1704–1735).

Sander, Nicholas, *The Rise and Growth of the Anglican Schism*, ed. D. Lewis (1877).

Scheurer, R., *Correspondence du Cardinal Jean du Bellay* (1969).

Sharp, Sir Cuthbert, *The 1569 Rebellion* (reprinted 1965).

Sharpe, R., *Letter Books of the City of London* (1894–9).

Spont, Alfred, *Letters and Papers Relating to the War with France, 1512–1513* (Navy Records Society, 1897).

*State Papers of Henry VIII* (1830–52).

*Statutes of the Realm*, ed. A. Luders et al. (1810–28).

*The Love Letters of Henry VIII*, ed. H. Savage (1949).

*Two Early Tudor Lives*, ed. R. S. Sylvester and D. P. Harding (1962).

Vergil, Polydore, *Anglica Historia*, ed D. Hay (Camden Society, 3rd series, 74, 1950).

Wilkins, David, *Concilia Magnae Brittanniae et Hiberniae* (1737).

Wriothesley, Charles, *A Chronicle of England, 1485–1559*, ed. W. D. Hamilton (Camden Society, 2nd series, 11, 1875).

## Secondary Works: Books

Adams, S., *Leicester and the Court* (2002).

Anglo, S., *Spectacle, Pageantry and Early Tudor Policy* (1969).

Beaven, A. B., *The Aldermen of the City of London* (1904).

Bedouelle, Guy, and Le Gal, Patrick, *Le 'Divorce' du roi Henry VIII* (1987).

Bernard, G. W., *Taxation and Rebellion in Early Tudor England* (1986).

Bernard, G. W., *The King's Reformation* (2005).

Bernard, G. W., *Anne Boleyn: Fatal Attractions* (2010).

Berry, Philppa, *Of Chastity and Power: Elizabethan Literature and the Unmarried Queen* (1989).

Bindoff, S. T., *The House of Commons, 1509–1558* (1982).

Boom, G de, *Marguerite d'Autriche-Savoie et la Pre-Renaissance* (1935).

Boynton, L. O., *The Elizabethan Militia* (1967).

Brown, M. P., and MacKendirck, S., *Illuminating the Book* (1998).

Burnet, G., *The History of the Reformation of the Church of England* (1679–1715).

Bush, M. L., *The Government Policy of Protector Somerset* (1975).

Camden, W., *The History of the Most Renowned Princess Elizabeth, Late Queen of England* (1688).

Carley, J. P., *The Books of Henry VIII and his Wives* (2004).

Colvin, H. M., *The History of the King's Works*: Vol. IV, 1485–1660 (1982).

Cruickshank, Charles, *Henry VIII and the Invasion of France* (1990).

Dietz, F. C., *English Government Finance, 1558–1641* (1964).

Devereux, W. B., *Lives and Letters of the Devereux Earls of Essex, 1540–1646* (1853).

Doran, Susan, *Monarchy and Matrimony: the Courtships of Elizabeth I* (1996).

Ellis, S. G., *Tudor Ireland* (1985).

Elton, G. R., *The Tudor Revolution in Government* (1953).

Elton, G. R., *Reform and Renewal* (1973).

Fraser, Antonia, *Mary Queen of Scots* (1969).

Gunn, S. J., *Charles Brandon, Duke of Suffolk* (1988).

Gwynn, Peter, *The King's Cardinal* (1990).

Guy, J. A., *The Public Career of Sir Thomas More* (1980).

Hasler, P. W., *The House of Commons, 1558–1603* (1981).

Herbert, Edward, *History of England under Henry VIII*, ed. White Kennett (1870).

*History of Parliament: Biographies* (1936)

Hoyle, R. W., *The Pilgrimage of Grace and the Politics of the 1530s* (2001).

Ives, Eric, *The Life and Death of Anne Boleyn* (2004).

Jacobs, E. F., *The Fifteenth Century* (1961).

James, Susan, *Katheryn Parr: the Making of a Queen* (1999).

Kelly, H. A., *The Matrimonial Trials of Henry VIII* (1976).

Klarwill, Victor von, *Queen Elizabeth and Some Foreigners* (1928).

Knecht, R. J., *Francis I* (1982).

Knecht, R. J., *Renaissance Warrior and Patron: the Reign of Francis I* (1994).

Knowles, D., *The Religious Orders in England; The Tudor Age* (1959).

Lehmberg, S. E., *The Reformation Parliament* (1970).

Lehmberg, S. E., *The Later Parliaments of Henry VIII* (1977).

Loach, J., *Parliament and the Crown in the Reign of Mary Tudor* (1986).

Loades, D, *Mary Tudor: A Life* (1989).

Loades, D., *The Tudor Navy* (1992).

Loades, D., *John Dudley, Duke of Northumberland* (1996).

Loades, D., *Elizabeth I* (2003).

Loades, D., *Mary Tudor* (2011).

Loades, D., *Henry VIII: Court, Church and Conflict* (2007).

Loades, D., *The Cecils: Privilege and Power behind the Throne* (2007).

Loades, D., *The Life and Career of William Paulet* (2008).

Loades, D., *The Tudor Queens of England* (2009).

Loades, D., *The Six Wives of Henry VIII* (2009).

Loades, D., *The Fighting Tudors* (2009).

Loades, D., *Henry VIII* (2011).

MacCaffrey, W., *The Shaping of the Elizabethan Regime* (1969).

MacCaffrey, W., *Queen Elizabeth and the Making of Policy, 1572–1588* (1981).

MacCaffrey, W., *War and Politics, 1588–1603* (1992).

MacCulloch, D., *Thomas Cranmer* (1996).

MacFarlane, K. B., *The Nobility of Later Medieval England* (1973).

Mattingly, Garrett, *Catherine of Aragon* (1963).

Mayer, T. F., *Reginald Pole: Prince and Prophet* (2000).

Miller, Helen, *Henry VIII and the English Nobility* (1986).

Mowat, Philip, *History and Antiquities of the County of Essex* (1768).

Murphy, Beverley, *Bastard Prince: Henry VIII's Lost Son* (2001).

Nitti, F., *Leo X e la Sua Politica* (1892).

*Oxford Dictionary of National Biography*.

Pollen, J. H., *Mary Queen of Scots and the Babington Plot* (1922).

Read, Conyers, *Mr. Secretary Cecil and Queen Elizabeth* (1965).

Read, Conyers, *Lord Burghley and Queen Elizabeth* (1965).

Redworth, G., *In Defence of the Church Catholic: the Life of Stephen Gardiner* (1990).

Rodger, N. A. M., *The Safeguard of the Sea* (1997).

Ross, Charles, *Edward IV* (1974).

Russell, J. G., *The Field of Cloth of Gold* (1969).

Scarisbrick. J. J., *Henry VIII* (1968).

Simon, Joan, *Education and Society in Tudor England* (1966).

Smith, L. B., *A Tudor Tragedy* (1961).

Smith L. B., *Treason in Tudor England* (1986).

Starkey, D., ed., *The English Court from the Wars of the Roses to the Civil War* (1987).

Stone, L., *The Crisis of the Aristocracy* (1965).

Strong, Roy, *The Cult of Elizabeth* (1977). '

Usherwood, S. and E., *The Counter Armada, 1596: the journal of the Mary Rose* (1983).

Walker, G., *John Skelton and Politics of the 1520s* (1988).

Warnicke, Retha, *The Rise and Fall of Anne Boleyn* (1989).

Weir, Alison, *Mary Queen of Scots and the Murder of Lord Darnley* (2008).

Weir, Alison, *Mary Boleyn* (2011).

Wernham, R. B., *The Expedition of Sir John Norris and Sir Francis Drake to Spain and Portugal, 1589* (Navy Record Society, 1988).

Wilson, Derek, *Sweet Robin: a Biography of Robert Dudley, Earl of Leicester* (1981).

Wormald, J., *Mary Queen of Scots: a Study in Failure* (1988).

Young, Alan, *Tudor and Jacobean Tournaments* (1987).

## *Secondary Works: Articles and shorter works.*

Aird, Ian, 'The death of Amy Robsart', *English Historical Review*, 71, 1956.

Bernard, G. W., 'The Downfall of Sir Thomas Seymour', in *The Tudor Nobility*, ed Bernard (1992).

Cheyney, A. D., 'The Holy Maid of Kent', *Transactions of the Royal Historical Society*, 2nd series, 18, 1904.

Dowling, M., 'Anne Boleyn and Reform', *Journal of Ecclesiastical History*, 35, 1984.

Elton, G. R., ed. D. Loades, *Thomas Cromwell* (2008).

Freeman, T. S., 'Research, Rumour and Propaganda; Anne Boleyn in Foxe's "Book of Martyrs"', *Historical Journal*, 38, 1995.

Gairdner, J. 'Mary and Anne Boleyn', *English Historical Review*, 8, 1893.

Gairdner, J., 'The age of Anne Boleyn', *English Historical Review*, 10, 1895.

Gunn, S. J., 'The Duke of Suffolk's march on Paris, 1523', *English Historical Review*, 101, 1986.

Haugaard, W. P., 'Elizabeth Tudor's Book of Devotions: a neglected clue to the Queen's life and character', *Sixteenth Century Journal*, 12, 1981.

Hoyle, R. W., 'The origin of the dissolution of the monasteries', *Historical Journal*, 38, 1995.

Ives, E. W., 'Stress, Faction, and Ideology in early-Tudor England', *Historical Journal*, 34, 1991.

Kelly, A., 'Eleanor of Acquitaine and her Courts of Love', *Speculum*, 12, 1937.

Knowles, D., 'The Matter of Wilton', *Bulletin of the Institute of Historical Research*, 31, 1958.

Loades, D., *Cardinal Wolsey, 1472–1530: Tudor Statesman and Chancellor* (2008).

Nicholson, G., 'The Act of Appeals and the English Reformation', in *Law and Government under the Tudors*, ed. C. Cross, D. Loades,

J. Scarisbrick (1988).

Paget, Hugh, 'The Youth of Anne Boleyn', *Bulletin of the Institute of Historical Research,* 54, 1981.

Quinn, D. B., 'Henry VIII and Ireland, 1509–1534', *Irish Historical Studies*, 12, 1961.

Read, Conyers, 'Queen Elizabeth's seizure of Alba's pay ships', *Journal of Modern History,* 5, 1933.

Rowley Williams, J., *Mary, Countess of Northumberland* (2011).

Rowley Williams, J., *Jane, Lady Rochford* (2011).

Rowley Williams, J., *Susan Clarencius* (2011).

Rowley Williams, J., *Honor, Lady Lisle* (2011).

Rowley Williams, J., *Sabine Johnson* (2012).

Weikel, A., 'The Marian Council re-visited', in *The Mid-Tudor Polity, 1540–1560,* ed. J. Loach and R. Tittler (1980).

# More Tudor History from Amberley Publishing

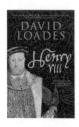

## HENRY VIII
David Loades

'David Loades Tudor biographies are both highly enjoyable and instructive, the perfect combination' *ANTONIA FRASER*

£25.00        978-1-84868-532-1        512 pages HB  113 illus, 49 col

## ANNE BOLEYN
Elizabeth Norton

'Meticulously researched and a great read' *THEANNEBOLEYNFILES.COM*

£9.99        978-1-84868-514-7        264 pages PB  47 illus, 26 col

## THE TUDORS VOL 1
G. J. Meyer

'His style is crisp and popular' *PROFESSOR DAVID LOADES*

£12.99        978-1-4456-0143-4        384 pages PB  72 illus, 54 col

## THE TUDORS VOL 2
G. J. Meyer

'A sweeping history of the gloriously infamous Tudor era' *KIRKUS REVIEW*

£12.99        978-1-4456-0144-1        352 pages PB  53 illus, 15 col

## ANNE BOLEYN
P. Friedmann

'A compelling and lively biography... meticulously researched and supremely readable classic of Tudor biography' *DR RICHARD REX*
'The first scholarly biography' *THE FINANCIAL TIMES*

£20.00        978-1-84868-827-8        352 pages HB  47 illus, 20 col

## MARY TUDOR
David Loades

£20.00        978-1-4456-0305-6        352 pages HB  40 illus, 25 col

## CATHERINE PARR
Elizabeth Norton

'Norton cuts an admirably clear path through tangled Tudor intrigues' *JENNY UGLOW*
'Wonderful... a joy to read' *HERSTORIA*

£18.99        978-1-84868-582-6        384 pages HB  40 illus, 20 col

## MARGARET BEAUFORT
Elizabeth Norton

£20.00        978-1-4456-0142-7        256 pages HB  70 illus, 40 col

# Forthcoming

## BESSIE BLOUNT
Elizabeth Norton

£20.00        978-1-84868-870-4        288 pages HB  40 illus, 20 col

## CATHERINE OF ARAGON
Patrick Williams

£25.00        978-1-84868-108-8        512 pages HB  80 illus, 40 col

Available from all good bookshops or to order direct
Please call **01453-847-800 www.amberleybooks.com**

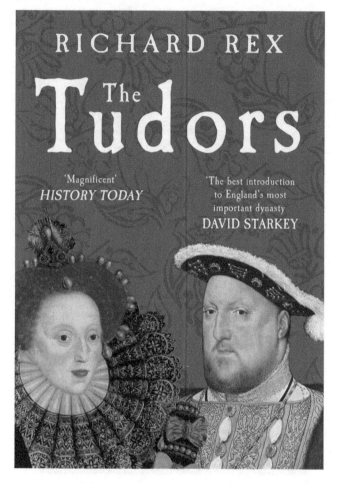

# Also available from Amberley Publishing

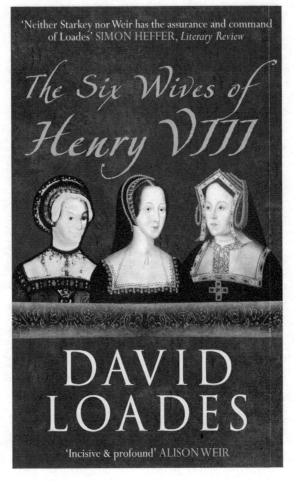

*The marital ups and downs of England's most infamous king*

'Neither Starkey nor Weir has the assurance and command of Loades'
SIMON HEFFER, LITERARY REVIEW

'Incisive and profound... I warmly recommend this book' ALISON WEIR

The story of Henry VIII and his six wives has passed from history into legend – taught in the cradle as a cautionary tale and remembered in adulthood as an object lesson in the dangers of marrying into royalty. The true story behind the legend, however, remains obscure to most people, whose knowledge of the affair begins and ends with the aide memoire 'Divorced, executed, died, divorce, executed, survived'.

£9.99 Paperback
55 illustrations (31 colour)
224 pages
978-1-4456-004-9

Available from all good bookshops or to order direct
Please call **01453-847-800**
**www.amberleybooks.com**

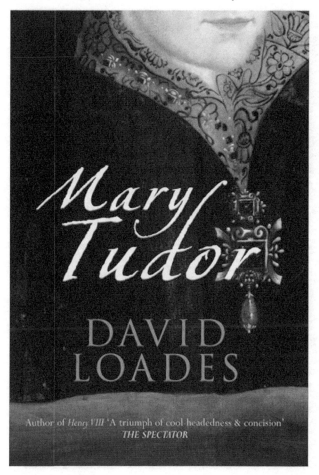

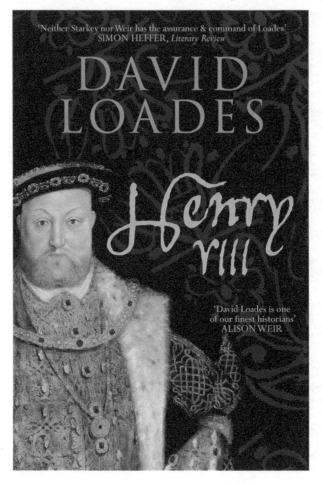

# INDEX